Start a Business in Illinois

Fifth Edition

Linda H. Connell

Mark Warda

Attorneys at Law

SPHINX® PUBLISHING
AN IMPRINT OF SOURCEBOOKS, INC.®
NAPERVILLE, ILLINOIS
www.SphinxLegal.com

Fifth Edition: 2007

Published by: **Sphinx® Publishing, An Imprint of Sourcebooks, Inc.®**

<u>Naperville Office</u>
P.O. Box 4410
Naperville, Illinois 60567-4410
630-961-3900
Fax: 630-961-2168
www.sourcebooks.com
www.SphinxLegal.com

This publication is designed to provide accurate and authoritative information in regard to the subject matter covered. It is sold with the understanding that the publisher is not engaged in rendering legal, accounting, or other professional service. If legal advice or other expert assistance is required, the services of a competent professional person should be sought.
From a Declaration of Principles Jointly Adopted by a Committee of the American Bar Association and a Committee of Publishers and Associations

This product is not a substitute for legal advice.

Disclaimer required by Texas statutes.

Library of Congress Cataloging-in-Publication Data
Connell, Linda H.
  Start a business in Illinois / by Linda H. Connell and Mark Warda. -- 5th ed.
      p. cm.
  Previously published as How to start a business in Illinois.
  Includes index.
  ISBN-13: 978-1-57248-593-8 (pbk. : alk. paper)
  ISBN-10: 1-57248-593-0 (pbk. : alk. paper)
  1. Business enterprises--Law and legislation--Illinois--Popular works. 2. Business law--Illinois. I. Warda, Mark. II. Connell, Linda H. How to start a business in Illinois. III. Title.

KFI1405.Z9G36 2007
346.773'065--dc22

2006102311

Printed and bound in the United States of America.
SB — 10 9 8 7 6 5 4 3 2 1

Contents

Hazard Insurance
Home Business Insurance
Automobile Insurance
Health Insurance
Employee Theft

Using Self-Help Law Books

Before using a self-help law book, you should realize the advantages and disadvantages of doing your own legal work and understand the challenges and diligence that this requires.

Rest assured that you will not be the first or only person handling your own legal matter. For example, in some states, more than 75% of the people in divorces and other cases represent themselves. Because of the high cost of legal services, this is a major trend, and many courts are struggling to make it easier for people to represent themselves. However, some courts are not happy with people who do not use attorneys and refuse to help them in any way. For some, the attitude is, "Go to the law library and figure it out for yourself."

The Growing Trend

We write and publish self-help law books to give people an alternative to the often complicated and confusing legal books found in most law libraries. We have made the explanations of the law as simple and easy to understand as possible. Of course, unlike an attorney advising an individual client, we cannot cover every conceivable possibility.

Cost/Value Analysis

Whenever you shop for a product or service, you are faced with various levels of quality and price. In deciding what product or service to buy, you make a cost/value analysis on the basis of your willingness to pay and the quality you desire.

When buying a car, you decide whether you want transportation, comfort, status, or sex appeal. Accordingly, you decide among choices such as a Neon, a Lincoln, a Rolls Royce, or a Porsche. Before making a decision, you usually weigh the merits of each option against the cost.

When you get a headache, you can take a pain reliever (such as aspirin) or visit a medical specialist for a neurological examination. Given this choice, most people, of course, take a pain reliever, since it costs only pennies; whereas a medical examination costs hundreds of dollars and takes a lot of time. This is usually a logical choice because it is rare to need anything more than a pain reliever for a headache. But in some cases, a headache may indicate a brain tumor, and failing to see a specialist right away can result in complications. Should everyone with a headache go to a specialist? Of course not, but people treating their own illnesses must realize that they are betting, on the basis of their cost/value analysis of the situation, that they are taking the most logical option.

The same cost/value analysis must be made when deciding to do one's own legal work. Many legal situations are very straightforward, requiring a simple form and no complicated analysis. Anyone with a little intelligence and a book of instructions can handle the matter without outside help.

But there is always the chance that complications are involved that only an attorney would notice. To simplify the law into a book like this, several legal cases often must be condensed into a single sentence or paragraph. Otherwise, the book would be several hundred pages long and too complicated for most people. However, this simplification necessarily leaves out many details and nuances that would apply to special or unusual situations. Also, there are many ways to interpret most legal questions. Your case may come before a judge who disagrees with the analysis of our authors.

Therefore, in deciding to use a self-help law book and to do your own legal work, you must realize that you are making a cost/value analysis. You have decided that the money you will save in doing it yourself outweighs the chance that your case will not turn out to your satisfaction. Most people handling their own simple legal matters never have a problem, but occasionally people find that it ended up costing them more to have an attorney straighten out the situation than it would have if they had hired an attorney in the beginning. Keep this in mind while handling your case, and be sure to consult an attorney if you feel you might need further guidance.

Local Rules   The next thing to remember is that a book which covers the law for the entire nation, or even for an entire state, cannot possibly include every procedural difference of every jurisdiction. Whenever possible, we provide the exact form needed; however, in some areas, each county, or even each judge, may require unique forms and procedures. In our state books, our forms usually cover the majority of counties in the state or provide examples of the type of form that will be required. In our national books, our forms are sometimes even more general in nature but are designed to give a good idea of the type of form that will be needed in most locations. Nonetheless, keep in mind that your state, county, or judge may have a requirement, or use a form, that is not included in this book.

You should not necessarily expect to be able to get all of the information and resources you need solely from within the pages of this book. This book will serve as your guide, giving you specific information whenever possible and helping you to find out what else you will need to know. This is just like if you decided to build your own backyard deck. You might purchase a book on how to build decks. However, such a book would not include the building codes and permit requirements of every city, town, county, and township in the nation; nor would it include the lumber, nails, saws, hammers, and other materials and tools you would need to actually build the deck. You would use the book as your guide, and then do some work and research involving such matters as whether you need a permit of some kind, what type and grade of wood is available in your area, whether to use hand tools or power tools, and how to use those tools.

Before using the forms in a book like this, you should check with your court clerk to see if there are any local rules of which you should be aware or local forms you will need to use. Often, such forms will require the same information as the forms in the book but are merely laid out differently or use slightly different language. They will sometimes require additional information.

Changes in the Law   Besides being subject to local rules and practices, the law is subject to change at any time. The courts and the legislatures of all fifty states are constantly revising the laws. It is possible that while you are reading this book, some aspect of the law is being changed.

In most cases, the change will be of minimal significance. A form will be redesigned, additional information will be required, or a waiting period will be extended. As a result, you might need to revise a form, file an extra form, or wait out a longer time period. These types of changes will not usually affect the outcome of your case. On the other hand, sometimes a major part of the law is changed, the entire law in a particular area is rewritten, or a case that was the basis of a central legal point is overruled. In such instances, your entire ability to pursue your case may be impaired.

Introduction

Each year, tens of thousands of new corporations are registered in Illinois, and thousands more partnerships and proprietorships open for business. The demand for new businesses keeps growing, and Illinois continues to be a desirable place to start a business.

Be your own boss and be as successful as you dare. However, if you do not follow the laws of the state, your progress can be slowed or stopped by government fines, civil judgments, or criminal penalties.

This book is intended to give you the framework for legally opening and operating a business in Illinois. It also includes information on where to find special rules for each type of business. If you have problems that are not covered by this book, you should seek out an attorney who can be available for your ongoing needs.

In order to cover all of the aspects of any business you are thinking of starting, read through this entire book instead of skipping to the parts that look most important. There are many laws that may not sound like they apply to you, but do have provisions that will affect your business.

The forms included in this book were the most recent ones available at the time of publication. It is possible that some may be revised by the time you read this book, but in most cases, they will be similar and require the same information.

Deciding to Start a Business

If you are reading this book, then you have probably made a serious decision to take the plunge and start your own business. You need to know why some succeed while others fail. Knowledge can only help your chances of success. Some of what follows may seem obvious, but to someone wrapped up in a new business idea, some of this information is occasionally overlooked.

KNOW YOUR STRENGTHS

You should consider all the skills and knowledge that running a successful business needs, and decide if you have what it takes. If you do not, it does not necessarily mean you are doomed to be an employee all your life. Perhaps you just need a partner who has the skills you lack. You can also hire people with the skills you need or structure your business to avoid areas where you are weak. If those suggestions do not work, maybe you can learn the skills you are lacking.

For example, if you are not good at dealing with employees (either you are too passive and get taken advantage of or too tough and scare them off), you can:

- ✪ handle product development yourself and have a partner or manager deal with employees;

- ✪ take seminars in employee management; or,

- ✪ structure your business so that you do not need employees. (Either use independent contractors or set yourself up as an independent contractor.)

The following are some of the factors to consider when planning your business.

- ✪ *If it takes months or years before your business turns a profit, do you have the resources to hold out?* Businesses have gone under or been sold just before they were about to take off.

- ✪ *Are you willing to put in a lot of overtime to make your business a success?* Owners of businesses do not set their own hours—the businesses set the hours for the owners. Many business owners work long hours seven days a week.

- ✪ *Are you willing to do the dirtiest or most unpleasant work of the business?* Emergencies come up and employees are not always dependable. You might need to mop up a flooded room, spend a weekend stuffing ten thousand envelopes, or work a holiday if someone calls in sick.

- ✪ *Do you know enough about the product or service?* Are you aware of the trends in the industry and what changes new technology might bring?

- ✪ *Do you know enough about accounting and inventory to manage the business?* Do you have a good head for business? Some people naturally know how to save money and do things profitably, while others are in the habit of buying the best and the most expensive of everything. The latter can be fatal to a struggling new business.

✪ *Are you good at managing employees?* If your business has employees (or will have in the future), managing them is an unavoidable part of running the business.

✪ *Do you know how to sell your product or service?* You can have the best product on the market, but people will not beat a path to your door if they do not know about it. If you are a wholesaler, shelf space in major stores is hard to get—especially for a new company without a track record, a large line of products, or a large advertising budget.

✪ *Do you know enough about getting publicity?* The media receive thousands of press releases and announcements each day, and most are thrown away. Do not count on free publicity to put your name in front of the public.

KNOW YOUR BUSINESS

You need the experience of working in a business as well as the concept of a business. Maybe you always dreamed of running a bed and breakfast or having your own pizza place. Have you ever worked in such a business? If not, you may have no idea of the day-to-day headaches and problems of the business. Do you really know how much to allow for theft, spoilage, and unhappy customers?

You might feel silly taking an entry level job at a pizza place when you would rather start your own, but it might be the most valuable preparation you could have. A few weeks of seeing how a business operates could mean the difference between success and failure in your new business.

Working in a business as an employee is one of the best ways to be a success at running such a business. New people with new ideas who work in older industries have been known to revolutionize those industries with obvious improvements that no one before dared to try.

SOURCES OF FURTHER GUIDANCE

There are many things to consider as you prepare to start your own business. Most likely, you will have numerous questions that need to be answered before opening your doors for the first time. Luckily, there are many resources available for help. The sources discussed in this section offer free or low-cost guidance for new businesses.

SCORE   The *Service Corps of Retired Executives* (SCORE) is a nonprofit group of retired people who volunteer to give guidance to businesses. Its website, **www.score.org**, offers multiple resources for a new business. You can also contact a local chapter at one of the following locations.

Central Illinois SCORE
402 North Hershey Road
Bloomington, IL 61704
309-664-0549
Fax: 309-663-8270

Chicago SCORE
Citicorp Center
500 West Madison Street
#1250
Chicago, IL 60661
312-353-7724
Fax: 312-886-4879

Decatur SCORE
Milliken University
1184 West Main Street
Decatur, IL 62522
217-424-6297
Fax: 217-424-3523

East Central Illinois SCORE
c/o Chamber of Commerce
1817 South Neil
Suite 201
Champaign, IL 61820
217-359-1791
Fax: 217-359-1809

Fox Valley SCORE
1444 North Farnsworth
Room 504
Aurora, IL 60505
630-692-1162
Fax: 630-852-3127

Kankakee Valley SCORE
1690 Newtowne Drive
Bradley, IL 60915
815-427-9818
Fax: 815-427-9818

Northern Illinois SCORE
c/o EIGER Lab
605 Fulton Avenue
Rockford, IL 61103
815-962-0122
Fax: 815-962-0806

Peoria SCORE
c/o Peoria Chamber of Commerce
124 Southwest Adams
Suite 300
Peoria, IL 61602
309-676-0755
Fax: 309-676-7534

Quad Cities SCORE
c/o Chamber of Commerce
622 19th Street
Moline, IL 61265
309-797-0082
Fax: 309-757-5435

Southern Illinois SCORE
150 East Pleasant Hill Road
Box 1
Carbondale, IL 62901
618-453-6654
Fax: 618-453-5040

Quincy Tri-State SCORE
c/o Chamber of Commerce
300 Civic Center Plaza
Suite 245
Quincy, IL 62301
217-222-8093
Fax: 217-222-3033

Southwest Illinois SCORE
5800 Godfrey Road
Alden Hall
Godfrey, IL 62035
618-467-2280
Fax: 618-466-8289

Springfield SCORE
3330 Ginger Creek Drive
Suite B South
Springfield, IL 62711
217-793-5020
Fax: 217-793-5025

Small Business Development Centers

Educational programs for small businesses are offered through the Small Business Development Centers at many Illinois colleges and universities. For further details visit **www.ilsmallbiz.biz**.

Check their programs for courses in any areas in which you are weak. (The development centers are listed in alphabetical order.)

Asian American Alliance Small Business Development Center
2169B South China Place
Chicago, IL 60616
312-225-9320
Fax: 312-225-9340

Black Hawk College Small Business Development Center
4703 16th Street
Suite G
Moline, IL 61265
309-764-2213

Bradley University Small Business Development Center
141 North Jobst Hall
First Floor
1501 West Bradley Avenue
Peoria, IL 61625
309-677-2992

Chicagoland Entrepreneurial Center at the Chicagoland Chamber of Commerce
200 East Randloph Street
Suite 2200
Chicago, IL 60601
312-494-6736
Fax: 312-494-0196

College of DuPage Small Business Development Center
425 Fawell Boulevard
Glen Ellyn, IL 60137
630-942-2771
Fax: 630-942-3789

College of Lake County Small Business Development Center
19351 West Washington Street
Room T-302
Grayslake, IL 60030
847-543-2033

Danville Area Community College Small Business Development Center
28 West North Street
Danville, IL 61832
217-442-7232
Fax: 217-442-1897

Elgin Community College Small Business Development Center
1700 Spartan Drive
Elgin, IL 60123
847-214-7488
Fax: 847-931-3911

Evanston Technology Innovation Center Small Business Development Center
820 Davis Street
Suite 137
Evanston, IL 60201
847-866-1817
Fax: 847-866-1808

Governors State University Small Business Development Center
College of Business
Room 3300
University Park, IL 60466
708-534-4929
Fax: 708-534-1646

Greater North Chicago Development Corporation Small Business Development Center
6600 West Armitage
Chicago, IL 60607
773-637-2768
Fax: 773-637-2698

Greater Southside Small Business Development Center
9501 South King Drive
BHS 601
Chicago, IL 60628
773-995-3938
Fax: 773-821-2841

Illinois Eastern Community College
Small Business Development Center
702 High Street
Olney, IL 62450
618-395-3011
Fax: 618-395-1922

Illinois Hispanic Chamber of Commerce
Morton College
3801 South Central Avenue
Suite# 101 D
Cicero, IL 60804
708-780-7876
Fax: 708-780-7850

Illinois Valley Community College
Small Business Development Center
815 North Orlando Smith
  Avenue
Building 11
Oglesby, IL 61348
815-224-0212
Fax: 815-223-1780

Industrial Council of Near West Chicago
2010 West Fulton
Suite 280
Chicago, IL 60612
312-433-2373
Fax: 312-421-1871

Jane Addams Hull House Association
Parkway Community House
500 East 67th Street
Chicago, IL 60637
773-955-8027
Fax: 773-955-8028

Joliet Junior College
Small Business Development Center
City Center Campus
Room 400
214 North Ottawa Street
Joliet, IL 60432
815-280-1400
Fax: 815-280-1292

Joseph Center
7600 West Roosevelt
Forest Park, IL 60130
708-697-6200
Fax: 708-488-2290

Kankakee Community College
Small Business Development Center
P.O. Box 888
River Road
Kankakee, IL 60901
815-933-0376

Fax: 815-933-0217
Kaskaskia College
Small Business Development
Center
Salem Center
206 West Main
Salem, IL 62881
618-548-9001
Fax: 618-548-9007

Kishwaukee College
Small Business Development
Center
21193 Malta Road
Malta, IL 60150
815-825-2086
Fax: 815-825-2305

Latin American Chamber of
Commerce Small Business
Development Center
3512 West Fullerton
Chicago, IL 60647
773-252-5211
Fax: 773-252-7065

Lincoln Land Community
College
Small Business Development
Center
c/o Greater Springfield Chamber
   of Commerce
3 South Old State
Capitol Place
Springfield, IL 62703
217-789-1017
Fax: 217-522-3512

McHenry County College
Small Business Development
Center
8900 U.S. Highway 14
Crystal Lake, IL 60012
815-455-6098
Fax: 815-455-9319

Moraine Valley College
Small Business Development
Center
10900 South 88th Avenue
Palos Hills, IL 60465
708-974-5412

North Business and
Industrial Council
Small Business Development
Center
5353 West Armstrong
Chicago, IL 60646
773-594-9292
Fax: 773-594-9416

Rend Lake College
Small Business Development
Center
327 Potomac Boulevard
Suite A
Mt. Vernon, IL 62864
618-242-5813
Fax: 618-242-8220

Rock Valley College
Technology Center
EIGER Lab
605 Fulton
Room E109
Rockford, IL 61103
815-921-2081
Fax: 815-921-2089

Sauk Valley Community College
Small Business Development Center
173 Illinois Route #2
Dixon, IL 61021
815-288-5511
Fax: 815-288-5958

Shawnee Community College
Small Business Development Center
8364 Shawnee College Road
Ullin, IL 62992
618-634-3371
Fax: 618-634-2347

Southeastern Illinois College
Small Business Development Center
303 South Commercial Street
Harrisburg, IL 62946
618-252-5001
Fax: 618-252-0210

Southern Illinois University at Carbondale
Small Business Development Center
150 East Pleasant Hill Road
Carbondale, IL 62901
618-536-2424
Fax: 618-453-5040

Southern Illinois University at East St. Louis
Small Business Development Center
601 James R. Thompson
  Boulevard
Building D
Room 1017
East St. Louis, IL 62201
618-482-8330
Fax: 618-482-8341

Southern Illinois University at Edwardsville
Small Business Development Center
Campus Box 1107
Alumni Hall 2126
Edwardsville, IL 62026
Phone: 618-650-2929
Fax: 618-650-2647

University of Illinois
Small Business Development Center
1817 South Neil Street
Suite 201
Champaign, IL 61820
217-378-8535
Fax: 217-359-1809

University of Illinois at Chicago
Small Business Development Center
601 South Morgan
Suite B4UH
Chicago, IL 60607
312-413-8130
Fax: 312-355-3604

**University of Illinois
Extension
Small Business Development
Center**
2525 Federal Drive
Suite #1105
Decatur, IL 62526
217-875-4004
Fax: 217-875-4334

**Waubonsee Community
College
Small Business Development
Center**
Aurora Campus
5 East Galena Boulevard
Aurora, IL 60506
630-906-4143
Fax: 630-892-4668

**Western Illinois University
Small Business Development
Center**
510 North Pearl Street
Suite 1400
Macomb, IL 61455
309-836-2640
Fax: 309-837-4688

**William Rainey Harper
College
Business and Professional
Development**
650 East Higgins Road
Suite 106
Schaumburg, IL 60173
847-925-6570
Fax: 847-925-6109

**Women's Business
Development Center
Small Business Development
Center**
8 South Michigan
Suite 400
Chicago, IL 60603
312-853-3477
Fax: 312-853-0145

Choosing the Form of Your Business

An important decision that needs to be made at the outset is the choice of legal structure for your business. There are numerous factors that will need to be considered to make the correct decision for your particular business. The most important consideration is that the corporate form will limit your liability for business debts and adverse judgments solely to the corporate assets, as opposed to your own personal assets.

BASIC FORMS OF DOING BUSINESS

The four most popular forms for a business in Illinois are sole proprietorship, partnership, corporation, and limited liability company. However, bear in mind that limited liability will only hold up if the corporate entity is maintained separate and apart from the owner. If there is an intermingling of monies between the corporate and the owner's individual accounts, then the owner may become personally liable for business debts, despite the corporate form. The characteristics, advantages, and disadvantages of each form of business are described in this chapter.

Proprietorship A proprietorship is one person doing business in his or her own name or under a fictitious name.

Advantages. Simplicity is a proprietorship's greatest advantage. There is also no organizational expense and no extra tax forms or reports.

Disadvantages. The proprietor is personally liable for all debts and obligations. There is also no continuation of the business after death. All profits are directly taxable, which is certainly a disadvantage for the proprietor, and business affairs are easily mixed with personal affairs.

General Partnership

A general partnership involves two or more people carrying on a business together to share the profits and losses.

Advantages. Partners can combine expertise and assets. A general partnership allows liability to be spread among more persons. Also, the business can be continued after the death of a partner, if the partnership agreement so provides, and if the deceased partner's share is bought out by a surviving partner.

Disadvantages. Each partner is liable for acts of other partners within the scope of the business. This means that if your partner harms a customer or signs a million-dollar credit line in the partnership's name, you can be personally liable. Even if you leave all profits in the business, those profits are taxable. Control is shared by all parties, and the death of a partner may result in liquidation. In a general partnership, it is often hard to get rid of a bad partner.

Limited Partnership

A limited partnership has characteristics similar to both a corporation and a partnership. There are *general partners* who have the control and personal liability, and there are *limited partners* who only put up money and whose liability is limited to what they paid for their share of the partnership (like corporate stock). A new type of limited partnership, a *limited liability limited partnership*, allows all partners to avoid liability.

Advantages. Capital can be contributed by limited partners who have no control of the business or liability for its debts.

Disadvantages. A great disadvantage is high start-up costs. Also, an extensive partnership agreement is required, because general partners are personally liable for partnership debts and for the acts of each other. (One solution to this problem is to use a corporation as the general partner.)

Corporation A corporation is an artificial, legal person that conducts the business through its officers for its shareholders. In Illinois, one person may form a corporation and be the sole shareholder and officer. Laws governing corporations are contained in Illinois Compiled Statutes (ILCS) Chapter 805, Section 5.

> **NOTE:** *Illinois Compiled Statutes are cited by the chapter number of the Illinois Compiled Statutes, followed by the section number. For example, the citation for the previously referenced section would be 805 ILCS 5.*

An *S corporation* is a corporation that has filed IRS Form 2553, choosing to have all profits taxed to the shareholders, rather than to the corporation. An S corporation files a tax return, but pays no federal or state tax. The profit shown on the S corporation tax return is reported on each owner's tax returns.

A *C corporation* is any corporation that has not elected to be taxed as an S corporation. A C corporation pays income tax on its profits. The effect of this is that when dividends are paid to shareholders, they are taxed twice—once by the corporation and once when they are paid to the shareholders. In Illinois, a C corporation must also pay corporate income tax.

A *professional service corporation* is a corporation formed by a professional, such as a doctor or accountant. Illinois has special rules for professional service corporations that differ slightly from those of other corporations. These are included in 805 ILCS 10. There are also special tax rules for professional service corporations.

A *nonprofit corporation* is usually used for organizations such as churches and condominium associations. However, with careful planning, some types of businesses can be set up as nonprofit corporations and save quite a bit in taxes. While a nonprofit corporation cannot pay dividends, it can pay its officers and employees fair salaries. Some of the major American nonprofit organizations pay their officers well over $100,000 a year. Illinois' special rules for nonprofit corporations are included in 805 ILCS 105.

Advantages. If a corporation is properly organized, shareholders have no liability for corporate debts and lawsuits. Officers usually have no personal liability for their corporate actions. The existence of a corporation may be perpetual. There are tax advantages allowed only to corporations. There is prestige in owning a corporation. Capital may be raised by issuing stock and it is easy to transfer ownership upon death. A small corporation can be set up as an S corporation to avoid corporate taxes, but still retain corporate advantages. Some types of businesses can be set up as nonprofit corporations, which provide significant tax savings.

Disadvantages. The start-up costs for forming a corporation are a disadvantage. There are also certain formalities, such as annual meetings, separate bank accounts, and tax forms. Unless a corporation registers as an S corporation, it must pay federal income tax separate from the tax paid by the owners, and it must pay Illinois income tax.

Limited Liability Company

Illinois was the eighteenth state in the United States to allow a limited liability company (LLC). The *Limited Liability Company Act* is found at 805 ILCS 180. This relatively new invention is like a limited partnership without general partners, and has characteristics of both a corporation and a partnership. It is fast becoming the first choice of small business owners. In general, none of the partners have liability and all can have some control. Keep in mind that, just as in any corporation, an LLC member may be held personally liable if he or she does not keep the LLC's affairs separate from his or her own personal business.

Advantages. The limited liability company offers the tax benefits of a partnership with the protection from liability of a corporation. It offers more tax benefits than an S corporation because it may pass through more depreciation and deductions, have different classes of ownership, have an unlimited number of members, and have aliens as members.

Disadvantages. Start-up and annual fees are higher for an LLC than for a corporation. Limited liability companies pay Social Security tax on all profits (up to a limit), whereas S corporation profits are exempt from Social Security tax. Limited liability companies must also pay Illinois corporate income tax. Because a limited liability company is a new invention, there are not a lot of answers to legal questions that may arise. (However, the courts will probably rely on corporation and limited partnership law.)

Limited Liability Partnership

The limited liability partnership (LLP) is like a general partnership without personal liability. It was devised to allow partnerships of lawyers and other professionals to limit their personal liability without losing their partnership structure. This was important because converting to an LLC could have tax consequences, and some states do not allow professionals to operate as LLCs. Both general and limited partnerships can register as LLPs.

Advantages. The limited liability partnership offers the flexibility and tax benefits of a partnership with the protection from liability of a corporation.

Disadvantages. Start-up and annual fees are higher for LLPs than for corporations. Also, the law requires the partnership to maintain certain minimum insurance.

Which to Choose

The selection of a form of doing business is best made with the advice of an accountant and an attorney. If you were selling harmless objects by mail, a sole proprietorship would be the easiest way to get started. However, if you own a taxi service, it would be important to incorporate to avoid losing your personal assets if one of your drivers injured someone in an accident in which the damages could exceed your insurance. If you can expect a high cash buildup the first year, then a corporation may be the best way to keep taxes low. If you expect the usual start-up losses, then a proprietorship, partnership, or S corporation would probably be best.

While the above list may seem overwhelming at first, as a practical matter, the majority of Illinois' nearly seven hundred thousand businesses are either a sole proprietorship or corporation. Keep in mind that you can change the structure of your business at any time if needed. It is best to keep things simple at first and wait for a clear need to develop before adopting a more complex business structure.

START-UP PROCEDURES

Except for a sole proprietorship, you must prepare some paperwork to start your business, and for some types, you must file the paperwork and pay a registration fee.

Proprietorship

In a proprietorship, all accounts, property, and licenses are taken in the name of the owner. (See Chapter 3 for information about using an assumed name.)

Partnership

To form a partnership, a written agreement should be prepared to spell out the rights and obligations of the parties. In most cases, licenses can be in either the name of the partnership or in the names of the partners.

Corporation

Articles of incorporation must be filed with the secretary of state in Springfield, along with $150 in filing fees and an additional amount for the franchise tax. An organizational meeting is then held. At the meeting, officers are elected, stock is issued, and other formalities are complied with to avoid the corporate entity being set aside later. It is very important to maintain the corporation as a separate entity from its owners in order to preserve limited liability. Licenses and accounts are titled in the name of the corporation.

Limited Partnership

A written limited partnership agreement must be drawn up and registered with the secretary of state in Springfield, and a lengthy disclosure document must be given to all prospective limited partners. Because of the complexity of securities laws and the criminal penalties for violation, it is advantageous to have an attorney organize a limited partnership.

Limited Liability Company

One or more persons may form a limited liability company by filing *articles of organization* with the secretary of state in Springfield. Licenses and accounts are in the name of the company.

Limited Liability Partnership

Two or more persons may form a limited liability partnership by filing a *Limited Liability Partnership Statement of Registration* with the secretary of state in Springfield. Licenses and accounts are in the name of the company.

BUSINESS COMPARISON CHART

	Sole Proprietorship	General Partnership	Limited Partnership	Limited Liability Co.	Corporation C or S	Nonprofit Corporation
Liability Protection	No	No	For limited partners	For all members	For all shareholders	For all members
Taxes	Pass through (complete Schedule C)	Pass through	Pass through	Pass through	S corporations pass through, C corporations pay tax	None on income Employees pay on wages
Minimum Number of Members	1	2	2	1	1	3
Start-Up Fee	None	None	$150	$500	$150	$50
Annual Fee	None	None	$100	$250	$75	$5
Different Classes of Ownership	No	Yes	Yes	Yes	S corps. No C corps. Yes	No ownership Diff. classes of membership
Survives after Death	No	No	Yes	Yes	Yes	Yes
Best for	1 person, low-risk business or no assets	Low-risk business	Low-risk business with silent partners	All types of businesses	All types of businesses	Educational, charitable

Registering the Name of Your Business

For some businesses, the single greatest asset that the business has may be its name. Companies spend billions of dollars each year on advertising in an effort to enhance the public's awareness of their names. Often, as a business matures, the name will attract business because it is associated with quality and good practices.

PRELIMINARY CONSIDERATIONS

Before deciding on a name for your business, be sure that it is not already being used by someone else. Many business owners have spent thousands of dollars on publicity and printing only to throw it all away because another company already owned the name. A company that owns a name can take you to court and force you to stop using that name. It can also sue you for damages if it thinks your use of the name caused it a financial loss.

Even if you will be running a small local shop with no plans for expansion, check if the name has been trademarked. If another company is using the same name anywhere in the country and has registered it as a federal trademark, that company can sue you. If you plan to expand or to deal nationally, do a thorough search of the name.

The first places to look are the local phone books and official records of your county. Next, you should check with the secretary of state's office in Springfield to see if someone has registered a fictitious name or corporate name the same as, or confusingly similar to, the one you have chosen. This can be done either by calling them or by visiting their Internet site at **www.ilsos.gov/corporatellc**.

To do a national search, you should check trade directories and phone books of major cities. These can be found at many libraries and are usually reference books that cannot be checked out. The *Trade Names Directory*, published by Gale Group Co., is a two-volume set of names compiled from many sources.

Using the Internet, you can search all of the Yellow Pages listings in the United States at a number of sites for no charge. One website, **www.yellowpages.com**, offers free searches of Yellow Pages for all states at once.

To be sure that your use of the name does not violate someone else's trademark rights, have a trademark search done in the United States Patent and Trademark Office. In the past, this required a visit to their offices or the hiring of a search, which can cost over a hundred dollars. Now, the USPTO trademark records can be searched online at **www.uspto.gov**.

If you do not have access to the Internet, you might be able to perform a search at a public library or to have one of its employees order an online search for you for a small fee. If this is not available to you, you can have the search done through a firm. One such firm is:

Government Liaison Services, Inc.
200 North Glebe Road
Suite 321
Arlington, VA 22203

The firm can be reached at 800-642-6564. It also offers searches of hundreds of sources.

No matter how thorough your search is, there is no guarantee that there is not a local user somewhere with rights to the mark. If, for example, you register a name for a new chain of restaurants and later find out that someone in Tucumcari, New Mexico has been using the name longer than you, that person will still have the right to use the name, but just in his or her local area. If you do not want his or her restaurant to cause confusion with your chain, you can try to buy him or her out. Similarly, if you are operating a small business under a unique name and a law firm in New York writes and offers to buy the right to your name, you can assume that some large corporation wants to start a major expansion under that name.

The best way to make sure a name you are using is not already owned by someone else is to make up a name. Such names as Xerox, Kodak, and Exxon were made up and did not have any meaning prior to their use. Remember that there are millions of businesses, and even something you make up may already be in use. Your best bet is to do a search.

ASSUMED NAMES

In Illinois, as in most states, unless you do business in your own legal name, you must register the name you are using. The name must be registered in each county where you intend to conduct business. The registration costs only $5 and does not have to be renewed.

It is a misdemeanor to fail to register an assumed name, and you may not sue anyone unless you are registered. If someone sues you and you are not registered, that person may be entitled to attorney's fees and court costs.

If your name is John Doe and you are operating a masonry business, you may operate your business as *John Doe, Mason* without registering it. However, any other use of a name should be registered, such as:

Doe Masonry	Doe Masonry Company
Doe Company	Illinois Masonry

You cannot use the words "Corporation," "Incorporated," "Corp.," or "Inc." unless you are a corporation. However, corporations do not have to register the name they are using unless it is different from their registered corporate name.

When you use an assumed name you are *doing business as* (d/b/a) whatever name you are using. Legally, you would use the name *John Doe d/b/a Doe Masonry*.

Professionals licensed by the Illinois Department of Professional Regulation do not have to register the names under which they practice their profession.

For a sole proprietorship or partnership to register an assumed name, it must first file an application with the county clerk. (Your county clerk should be able to provide the form.) Unlike corporate names and trademarks, which are carefully screened by the secretary of state to avoid duplication, fictitious name registrations are accepted without regard to who else is using the name. If you apply for registration of a trademark or corporate name, the secretary of state will check all other registrations and refuse registration if the name or a similar name is already registered. A sample, filled-in **APPLICATION TO ADOPT, CHANGE, OR CANCEL AN ASSUMED CORPORATE NAME** is included in Appendix C. A blank form is included in Appendix D. (see form 2, p.231.)

The registration of a fictitious name does not bestow any rights to the name upon the registrant; it is merely notice to the world of who is behind the business. The county clerk will allow anyone to register any name, even if one hundred others have already registered that name.

As discussed in Chapter 3, you should do some research to see if the name you intend to use is already being used by anyone else. Even persons who have not registered a name can acquire some legal rights to the name simply through use.

Some businesses have special requirements for registration of their fictitious names. For example, a private investigative agency must obtain permission from the Department of Business and Professional Regulation for the use of its proposed name prior to obtaining its license from the state. Other businesses may have similar requirements. (See Chapter 7 for a list of state-regulated professions with references to the laws that apply to them.)

Next, you must place an ad in a newspaper of general circulation in the county in which you will be maintaining your principal place of business, announcing your intent to use the name. The ad only has to be run once a week for three consecutive weeks, and would usually be placed in the classified section under *Legal Notices*. It could be worded as follows.

> Notice is hereby given, pursuant to "An Act in relation to the use of an Assumed Business Name in the conduct or transaction of Business in the State," as amended, that a certification was filed by the undersigned with the Recorder of Deeds, Cook County.
>
> Under the Assumed Name of <u>DOE COMPANY</u> with the business located at <u>1234 West Main Street, Chicago, IL 60601.</u>
>
> The true name(s) and residence address of the owner(s) are:
> <u>JOHN DOE</u>   <u>1234 West Main Street, Chicago, IL 60601</u>
>
> <u>JIM DOE</u>   <u>2550 West Maple Street, Chicago, IL 60601</u>

You should compare rates before placing the ad. Many counties have weekly newspapers that specialize in legal ads and charge a third of what the large newspapers charge. In Chicago, or anywhere in Cook County, you may place an ad in the *Chicago Law Bulletin*. To do so, visit **www.lawbulletin.com** or call 312-644-7800.

CORPORATE NAMES

A corporation does not have to register as an assumed name because it already has a legal name, unless it is using another name than that listed on its articles of incorporation. The name of a corporation must contain one of the following words.

Incorporated	Inc.
Company	Co.
Corporation	Corp.
Limited	Ltd.

It is not advisable to use only the word "Company" or "Co." because unincorporated businesses also use these words. A person dealing with you might not realize you are incorporated. If this happens, you might end up with personal liability for corporate debts. Instead, you can use a combination of two of the words, such as "ABC Co., Inc."

If the name of the corporation does not contain one of the previously mentioned words, it will be rejected by the secretary of state. It will also be rejected if the name is already taken, is similar to the name of another corporation, or it uses a forbidden word such as *Bank* or *Trust*. To check on a name, call the corporate name information number in Springfield, 217-782-9521, or check the website listed on page 20.

NOTE: *To check on the name of an LLC, call 217-524-8008.*

If a name you pick is taken by another company, you may be able to change it slightly and have it accepted. For example, if there is already a Tri-City Upholstery, Inc. and it is in a different county, you may be allowed to use Tri-City Upholstery of Cook County, Inc. However, even if this is approved by the secretary of state, you might get sued by the other company if your business is close to theirs or there is a likelihood of confusion.

Do not have anything printed until your corporate papers are returned to you. Sometimes a name is approved over the phone and rejected when submitted. Once you have chosen a corporate name and know it is available, you should immediately register your corporation. A name can be reserved for ninety days for a fee ($25 for corporations and $300 for LLCs). Still, it is easier to register the corporation than to waste time on the name reservation.

If a corporation wants to do business under a name other than its corporate name, it can register a fictitious name such as "Doe Corporation d/b/a Doe Industries." However, if the name used leads people to believe that the business is not a corporation, the right to limited liability may be lost. If such a name is used it should always be accompanied by the corporate name.

PROFESSIONAL SERVICE CORPORATIONS

Professional service corporations are corporations formed by professionals such as attorneys, doctors, dentists, and architects. Under Illinois law, a professional corporation cannot use the usual corporate designations, "Inc.," "Corp.," or "Co.," but instead must use one of the following words or abbreviations.

Chartered	P.C.
Limited	Ltd.
Professional Corporation	Prof. Corp.

DOMAIN NAMES

With the Internet changing so rapidly, all of the rules for Internet names have not yet been worked out. Originally, the first person to reserve a name owned it, and enterprising souls bought up the names of most of the Fortune 500 corporations. Then a few of the corporations went to court and the rule was developed that if a company had a trademark for a name, that company could stop someone else from using it if the other person did not have a trademark. More recently, Congress made it illegal for cybersquatters to register the names of famous persons and companies. Once you have a valid trademark, you will be safe using it for your domain name.

In recent years, several new top-level domains (TLDs) have been created. Top-level domains are the last letters of the URL (uniform resource locator), such as ".com," ".org," and ".net." Now you can also register names with the following TLDs.

.biz	.pro
.cc	.aero
.info	.coop
.name	.museum

One of the best places to register a domain name is **www.registerfly.com**. If your name is taken, they automatically suggest related names that might work for you, and their registration fees are lower than most other sites.

To find out if a domain name is available, go to **www.whois.net**.

TRADEMARKS

As your business builds goodwill, its name will become more valuable and you will want to protect it from others who may wish to copy it. To protect a name used to describe your goods or services, you can register it as a trademark (for goods) or a service mark (for services) with either the Illinois secretary of state or with the United States Patent and Trademark Office.

You cannot obtain a trademark for the name of your business, but you can trademark the name you use on your goods and services. In most cases, you use your company name on your goods as your trademark. In effect, it protects your company name. Another way to protect your company name is to incorporate, because a particular corporate name can only be registered by one company in Illinois.

State registration is useful if you only expect to use your trademark within the state of Illinois. Federal registration protects your mark anywhere in the country. The registration of a mark gives you exclusive use of the mark for the types of goods for which it is registered. The only exception is those who have already been using the mark— you cannot stop people who have been using the mark prior to your registration. It is much cheaper to register with the secretary of state, and the protection provided is adequate within the state.

Illinois Registration

The procedure for state registration is simple and costs only $10. First, you should write to the secretary of state's office to ask them to search your name and tell you if it is available.

Secretary of State
Department of Business Services—Trademarks
501 South 2nd Street
Room 328
Springfield, IL 62756
217-782-6961

Before a mark can be registered, it must be used in Illinois. For goods, it must be used on the goods themselves or on containers, tags, labels, or displays of the goods. For services, it must be used in the sale or advertising of the services. The use must be in an actual transaction with a customer. A sample mailed to a friend is not considered an acceptable use.

The $10 fee will register the mark in only one class of goods. If the mark is used on more than one class of goods, a separate registration must be filed. The registration is good for ten years. Six months prior to its expiration it must be renewed. The renewal fee is $5 for each class of goods.

A sample **TRADEMARK OR SERVICEMARK APPLICATION** is in Appendix C and a blank copy in Appendix D. (see form 3, p.233.) You can also get information and forms from the Illinois secretary of state's office. Visit the website at **www.cyberdriveillinois.com/departments/ business_services/publications_and_forms/trademrk.html**, or write one of their offices:

Springfield Office:
Howlett Building
Room 328
Springfield, IL 62756
Hours: M–F 8:00 a.m.–4:30 p.m.

Chicago Office:
69 West Washington
Suite 1240
Chicago, IL 60602
Hours: M–F 8:00 a.m.–5:00 p.m.

Federal Registration

For federal registration, the procedure is a little more complicated. There are two types of applications, depending on whether you have already made *actual use* of the mark or whether you merely have an *intention to use* the mark in the future.

For a trademark that has been in use, you must file an application form along with specimens showing actual use and a drawing of the mark that complies with all of the rules of the United States Patent and Trademark Office.

For an intent to use application, you must file two separate forms: one when you make the initial application and the other after you have made actual use of the mark, along with the specimens and drawing.

Before a mark can be entitled to federal registration, the use of the mark must be in *interstate commerce*, or in commerce with another country. The fee for registration is $375 ($325 if filing electronically), but if you file an intent to use application, there is a second fee of $100 for the filing after actual use.

Preparing a Business Plan

Not everyone needs a business plan to start a business, but if you have one it might help you avoid mistakes and make better decisions. For example, if you think it would be a great idea to start a candle shop in a little seaside resort, you might find out after preparing a business plan that, considering the number of people who might stop by, you could never sell enough candles to pay the rent.

A business plan lets you look at the costs, expenses, and potential sales, and see whether or not your plan can be profitable. It also allows you to find alternatives that might be more profitable. In the candle shop example, you might find that if you chose a more populous location or if you sold something else in addition to the candles, you would be more likely to make a profit.

ADVANTAGES AND DISADVANTAGES OF A BUSINESS PLAN

If your idea is truly unusual, a business plan may discourage you from starting your business. A business idea might look like a failure on paper, but if in your gut you know it would work, it might be worth trying without a business plan.

Example:

When Chester Carlson invented the first photocopy machine, he went to IBM. They spent $50,000 to analyze the idea and concluded that nobody needed a photocopy machine because people already had carbon paper—which was cheaper. However, he believed in his machine and started Xerox Corporation, which became one of the biggest and hottest companies of its time.

However, even with a great concept, you need to at least do some basic calculations to see if the business can make a profit.

- If you want to start a retail shop, figure out how many people are close enough to become customers and how many other stores will be competing for those customers. Visit some of those other shops and see how busy they are. Without giving away your plans to compete, ask some general questions like "how's business?" and maybe they will share their frustrations or successes.

- Whether you sell a good or a service, do the math to find out how much profit is in it. For example, if you plan to start a house painting company, find out what you will have to pay to hire painters, what it will cost you for all of the insurance, what bonding and licensing you will need, and what the advertising will cost you. Figure out how many jobs you can do per month and what other painters are charging. In some industries, in different areas of the state there may be a large margin of profit, while in other areas there may be almost no profit.

- Find out if there is a demand for your product or service. Suppose you have designed a beautiful new kind of candle and your friends all say you should open a shop because "everyone will want them." Before making a hundred of them and renting a store, bring a few to craft shows or flea markets and see what happens.

- Figure out what the income and expenses would be for a typical month of your new business. List monthly expenses, such as rent, salaries, utilities, insurance, taxes, supplies, advertising, services, and other overhead. Then, figure out how much profit you will average from each sale. Next, figure out how many sales you will need to cover your overhead and divide by the number of business days in the month. Can you reasonably expect that many sales? How will you get those sales?

Most types of businesses have trade associations, which often have figures on how profitable its members are. Some even have start-up kits for people wanting to start businesses. One good source of information on such organizations is the *Encyclopedia of Associations* published by Gale Research Inc., available in many library reference sections. Suppliers of products to the trade often give assistance to small companies getting started, to win their loyalty. Contact the largest suppliers of the products your business will be using and see if they can be of help.

OUTLINE FOR YOUR BUSINESS PLAN

While you may believe that you do not need a business plan, conventional wisdom says you do and it only makes good business sense to have one. A typical business plan has sections that cover topics such as the following:

- executive summary;

- product or service;

- market;

- competition;

- marketing plan;

- production plan;

- organizational plan;

- financial projections;

✪   management team; and,

✪   risks.

The following is an explanation of each.

Executive Summary   The executive summary is an overview of what the business will be and why it is expected to be successful. If the business plan will be used to lure investors, this section is the most important, since many might not read any further if they are not impressed with the summary.

Product or Service   This is a detailed description of what you will be selling. You should describe what is different about it and why people would need it or want it.

Market   The market section should analyze who the potential buyers of your product or service are. Describe both the physical location of the customers and their demographics. For example, a bodybuilding gym would probably mostly appeal to males in the 18 to 40 age bracket in a ten to twenty mile radius, depending on the location.

If you will sell things from a retail shop, you might also want to sell from mail order catalogs or over the Internet if your local customer base would not be large enough to support the business. Describe what you will be doing for those ventures.

If you are manufacturing things, you should find out who the wholesalers and distributors are, and their terms. This information should also be included in this section.

Competition   Before opening your business, you should know who and where your competitors are. If you are opening an antique shop, you might want to be near other antique shops so more customers come by your place, since antiques are unique and do not really compete with other antiques. However, if you open a florist shop, you probably do not want to be near other florist shops, since most florists sell similar products and a new shop would just dilute the customer base.

If you have a truly unique way of selling something, you might want to go near other similar businesses to grab their existing customer base and expand your market share. However, if they could easily copy your idea, you might not take away the business for long and end up diluting the market for each business. (see Chapter 6.)

Marketing Plan

Many a business has closed just a few months after opening because not enough customers showed up. How do you expect customers to find out about your business? Even if you get a nice write-up in the local paper, not everyone reads the paper, many people do not read every page, and lots of people forget what they read.

Your marketing plan describes how you will advertise your business. List how much the advertising will cost, and describe how you expect people to respond to the advertising.

Production Plan

The production plan needs to address and answer questions such as the following.

- If you are manufacturing a product, do you know how you will be able to produce a large quantity of them?

- Do you know all the costs and the possible production problems that could come up?

- If Wal-Mart orders 100,000 of them, could you get them made in a reasonable time?

The production plan needs to anticipate the normal schedule you intend to use, as well as how to handle any changes, positive or negative, to that schedule.

If you are selling a service and will need employees to perform those services, your production plan should explain how you will recruit and train those employees.

Organizational Plan

If your business will be more than a mom-and-pop operation, what will the organizational plan be? How many employees will you need and who will supervise whom? How much of the work will be done by employees and how much will be hired out to other businesses and independent contractors? Will you have a sales force? Will you need manufacturing employees? Will your accounting, website maintenance, and office cleaning and maintenance be contracted out or done by employees?

Financial Projections

Tying all the previously discussed topics together is what your financial plan will discuss. You should know how much rent, utilities, insurance, taxes, marketing, and product costs or wages for labor will cost you for the first year. Besides listing known, expected expenses, you should calculate your financial well-being under a number of different possible scenarios. Some of the questions to think about and answer will be: how long would you be in business if you have very few customers the first few months, and, if Wal-Mart does order 100,000 of your products, could you afford to manufacture them, knowing you won't be paid for months?

Management Team

If you will be seeking outside funding, you will need to list the experience and skills of the management of the business. Investors want to know that the people have experience and know what they are doing.

Risks

A good business plan weighs all the risks of the new enterprise. Is new technology in the works that will make the business obsolete? Would a rise in the price of a particular needed supply eliminate all your profits? What are the chances of a new competitor entering the market if you show some success, and what are you going to do about it? Part of your analysis should be to look at all of the possible things that could happen in the field you chose and to gauge the likelihood of success.

Gathering Information

Some of the sections of your business plan require a lot of research. People sometimes take years to prepare them. Today, the Internet puts a nearly infinite amount of information at your fingertips, but you might also want to do some personal research.

Sometimes the best way to get the feel for a business is to get a job in a similar business. At a minimum, you should visit similar businesses and perhaps sit outside of one, and see how many customers they have and how much business they do. There are start-up guides for many types of businesses, which can be found at Amazon.com, as well as your local bookstores and library. Your local chamber of commerce, business development office, or SCORE office might also have materials to help your research.

SAMPLE BUSINESS PLAN

The following plan is one for a simple, one-person business that will use its owner's assets to start. Of course, a larger business, or one that needs financing, will need a much longer and more detailed plan.

A website with sixty sample business plans and information on business plan software is **www.bplans.com**.

Executive Summary

This is the plan for a new business, Reardon Computer Repair, LLC by Henry Reardon, to be started locally and then expanded throughout the state and perhaps further if results indicate this is feasible.

The mission of Reardon Computer Repair (RCR) is to offer fast, affordable repairs to office and home computers. The objective is to become profitable within the first three months and to grow at a quick but manageable pace.

In order to offer customers the quickest service, RCR will rely on youthful computer whizzes who are students and have the time and expertise to provide the service. They will also have the flexibility to arrive quickly and the motivation to show off their expertise.

To reach customers, we will use limited advertising, but primarily the Internet and word of mouth from happy customers.

With nearly every business and family having several computers and lack of fast service currently available, it is expected this business could be successful quickly and could grow rapidly.

Product or Service

The company will offer computer repair services both at its shop and at customers' offices and homes. It will sell computer parts as necessary to complete the repairs and it will also carry upgrades, accessories, and peripherals, which will most likely be of value to customers needing repairs.

Market

The market would be nearly every business and family at every address in the city, state, and country, since today nearly everyone has a computer. Figures show nearly 250 million computers in use in America, and that number is expected to grow to over 300 million in five years.

The market for the initial shop would be a fifteen-mile radius, which is a reasonable driving distance for our employees. The population in that area is 300,000, people which would mean 240,000 potential customers, based on the current level of 800 computers per 1,000 people.

The market would not include new computers, which typically come with a one-year guarantee. It would also not include people who bought extended guarantees.

The growth trend for the industry is 8–10% for the next decade.

Competition

The competition would be the authorized repair shops working with the computer manufacturers. While these have the advantage of being authorized, research and experience has shown that they are slow and do not meet customers' need for an immediate repair.

There is one computer repair shop within a ten-mile radius of the proposed shop and two more within a twenty-five-mile radius. Average wait time for a dropped off repair is one week. The two closest repair services offer no on-site repair. Shipping a computer to a dealer for repair takes one to two weeks. Most customers need their computer fixed within a day or two.

One potential source for competition would be from employees or former employees who are asked to work for customers "on the side" at a reduced rate. To discourage this, the company will have a contract with employees with a non-compete agreement that specifies that they will pay the company three times what they earn. Also, agreements with customers will include a clause that they have the option to hire away one of our employees for a one-time $2,000 fee.

Marketing Plan

The business will be marketed through networking, Internet marketing, advertising, and creative marketing.

Networking will be through the owner's contacts and local computer clubs and software stores. Some local retailers do not offer service and they have already indicated that they would promote a local business that could offer fast repairs.

A website would be linked to local businesses and community groups, and to major computer repair referral sites.

Advertising would include the Yellow Pages and local computer club newsletters. Studies have shown that newspaper and television advertising would be too expensive and not cost effective for this type of business.

Creative advertising would include vinyl lettering on the back window of owner's vehicle.

Production Plan

The company will be selling the services of computer technicians and computer parts. The owner will supply most of the services in the beginning and then add student technicians as needed.

The parts will all be purchased ready-made from the manufacturers, except for cables, which can be made on an as-needed basis much cheaper than ready-made ones.

Employees

The employees will be students who are extremely knowledgeable about computers. Some would call them computer "geeks"—in a nice way. They have extensive knowledge of the workings of computers, have lots of free time, need money, and would love to show off how knowledgeable they are.

As students, they already have health insurance and do not need full-time work. They would be available as needed. The company would pay them $12 an hour plus mileage, which is more than any other jobs available to students, but is not cost prohibitive, considering the charge to customers of $50 per hour.

Financial Projections

The minimum charge for a service call will be $75 on-site and $50 in-shop, which will include one hour of service. The parts markup will be the industry standard of 20%. The average customer bill will be estimated to be $100 including labor and markup.

The labor cost is estimated to be $30 per call including time, taxes, insurance, and mileage. The owner will be estimated to handle 75% of the work the first six months and 50% the second six months.

Rent, utilities, insurance, taxes, and other fixed costs is estimated to be $3,000 per month.

Advertising and promotion expenses are expected to be $3,000 per month.

Estimated number of customers will be:

First three months:	10 per week
Second three months:	20 per week
Third three months:	35 per week
Fourth three months:	50 per week

Estimated monthly revenue:

First three months:	$4,000
Second three months:	$8,000
Third three months:	$14,000
Fourth three months:	$20,000

Monthly income and expense projection:
First three months:

Income	$4,000
Labor	$300
Fixed costs	$3,000
Advertising	$3,000
Net	$2,300 loss per month

Second three months:

Income	$8,000
Labor	$600
Fixed costs	$3,000
Advertising	$3,000
Net	$1,400 profit per month

Third three months:

Income	$14,000
Labor	$2,100
Fixed costs	$3,000
Advertising	$3,000
Net	$5,900 profit per month

Fourth three months:

Income	$20,000
Labor	$3,000
Fixed costs	$3,000
Advertising	$3,000
Net	$11,000 profit per month

Organization Plan

The business will start with the owner, Henry Reardon, and three students who are experts at computer repair and available as part time workers on an as-needed basis.

The owner will manage the business and do as many repairs as are possible with the time remaining in the week.

One of the students, Peter Galt, will work after school in the shop, and the others, Dom Roark and Howard Taggert, are willing to work on an on-call basis, either at the shop or at customers' homes.

As business grows, the company will recruit more student employees through the school job placement offices and at computer clubs.

Management Team

The owner, Henry Reardon, will be the sole manager of the company. He will use the accounting services of his accountant, Dave Burton.

The owner anticipates being able to supervise up to ten employees. When there are more than ten, the company will need a manager to take over scheduling and some of other management functions.

Risks

Because the business does not require a lot of capital, there will be a low financial risk in the beginning. The biggest reason for failure would be an inability to get the word out that the company exists and can fill a need when it arises. For this reason, the most important task in the beginning will be marketing and promotion.

As the company grows, the risk will be that computers will need fewer repairs, become harder to repair, and become so cheap they are disposable. To guard against this possibility, the company will add computer consulting services as it grows so that it will always have something to offer computer owners.

Financing Your Business

The way to finance your business is determined by how fast you want your business to grow and how much risk of failure you are able to handle. Letting the business grow with its own income is the slowest but safest way to grow. Taking out a personal loan against your house to expand quickly is the fastest but riskiest way to grow.

GROWING WITH PROFITS

Many successful businesses have started out with little money and used the profits to grow bigger and bigger. If you have another source of income to live on (such as a job or a spouse's job), you can plow all the income of your fledgling business into growth.

Some businesses start as hobbies or part-time ventures on the weekend while the entrepreneur holds down a full-time job. Many types of goods or service businesses can start this way. Even some multimillion dollar corporations, such as Apple Computer, started out this way.

This allows you to test your idea with little risk. If you find you are not good at running that type of business, or the time or location was not right for your idea, all you are out is the time you spent and your start-up capital.

However, a business can only grow so big from its own income. In many cases, as a business grows, it gets to a point where the orders are so big that money must be borrowed to produce the product to fill them. With this kind of order, there is the risk that if the customer cannot pay or goes bankrupt, the business will also go under. At such a point, a business owner should investigate the creditworthiness of the customer and weigh the risks. Some businesses have grown rapidly, some have gone under, and others have decided not to take the risk and stayed small. You can worry about that down the road.

USING YOUR SAVINGS

If you have savings you can tap to get your business started, that is the best source. You will not have to pay high interest rates and you will not have to worry about paying someone back. This section discusses some options for using your own savings to start your business, and potential pitfalls for each.

Home Equity

If you have owned your home for several years, it is possible that the equity has grown substantially and you can get a second mortgage to finance your business. If you have been in the home for many years and have a good record of paying your bills, some lenders will make second mortgages that exceed the equity. Just remember, if your business fails, you may lose your house.

Retirement Accounts

Be careful about borrowing from your retirement savings. There are tax penalties for borrowing from or against certain types of retirement accounts. Also, your future financial security may be lost if your business does not succeed.

Having too much Money

It probably does not seem possible to have too much money with which to start a business, but many businesses have failed for that reason. With plenty of start-up capital available, a business owner does not need to watch expenses and can become wasteful. Employees get used to lavish spending. Once the money runs out and the business must run on its own earnings, it fails.

Starting with the bare minimum forces a business to watch its expenses and be frugal. It necessitates finding the least expensive solutions to problems that crop up and creative ways to be productive.

BORROWING MONEY

It is extremely tempting to look to others to get the money to start a business. The risk of failure is less worrisome and the pressure is lower, but that is a problem with borrowing. If it is others' money, you do not have quite the same incentive to succeed as you do if everything you own is on the line.

Actually, you should be even more concerned when using the money of others. Your reputation is at risk, and if you do not succeed, you probably will still have to pay back the loan.

Family

Depending on how much money your family can spare, it may be the most comfortable or most uncomfortable source of funds for you. If you have been assured a large inheritance and your parents have more funds than they need to live on, you may be able to borrow against your inheritance without worry. It will be your money anyway, and you need it much more now than you will ten or twenty years from now. If you lose it all, it is your own loss.

However, if you are asking your widowed mother to cash in a CD she lives on to finance your get-rich-quick scheme, you should have second thoughts about it. Stop and consider all the real reasons your business might not take off and what your mother would do without the income.

Friends

Borrowing from friends is like borrowing from family members. If you know they have the funds available and could survive a loss, you may want to risk it, but if they would be loaning you their only resources, do not chance it.

Financial problems can be the worst thing for a relationship, whether it is a casual friendship or a long-term romantic involvement. Before you borrow from a friend, try to imagine what would happen if you could not pay it back and how you would feel if it caused the end of your relationship.

The ideal situation is if your friend were a co-venturer in your business, so the burden would not be totally on you to see how the funds were spent. Still, realize that such a venture will put extra strain on the relationship.

Banks   In a way, a bank can be a more comfortable party from which to borrow, because you do not have a personal relationship with them as you do with a friend or family member. If you fail, they will write your loan off rather than disown you. However, a bank can also be the least comfortable party to borrow from because they will demand realistic projections (your business plan) and be on top of you to perform. If you do not meet their expectations, they may call your loan just when you need it most.

The best thing about a bank loan is that they will require you to do your homework. You must have plans that make sense to a banker. If they approve your loan, you know that your plans are at least reasonable.

Bank loans are not cheap or easy. You will be paying a good interest rate, and you will have to put up collateral. If your business does not have equipment or receivables, the bank may require you to put up your house and other personal property to guarantee the loan.

Banks are a little easier to deal with when you get a Small Business Administration (SBA) loan. That is because the SBA guarantees that it will pay the bank if you default on the loan. These loans are obtained through local bank branches.

Credit Cards   Borrowing against a credit card is one of the fastest growing ways of financing a business, but it can be one of the most expensive ways. The rates can go higher than 20%, although many cards offer lower rates. Some people are able to get numerous cards. Some successful businesses have used credit cards to get off the ground or to weather through a cash crunch, but if the business does not begin to generate the cash to make the payments, you could soon end up in bankruptcy. A good strategy is to only use credit cards for a long-term asset, like a computer, or for something that will quickly generate cash, like buying inventory to fill an order. Do not use credit cards to pay expenses that are not generating revenue.

GETTING A RICH PARTNER

One of the best business combinations is a young entrepreneur with ideas and ambition, and a retired investor with business experience and money. Together, they can supply everything the business needs.

How to find such a partner? Be creative. You should have investigated the business you are starting and know others who have been in such businesses. Have any of them had partners retire over the last few years? Are any of the partners planning to phase out of the business?

SELLING SHARES OF YOUR BUSINESS

Silent investors are the best source of capital for your business. You retain full control of the business, and if it happens to fail, you have no obligation to them. Unfortunately, few silent investors are interested in a new business. It is only after you have proven your concept to be successful and built up a rather large enterprise that you will be able to attract such investors.

The most common way to obtain money from investors is to issue stock to them. For this, the best type of business entity is the corporation. It gives you almost unlimited flexibility in the number and kinds of shares of stock you can issue.

UNDERSTANDING SECURITIES LAWS

There is one major problem with selling stock in your business, and that is all of the federal and state regulations with which you must comply. Both the state and federal governments have long and complicated laws dealing with the sales of securities. There are also hundreds of court cases attempting to explain what these laws mean. A thorough explanation of this area of law is obviously beyond the scope of this book.

Basically, securities have been held to exist in any case in which a person provides money to someone with the expectation that he or she will get a profit through the efforts of that person. This can apply to any situation where someone buys stock in, or makes a loan to, your business. What the laws require is disclosure of the risks involved, and in some cases, registration of the securities with the government. There are some exemptions, such as for small amounts of money and for limited numbers of investors.

Penalties for violation of securities laws are severe, including triple damages and prison terms. You should consult a specialist in securities laws before issuing any security. You can often get an introductory consultation at a reasonable rate to learn your options.

USING THE INTERNET TO FIND CAPITAL

The Internet can also be a great resource for finding and marketing to investors. However, before attempting to market your company's shares on the Internet, be sure to get an opinion from a securities lawyer or do some serious research into securities law. The immediate accessibility of the Internet makes it very easy for you to get ahead of yourself and unintentionally violate state and federal securities laws. The Internet contains a wealth of information that can be useful in finding sources of capital. The following sites may be helpful.

America's Business Funding Directory
www.businessfinance.com

Small Business Administration
www.sba.gov

Inc. Magazine
www.inc.com

NVST
www.nvst.com

The Capital Network
www.thecapitalnetwork.com

Locating Your Business

The right location for your business will be determined by what type of business it is and how fast you expect it to grow. For some types of businesses, the location will not be important to your success or failure—in others, it will be crucial.

WORKING OUT OF YOUR HOME

Many small businesses get started out of the home. Chapter 7 discusses the legalities of home businesses. This section discusses the practicalities.

Starting a business out of your home can save you the rent, electricity, insurance, and other costs of setting up at another location. For some people this is ideal, and they can combine their home and work duties easily and efficiently. For other people it is a disaster. A spouse, children, neighbors, television, and household chores can be so distracting that no other work gets done.

Since residential rates are usually lower than business lines, many people use their residential telephone line or add a second residential line to conduct business. However, if you wish to be listed in the

Yellow Pages, you will need to have a business line in your home. If you are running two or more types of businesses, you can probably add their names as additional listings on the original number and avoid paying for another business line.

You also should consider whether the type of business you are starting is compatible with a home office. For example, if your business mostly consists of calling clients, then the home may be an ideal place to run it. If your clients need to visit you, or you will need daily pickups and deliveries by truck, then the home may not be a good location. This is discussed in more detail in the next chapter.

CHOOSING A RETAIL SITE

For most types of retail stores the location is of prime importance. Things to consider include how close it is to your potential customers, how visible it is to the public, and how easily accessible it is to both autos and pedestrians. The attractiveness and safety of the site should also be considered.

Location would be less important for a business that was the only one of its kind in the area. For example, if there was only one moped parts dealer or Armenian restaurant in a metropolitan area, people would have to come to wherever you are if they want your products or services. However, even with such businesses, keep in mind that there is competition. People who want moped parts can order them by mail and restaurant customers can choose another type of cuisine.

You should look up all the businesses similar to the one you plan to run in the phone book and mark them on a map. For some businesses, like a cleaners, you would want to be far from the others. However, for other businesses, like antique stores, you would want to be near the others. (Antique stores usually do not carry the same things, they do not compete, and people like to go to an antique district and visit all the shops.)

CHOOSING OFFICE, MANUFACTURING, OR WAREHOUSE SPACE

If your business will be the type where customers will not come to you, then locating it near customers is not as much of a concern, and you can probably save money by locating away from the high-traffic, central business districts. However, you should consider the convenience for employees, and not locate in an area that would be unattractive to them or too far from where they would likely live.

For manufacturing or warehouse operations, you should consider your proximity to a post office, trucking company, or rail line. When several sites are available, you might consider which one has the earliest or most convenient pickup schedule for the carriers you plan to use.

LEASING A SITE

A lease of space can be one of the biggest expenses of a small business, so you should do a lot of homework before signing one. There are a lot of terms in a commercial lease that can make or break your business. The most critical terms are discussed in the following pages.

Zoning Before signing a lease, you should be sure that everything that your business will need to do is allowed by the zoning of the property. Check the city and county zoning regulations.

Restrictions In some shopping centers, existing tenants have guarantees that other tenants do not compete with them. For example, if you plan to open a restaurant and bakery, you may be forbidden to sell carryout baked goods if the supermarket next door has a bakery and a noncompete clause.

Signs Business signs are regulated by zoning laws, sign laws, and property restrictions. If you rent a hidden location with no possibility for adequate signage, your chances for success are less than with a more visible site or much larger sign.

ADA Compliance The *Americans with Disabilities Act* (ADA) requires that reasonable accommodations be made to make businesses accessible to the disabled. When a business is remodeled, many more changes are required than if no remodeling is done. Be sure that the space you rent complies with the law, or that the landlord will be responsible for compliance. Be aware of the full costs you will bear.

Expansion   As your business grows, you may need to expand your space. The time to find out about your options is before you sign the lease. Perhaps you can take over adjoining units when those leases expire.

Renewal   Location is a key to success for some businesses. If you spend five years building up a clientele, you do not want someone to take over your locale at the end of your lease. Therefore, you should have a renewal clause on your lease. Usually, this allows an increase in rent based on inflation.

Guarantee   Most landlords of commercial space will not rent to a small corporation without a personal guarantee of the lease. This is a very risky thing for a new business owner to do. The lifetime rent on a long-term commercial lease can be hundreds of thousands of dollars, and if your business fails, the last thing you want to do is be personally responsible for five years of rent.

Where space is scarce or a location is hot, a landlord can get the guarantees he or she demands, and there is nothing you can do about it (except perhaps set up an asset protection plan ahead of time). However, where several units are vacant or the commercial rental market is soft, often you can negotiate out of the personal guarantee. If the lease is five years, maybe you can get away with a guarantee of just the first year.

Duty to Open   Some shopping centers have rules requiring all shops to be open certain hours. If you cannot afford to staff it the whole time required, or if you have religious or other reasons that make this a problem, you should negotiate it out of the lease or find another location.

Sublease   At some point, you may decide to sell your business, and in many cases the location is the most valuable aspect of it. For this reason, you should be sure that you have the right to either assign your lease or to sublease the property. If this is impossible, one way around a prohibition is to incorporate your business before signing the lease, and then when you sell the business, sell the stock. However, some lease clauses prohibit transfer of any interest in the business, so read the lease carefully.

BUYING A SITE

If you are experienced with owning rental property, you will probably be more inclined to buy a site for your business. If you have no experience with real estate, you should probably rent and not take on the extra cost and responsibility of property ownership.

One reason to buy your site is that you can build up equity. Rather than pay rent to a landlord, you can pay off a mortgage and eventually own the property.

Separating the Ownership

One risk in buying a business site is that if the business gets into financial trouble, the creditors may go after the building as well. For this reason, most people who buy a site for their business keep the ownership out of the business. For example, the business will be a corporation and the real estate will be owned personally by the owner or by a trust unrelated to the business.

Expansion

Before buying a site, you should consider the growth potential of your business. If it grows quickly, will you be able to expand at that site or will you have to move? Might the property next door be available for sale in the future if you need it? Can you get an option on it?

If the site is a good investment whether or not you have your business, then by all means buy it. However, if its main use is for your business, think twice.

Zoning

Some of the concerns when buying a site are the same as when renting. You will want to make sure that the zoning permits the type of business you wish to start, or that you can get a variance without a large expense or delay. Be aware that just because a business is now using the site does not mean that you can expand or remodel the business at that site. Check with the zoning department of your local government and find out exactly what is allowed.

Signs

Signs are another concern. Some cities have regulated signs and do not allow new or larger ones. Some businesses have used these laws to get publicity. A car dealer who was told to take down a large number of American flags on his lot filed a federal lawsuit and rallied the community behind him.

**ADA
Compliance**

Compliance with the ADA is another concern when buying a commercial building. Find out from the building department if the building is in compliance or what needs to be done to put it in compliance. If you remodel, the requirements may be more strict.

NOTE: *When dealing with public officials, keep in mind that they do not always know what the law is, or do not accurately explain it. They occasionally try to intimidate people into doing things that are not required by law. Read the requirements yourself and question the officials if they seem to be interpreting it incorrectly. Seek legal advice if officials refuse to reexamine the law or move away from an erroneous position.*

Also, consider that keeping them happy may be worth the price. If you are already doing something they have overlooked, do not make a big deal over a little thing they want changed, or they may subject you to a full inspection or audit.

CHECKING GOVERNMENTAL REGULATIONS

When looking for a site for your business, you should investigate the different governmental regulations in your area. For example, a location just outside the city or county limits might have a lower licensing fee, a lower sales tax rate, and less strict sign requirements.

Licensing Your Business

The federal, state, and local governments have an interest in protecting consumers from bad business practices. In order to ensure that consumers are protected from unscrupulous business people and to require a minimum level of service to the public, the federal, state, and local governments have developed hundreds of licensing requirements that cover occupations and services ranging from attorneys to barbers to day care providers and hundreds of others.

OCCUPATIONAL LICENSES AND ZONING

Before opening your business, you are supposed to obtain a county occupational license. If you are working in a city, you will need a city occupational license. Businesses that do work in several cities, such as builders, must obtain a license from each city in which they work. This does not have to be done until you actually begin a job in a particular city.

County occupational licenses usually can be obtained from the tax collector in the county administration building. City licenses are usually available at city hall. Be sure to find out if zoning allows your type of business before buying or leasing property, because the licensing departments will check the zoning before issuing your license.

If you will be preparing or serving food, you will need to check with the local health department to be sure the premises complies with health regulations. In some areas, if food has been served on the premises in the past, there is no problem getting a license. If food has never been served on the premises, the property must comply with all the newest regulations. Compliance can be very costly.

Home Businesses

Problems occasionally arise when people attempt to start a business in their homes. A small new business cannot afford to pay rent for commercial space and cities often try to forbid businesses in residential areas. Getting a county occupational license or advertising a fictitious name often gives notice to the city that a business is being conducted in a residential area.

Some people avoid the problem by starting their businesses without occupational licenses, figuring that the penalties are less expensive than the cost of office space. Others get the county license and ignore the city rules. If a person has commercial trucks and equipment all over his or her property, there will probably be complaints from neighbors and the city may take legal action. However, if a person's business consists merely of making phone calls out of the home and keeping supplies there, it may never become an issue.

If a problem does arise regarding a home business that does not disturb the neighbors, a good argument can be made that the zoning law that prohibits the business is unconstitutional. However, court battles with a city are expensive and probably not worth the effort for a small business. The best course of action is to keep a low profile. Using a post office box is sometimes helpful in diverting attention away from the residence.

STATE-REGULATED PROFESSIONS

Many professionals require special state licenses. You will probably be called upon to produce such a license when applying for an occupational license.

If you are in a regulated profession, be aware of the laws that apply to your profession. The following pages contain a list of professions and the state laws and regulations covering them. You can make copies of these laws at your local public library or court law library. If you do not think your profession is regulated, you should read through the list anyway. Some of those included may surprise you.

The following citations are to the Illinois Compiled Statutes (ILCS) and the Illinois Administrative Code (Ill. Admin. Code).

Profession/Activity	Statute Section
Accountancy	225 ILCS 450; Ill. Admin. Code Chapter 68, Section 1420.10
Aircraft, Pilots, and Airports	620 ILCS 5
Architecture and Structural Engineering	225 ILCS 305, 340
Attorneys	705 ILCS 205
Art Auction House	225 ILCS 405
Auctioneers	225 ILCS 407
Barbering	225 ILCS 410; Ill. Admin. Code Title 68, Section 1175.100
Cemeteries	760 ILCS 100/8
Chiropractic	225 ILCS 60
Clinical Social Workers	225 ILCS 20; Ill. Admin. Code Title 68, Section 1470.5
Cosmetology	225 ILCS 410; Ill. Admin. Code Title 68, Section 1175.100
Counseling and Psychotherapy	225 ILCS 15, 107; Ill. Admin. Code Title 68 , Section 1400.10
Day Care	225 ILCS 10/4; Ill. Admin. Code Title 89, Section 377.1
Dentistry	225 ILCS 25; Ill. Admin. Code Title 68, Section 1220.110
Detective Agencies	225 ILCS 447
Driving Schools	625 ILCS 5/6-401
Electrical Contracting	65 ILCS 5/11-33-1
Employment Agencies	225 ILCS 515; 68 Ill. Admin. Code Title, Section 680.100
Engineering	225 ILCS 325; Ill. Admin. Code Title 68, Section 1380.210
Financial Planning	205 ILCS 665
Funeral Directing and Embalming	225 ILCS 41
Health Testing Services	210 ILCS 25

Hearing Aid Sales	225 ILCS 50; Ill. Admin. Code Title 77, Section 3000.10
Interior Design	225 ILCS 310
Investigative Services	225 ILCS 447; Ill. Admin. Code Title 68, Section 1240.5
Land Surveying	225 ILCS 330; Ill. Admin. Code Title 68, Section 1270.10
Landscape Architects	225 ILCS 315; Ill. Admin. Code Title 68, Section 1275.60
Massage Practice	225 ILCS 57
Mortgage Brokers	205 ILCS 635
Nursing	225 ILCS 65; Ill. Admin. Code Title 68, Section 1300.10
Nursing Homes	225 ILCS 70; Ill. Admin. Code Title 68, Section 1310.20
Occupational Therapists	225 ILCS 75; Ill. Admin. Code Title 68, Section 1315.90
Optometry	225 ILCS 80; Ill. Admin. Code Title 68, Section 1320.20
Osteopathy	225 ILCS 60
Outdoor Advertising	225 ILCS 440
Pest Control	415 ILCS 60/10
Pharmacy	225 ILCS 85, 120; Ill. Admin. Code Title 68, Section 1330.10
Physical Therapy	225 ILCS 90; Ill. Admin. Code Title 68, Section 1340.20
Physicians	225 ILCS 60; Ill. Admin. Code Title 68, Section 1285.20
Plumbing	225 ILCS 320
Podiatry	225 ILCS 100; Ill. Admin. Code Title 68, Section 1360.10
Radiologic Technologists	420 ILCS 40/6
Real Estate Brokerage, Sales and Schools	225 ILCS 454; Ill. Admin. Code Title 68, Section 1450.10
Roofing	225 ILCS 335; Ill. Admin. Code Title 68, Section 1460.10
Speech Pathology and Audiology	225 ILCS 110; Ill. Admin. Code Title 68, Section 1465.10
Vendors (Transient or Itinerant)	225 ILCS 465
Veterinary Medicine	225 ILCS 115; Ill. Admin. Code Title 68, Section 1500.5

FEDERAL LICENSES

Few businesses require federal registration. If you are in any of the types of businesses in the following list, you should check with the federal agency connected with it.

✪ Radio or television stations or manufacturers of equipment emitting radio waves:

Federal Communications Commission
445 12th Street, SW
Washington, DC 20554
www.fcc.gov

✪ Manufacturers of alcohol, tobacco, or firearms:

Bureau of Alcohol, Tobacco, Firearms, and Explosives
Office of Public and Governmental Affairs
650 Massachusetts Avenue, NW
Room 8290
Washington, DC 20226
www.atf.treas.gov

✪ Securities brokers and providers of investment advice:

Securities and Exchange Commission
100 F Street, NW
Washington, DC 20549
www.sec.gov

✪ Manufacturers of drugs and processors of meat:

Food and Drug Administration
5600 Fishers Lane
Rockville, MD 20857
www.fda.gov

✪   Interstate carriers:

Surface Transportation Board
1925 K Street, NW
Washington, DC 20423
www.stb.dot.gov

✪   Exporters:

Bureau of Industry and Security
Department of Commerce
14th Street & Constitution Avenue, NW
Washington, DC 20230
www.bis.doc.gov

Contract Laws

As a business owner, you will need to know the basics of forming a simple contract for your transactions with both customers and vendors. There is a lot of misunderstanding about what the law is, and people may give you erroneous information. Relying on it can cost you money. This chapter gives you a quick overview of the principles that apply to your transactions and the pitfalls to avoid. If you face more complicated contract questions, consult a law library or an attorney familiar with small business law.

TRADITIONAL CONTRACT LAW

One of the first things taught in law school is that a contract is not legal unless three elements are present: offer, acceptance, and consideration. The rest of the semester dissects exactly what may be a valid offer, acceptance, and consideration. For your purposes, the important things to remember are as follows.

   ✪   If you make an offer to someone, it may result in a binding contract, even if you change your mind or find out it was a bad deal for you.

○ Unless an offer is accepted and both parties agree to the same terms, there is no contract.

○ A contract does not always have to be in writing. Some laws require certain contracts to be in writing, but as a general rule, an oral contract is legal. The problem is in proving that the contract existed in the first place.

○ Without *consideration* (the exchange of something of value or mutual promises), there is not a valid contract.

Basic Contract Rules

The most important rules for the business owner are as follows.

○ *An advertisement is not an offer.* Suppose you put an ad in the newspaper offering "New IBM computers only $1995," but there is a typo in the ad and it says $19.95. Can people come in and say, "I accept, here's my $19.95," creating a legal contract? Fortunately, no. Courts have ruled that the ad is not an offer that a person can accept. It is an invitation to come in and make offers, which the business can accept or reject.

○ *The same rule applies to the price tag on an item.* If someone switches price tags on your merchandise, or if you accidentally put the wrong price on it, you are not required by law to sell it at that price. However, many merchants honor a mistaken price, because refusing to do so would constitute bad will and probably lose a customer. If you intentionally put a lower price on an item, intending to require a buyer to pay a higher price, you may be in violation of *bait and switch* laws.

○ *When a person makes an offer, several things may happen.* It may be accepted, creating a legal contract. It may be rejected. It may expire before it has been accepted. It may be withdrawn before acceptance. A contract may expire either by a date made in the offer ("This offer remains open until noon on January 29, 2008") or after a reasonable amount of time. What is *reasonable* is a legal question that a court must decide. If someone makes you an offer to sell goods, clearly you cannot come back five years later and accept. Can you accept a week later or a month later and create a legal contract? That depends on the type of goods and the circumstances.

- *A person accepting an offer cannot add any terms to it.* If you offer to sell a car for $1,000 and the other party says he or she accepts as long as you put new tires on it, there is no contract. An acceptance with changed terms is considered a rejection and a counteroffer.

- *When someone rejects your offer and makes a counteroffer, a contract can be created by your acceptance of the counteroffer.*

These rules can affect your business on a daily basis. Suppose you offer to sell something to one customer over the phone and five minutes later another customer walks in and offers you more for it. To protect yourself, you should call the first customer and withdraw your offer before accepting the offer of the second customer. If the first customer accepts before you have withdrawn your offer, you may be sued if you sell the item to the second customer.

Exceptions

There are a few exceptions to the basic rules of contracts. They are as follows.

- *Consent to a contract must be voluntary.* If it is made under a threat, the contract is not valid. If a business refuses to give a person's car back unless he or she pays $500 for changing the oil, the customer could probably sue and get the $500 back.

- *Contracts to do illegal acts or acts against public policy are not enforceable.* If an electrician signs a contract to put some wiring in a house that is not legal, the customer could probably not force him or her to do it, because the court would refuse to require an illegal act.

- *If either party to an offer dies, then the offer expires and cannot be accepted by the heirs.* If a painter is hired to paint a portrait and dies before completing it, his wife cannot finish it and require payment. However, a corporation does not die, even if its owners die. If a corporation is hired to build a house and the owner dies, his or her heirs may take over the corporation, finish the job, and require payment.

- ✪ *Contracts made under misrepresentation are not enforceable.* For example, if someone tells you a car has 35,000 miles on it and you later discover it has 135,000 miles, you may be able to rescind the contract for fraud and misrepresentation.

- ✪ *If there was a mutual mistake, a contract may be rescinded.* For example, if both you and the seller thought the car had 35,000 miles on it, the contract could be rescinded. However, if the seller knew the car had 135,000 miles on it, but you assumed it had 35,000 and did not ask, you probably could not rescind the contract.

STATUTORY CONTRACT LAW

The previous section discussed the basics of contract law, which are principles not stated in the statutes, but decided by judges hundreds of years ago. In recent times, the legislatures have made numerous exceptions to these principles, and in most cases, these laws have been passed when the legislature felt that traditional law was not fair. The important laws that affect contracts follow.

Statutes of Fraud

The *statutes of fraud* state when a contract must be in writing to be valid. Some people believe a contract is not valid unless it is in writing, but that is not true. Only those types of contracts mentioned in the statutes of fraud must be in writing. Of course, an oral contract is much harder to prove in court than a written one. In Illinois, some of the contracts that must be in writing are:

- ✪ agreements that take over one year to complete (740 ILCS 80/1);

- ✪ sales of any interest in real estate (740 ILCS 80/2);

- ✪ leases of real estate over one year (740 ILCS 80/2);

- ✪ guarantees of debts of another person (740 ILCS 80/1);

- ✪ sales of goods of over $500 (810 ILCS 5/2–201/1); and,

- ✪ sales of securities (740 ILCS 80/1).

Consumer Protection Laws

Due to the alleged unfair practices by some types of businesses, laws have been passed controlling the types of contracts they may use. Most notable among these are health clubs and door-to-door solicitations. The laws covering these businesses usually give the consumer a certain time to cancel the contract. These laws are described in Chapter 13.

PREPARING YOUR CONTRACTS

Before you open your business, you should obtain or prepare the contracts or policies you will use in your business. In some businesses, such as a restaurant, you will not need much. Perhaps you will want a sign near the entrance stating, "shirt and shoes required" or "diners must be seated by 10:30 p.m."

However, if you are a building contractor or a similar business, you will need detailed contracts to use with your customers. If you do not clearly spell out your rights and obligations, you may end up in court and lose thousands of dollars in profits.

The best way to have an effective contract is to have one prepared by an attorney who is experienced in the subject. However, since this may be too expensive for your new operation, you may want to go elsewhere. Three sources for the contracts you will need are other businesses like yours, trade associations, and legal form books. Obtain as many different contracts as possible, compare them, and decide which terms are most comfortable for you.

Insurance Laws

There are few laws requiring you to have insurance. However, if you do not have insurance, you may face liability that could ruin your business. You should be aware of the types of insurance available and weigh the risks of a loss against the cost of a policy.

Be aware that there can be a wide range of prices and coverage in insurance policies. You should get at least three quotes from different insurance agents and ask each one to explain the benefits of his or her policy.

WORKERS' COMPENSATION

Workers' compensation is a system of benefits provided by law to most workers who have job-related injuries or diseases. The amount of benefits is limited by law and paid without regard to fault. Almost every employee in Illinois is covered under this system.

The employer is responsible for providing benefits, and does so either directly or through an insurance company that administers the program for the employer. This insurance can be obtained from most insurance companies, and in many cases is not expensive. If you have such coverage, you are protected against potentially ruinous suits by employees or their heirs in case of accidents.

There are other requirements of the workers' compensation law, such as reporting any on-the-job death of a worker within twenty-four hours. Also, it is unlawful to deduct the amount of the premiums from the employee's wages.

This law has been subject to frequent change, so check with the Industrial Commission of Illinois for the latest requirements. Ask for the *Handbook on Workers' Compensation and Occupational Diseases*. Call 866-352-3033 or write:

Illinois Industrial Commission
701 South Second Street
Springfield, IL 62704
www.state.il.us/agency/iic

LIABILITY INSURANCE

In most cases, you are not required to carry liability insurance. Liability insurance can be divided into two main areas: coverage for injuries on your premises or by your employees, and coverage for injuries caused by your products.

Coverage for the first type of injury is usually very reasonably priced. Injuries in your business or by your employees (such as in an auto accident) are covered by standard premises or auto policies. However, coverage for injuries by products may be harder to find and more expensive.

If insurance is unavailable or unaffordable, you can go without and use a corporation and other asset protection devices to protect yourself from liability.

The best way to find out if insurance is available for your type of business is to check with other businesses. If there is a trade group for your industry, their newsletter or magazine may contain ads for insurers.

Umbrella Policy

As a business owner, you will be more visible as a target for lawsuits, even if there is little merit to them. Lawyers know that a *nuisance suit* is often settled for thousands of dollars. Because of your greater exposure, you should consider getting a personal *umbrella policy*. This is a policy that covers you for claims of up to a certain dollar amount (possibly even two or five million) and is very reasonably priced.

HAZARD INSURANCE

One of the worst things that can happen to your business is a fire, flood, or other disaster. Due to lost customer lists, inventory, and equipment, many businesses have been forced to close after such a disaster.

The premium for hazard insurance is usually reasonable and could protect you from loss of your business. You can even get business interruption insurance, which will cover your losses while your business is getting back on its feet.

HOME BUSINESS INSURANCE

There is a special insurance problem for home businesses. Most homeowner and tenant insurance policies do not cover business activities. In fact, under some policies, you may be denied coverage if you use your home for a business.

You probably will not have a problem and will not need extra coverage if you merely use your home to make business phone calls and send letters. However, if you own equipment or have dedicated a portion of your home exclusively to the business, you could have a problem. Check with your insurance agent for the options that are available to you.

If your business is a sole proprietorship and you have a computer that you use both personally and for your business, it would probably be covered under your homeowners policy. However, if you incorporate your business and bought the computer in the name of the corporation, coverage might be denied. It is possible to get a special insurance policy in the company name covering just the computer if it is your main business asset. One company that offers such a policy is Safeware, which can be reached at 800-800-1492 or **www.safeware.com**. Other specialty insurance may be located on the Internet.

AUTOMOBILE INSURANCE

If you or any of your employees will be using an automobile for business purposes, be sure to have this use covered. Sometimes a policy may contain an exclusion for business use. Check to be sure your liability policy covers you if one of your employees causes an accident while running a business errand.

HEALTH INSURANCE

While new businesses can rarely afford health insurance for their employees, the sooner they can obtain it, the better chance they will have to find and keep good employees. Those starting a business usually need insurance for themselves, and they can sometimes receive a better rate if they obtain a small business package.

EMPLOYEE THEFT

If you fear employees may be able to steal from your business, you may want to have them *bonded*. This means that you pay an insurance company a premium to guarantee employees' honesty, and if they cheat you, the insurance company pays you damages. This can cover all existing and new employees.

Your Business and the Internet

The Internet has opened up a world of opportunities for businesses. It was not long ago that getting national visibility cost a fortune. Today, a business can set up a Web page for a few hundred dollars, and with some clever publicity and a little luck, millions of people around the world will see it.

This new world has new legal issues and new liabilities. Not all of them have been addressed by laws or by the courts. Before you begin doing business on the Internet, you should know the existing rules and the areas where legal issues exist.

DOMAIN NAMES

A *domain name* is the address of your website. For example, www.apple.com is the domain name of Apple Computer Company. The last part of the domain name, the ".com" (or "dot com") is the *top-level domain*, or TLD. Dot com is the most popular, but others are currently available in the United States, including .net and .org. (Originally, .net was only available to network service providers and .org only to nonprofit organizations, but regulations have eliminated those requirements.)

It may seem like most words have been taken as a dot-com name, but if you combine two or three short words or abbreviations, a nearly unlimited number of possibilities are available. For example, if you have a business dealing with automobiles, most likely someone has already registered automobile.com and auto.com. You can come up with all kinds of variations, using adjectives or your name, depending on your type of business:

autos4u.com	joesauto.com	autobob.com
myauto.com	yourauto.com	onlyautos.com
greatauto.com	autosfirst.com	usautos.com
greatautos.com	firstautoworld.com	4autos.com

One site that provides both low-cost registrations and suggestions for name variations is **www.registerfly.com**.

When the Internet first began, some individuals realized that major corporations would soon want to register their names. Since the registration was easy and cheap, people registered names they thought would ultimately be used by someone else.

At first, some companies paid high fees to buy their names from the registrants. One company, Intermatic, filed a lawsuit instead of paying. The owner of the domain name they wanted had registered numerous domain names, such as britishairways.com and ussteel.com. The court ruled that since Intermatic owned a trademark on the name, the registration of their name by someone else violated that trademark, and that Intermatic was entitled to it.

Since then, people have registered names that are not trademarks, such as CalRipkin.com, and have attempted to charge the individuals with those names to buy their domain. In 1998, Congress passed the *Anti-Cybersquatting Consumer Protection Act*, making it illegal to register a domain with no legitimate need to use it.

This law helped a lot of companies protect their names, but then some companies started abusing it and tried to stop legitimate users of names similar to theirs. This is especially likely against small companies. An organization that has been set up to help small companies protect their domains is the *Domain Name Rights Coalition*. Its website is **www.netpolicy.com**. Some other good information on domain names can be found at **www.bitlaw.com/internet/domain.html**.

Registering a domain name for your own business is a simple process. There are many companies that offer registration services. For a list of those companies, visit the site of the *Internet Corporation for Assigned Names and Numbers* (ICANN) at **www.icann.org**. You can link directly to any member's site and compare the costs and registration procedures required for the different top-level domains.

WEB PAGES

There are many new companies eager to help you set up a website. Some offer turnkey sites for a low, flat rate, while custom sites can cost tens of thousands of dollars. If you have plenty of capital, you may want to have your site handled by one of these professionals. However, setting up a website is a fairly simple process, and once you learn the basics, you can handle most of it in-house.

If you are new to the Web, you may want to look at **www.learnthenet.com** and **www.webopedia.com**, which will familiarize you with the Internet jargon and give you a basic introduction to the Web.

Site Setup There are seven steps to setting up a website: site purpose, design, content, structure, programming, testing, and publicity. Whether you do it yourself, hire a professional site designer, or employ a college student, the steps toward creating an effective site are the same.

Before beginning your own site, you should look at other sites, including those of major corporations and small businesses. Look at the sites of all the companies that compete with you. Look at hundreds of sites and click through them to see how they work (or do not work).

Site purpose. To know what to include on your site, you must decide what its purpose will be. Do you want to take orders for your products or services, attract new employees, give away samples, or show off your company headquarters? You might want to do several of these things.

Site design. After looking at other sites, you can see that there are numerous ways to design a site. It can be crowded, or open and airy; it can have several windows (frames) open at once or just one; and, it can allow long scrolling or just click-throughs.

You will have to decide whether the site will have text only; text plus photographs and graphics; or, text plus photos, graphics, and other design elements, such as animation or Java script. Additionally, you will begin to make decisions about colors, fonts, and the basic graphic appearance of the site.

Site content. You must create the content for your site. For this, you can use your existing promotional materials, new material just for the website, or a combination of the two. Whatever you choose, remember that the written material should be concise, free of errors, and easy for your target audience to read. Any graphics (including photographs) and written materials not created by you require permission. You should obtain such permission from the lawful copyright holder in order to use any copyrighted material. Once you know your site's purpose, look, and content, you can begin to piece the site together.

Site structure. You must decide how the content (text plus photographs, graphics, animation, etc.) will be structured—what content will be on which page, and how a user will link from one part of the site to another. For example, your first page may have the business name and then choices to click on, such as "about us," "opportunities," or "product catalog." Have those choices connect to another page containing the detailed information, so that a user will see the catalog when he or she clicks on "product catalog." Your site could also have an option to click on a link to another website related to yours.

Site programming and setup. When you know nothing about setting up a website, it can seem like a daunting task that will require an expert. However, *programming* here means merely putting a site together. There are inexpensive computer programs available that make it very simple.

Commercial programs such as Microsoft FrontPage, Dreamweaver, Pagemaker, Photoshop, MS Publisher, and PageMill allow you to set up Web pages as easily as laying out a print publication. These programs will convert the text and graphics you create into HTML, the programming language of the Web. Before you choose Web design software and design your site, you should determine which Web hosting service you will use. Make sure that the design software you use is compatible with the host server's system. The Web host is the provider who will give you space on their server and who may provide other services to you, such as secure order processing and analysis of your site to see who is visiting and linking to it.

If you have an America Online (AOL) account, you can download design software and a tutorial for free. You do not have to use AOL's design software in order to use this service. You are eligible to use this site whether you design your own pages, have someone else do the design work for you, or use AOL's templates. This service allows you to use your own domain name and choose the package that is appropriate for your business.

If you have used a page layout program, you can usually get a simple Web page up and running within a day or two. If you do not have much experience with a computer, you might consider hiring a college student to set up a Web page for you.

Site testing. Some of the website setup programs allow you to thoroughly check your new site to see if all the pictures are included and all the links are proper. There are also websites you can go to that will check out your site. Some even allow you to improve your site, such as by reducing the size of your graphics so they download faster. Use one of the major search engines listed on page 74 to look for companies that can test your site before you launch it on the Web.

Site publicity. Once you set up your website, you will want to get people to look at it. *Publicity* means getting your site noticed as much as possible by drawing people to it.

The first thing to do to get noticed is to be sure your site is registered with as many *search engines* as possible. These are pages that people use to find things on the Internet, such as Yahoo and Google. They do not automatically know about you just because you created a website. You must tell them about your site, and they must examine and catalog it.

For a fee, there are services that will register your site with numerous search engines. If you are starting out on a shoestring, you can easily do it yourself. While there are hundreds of search engines, most people use a dozen or so of the bigger ones. If your site is in a niche area, such as genealogy services, then you would want to be listed on any specific genealogy search engines. Most businesses should be mainly concerned with getting on the biggest ones.

By far the biggest and most successful search engine today is Google (**www.google.com**). Some of the other big ones are:

www.altavista.com	www.hotbot.com
www.excite.com	www.lycos.com
www.fastsearch.com	www.metacrawler.com
www.go.com	www.northernlight.com
www.goto.com	www.webcrawler.com

Most of these sites have a place to click to add your site to their system. Some sites charge hundreds of dollars to be listed. If your site contains valuable information that people are looking for, you should be able to do well without paying these fees.

Getting Your Site Known

A *meta tag* is an invisible subject word added to your site that can be found by a search engine. For example, if you are a pest control company, you may want to list all of the scientific names of the pests you control and all of the treatments you have available, but you may not need them to be part of the visual design of your site. List these words as meta tags when you set up your page so people searching for those words will find your site.

Some companies thought that a clever way to get viewers would be to use commonly searched names, or names of major competitors, as meta tags to attract people looking for those big companies. For example, a small delivery service that has nothing to do with UPS or FedEx might use those company names as meta tags so people looking for them would find the smaller company. While it may sound like a good idea, it has been declared illegal trademark infringement. Today many companies have computer programs scanning the Internet for improper use of their trademarks.

Once you have made sure that your site is passively listed in all the search engines, you may want to actively promote your site. However, self-promotion is seen as a bad thing on the Internet, especially if its purpose is to make money.

Newsgroups are places on the Internet where people interested in a specific topic can exchange information. For example, expectant mothers have a group where they can trade advice and experiences. If you have a product that would be great for expectant mothers, that would be a good place for it to be discussed. However, if you log into the group and merely announce your product, suggesting people order it from your website, you will probably be *flamed* (sent a lot of hate mail).

If you join the group, however, and become a regular, and in answer to someone's problem, mention that you "saw this product that might help," your information will be better received. It may seem unethical to plug your product without disclosing your interest, but this is a procedure used by many large companies. They hire *buzz agents* to plug their product all over the Internet and create positive *buzz* for the product. So, perhaps it has become an acceptable marketing method and consumers know to take plugs with a grain of salt. Let your conscience be your guide.

Keep in mind that Internet publicity works both ways. If you have a great product and people love it, you will get a lot of business. If you sell a shoddy product, give poor service, and do not keep your customers happy, bad publicity on the Internet can kill your business. Besides being an equalizer between large and small companies, the Internet can be a filtering mechanism between good and bad products.

Spamming   Sending unsolicited email advertising (called *spam*) started out as a mere breach of internet etiquette (*netiquette*), but has now become a state and federal crime. The ability to reach millions of people with advertising at virtually no cost was too good for too many businesses to pass up, and this resulted in the clogging of most users' email boxes and near shut down of some computer systems. Some people ended up with thousand of offers every day.

To prevent this, many states passed anti-spamming laws and Congress passed the CAN-SPAM Act. This law:

○ bans misleading or false headers on email;

○ bans misleading subject lines;

○ requires allowing recipients to opt out of future mailings;

○ requires the email be identified as advertising; and,

○ requires the email include a valid physical address.

Each violation can result in up to an $11,000 fine, and the fines can be raised if advertisers violate other rules such as not harvesting names and not using permutations of existing names. More information can be found on the Federal Trade Commission's website at **www.ftc.gov**.

Advertising   Advertising on the Internet has grown in recent years. At first, small, thin rectangular ads appeared at the top of websites; these are called *banner ads*. Lately they have grown bigger, can appear anywhere on the site, and usually blink or show a moving visual.

The fees can be based on how many people view an ad, how many click on it, or both. Some larger companies, such as Amazon.com, have affiliate programs in which they will pay a percentage of a purchase if a customer comes from your site to theirs and makes a purchase. For sites that have thousands of visitors, the ads have been profitable—some sites reportedly make over $100,000 a year.

Example:
One financially successful site is Manolo's Shoe Blog (http://shoeblogs.com). It is written by a man who loves shoes, has a great sense of humor, and writes in endearing broken English. Because he is an expert in his field, his suggestions are taken by many readers who click through to the products and purchase them.

LEGAL ISSUES

Before you set up a Web page, you should consider the many legal issues associated with it.

Jurisdiction   *Jurisdiction* is the power of a court in a particular location to decide a particular case. Usually, you have to have been physically present in a jurisdiction or have done business there before you can be sued there. Since the Internet extends your business's ability to reach people in faraway places, there may be instances when you could be subject to legal jurisdiction far from your own state (or country). There are a number of cases that have been decided in this country regarding the Internet and jurisdiction, but very few cases have been decided on this issue outside of the United States.

In most instances, U.S. courts use the pre-Internet test—whether you have been present in another jurisdiction or have had enough contact with someone in the other jurisdiction. The fact that the Internet itself is not a "place" will not shield you from being sued in another state when you have shipped you company's product there, have entered into a contract with a resident of that state, or have defamed a foreign resident with content on your website.

According to the court, there is a spectrum of contact required between you, your website, and consumers or audiences. (*Zippo Manufacturing Co. v. Zippo Dot Com, Inc.*, 952 F. Supp. 1119 (W.D. Pa 1997).) The more interactive your site is with consumers, the more you target an audience for your goods in a particular location, and the farther you reach to send your goods out into the world, the more it becomes possible for someone to sue you outside of your own jurisdiction—so weigh these risks against the benefits when constructing and promoting your website.

The law is not even remotely final on these issues. The American Bar Association, among other groups, is studying this topic in detail. At present, no final, global solution or agreement about jurisdictional issues with websites exists.

One way to protect yourself from the possibility of being sued in a far-away jurisdiction would be to state on your website that those using the site or doing business with you agree that "jurisdiction for any actions regarding this site" or your company will be in your home county.

For extra protection, you can have a preliminary page that must be clicked before entering your website. However, this may be overkill for a small business with little risk of lawsuits. If you are in any business for which you could have serious liability, you should review some competitors' sites and see how they handle the liability issue. They often have a place to click for "legal notice" or "disclaimer" on their first page.

You may want to consult with an attorney to discuss the specific disclaimer you will use on your website, where it should appear, and whether you should have users of your site actively agree to this disclaimer or just passively read it. However, these disclaimers are not enforceable everywhere in the world. Until there is global agreement on jurisdictional issues, this may remain an area of uncertainty for some time to come.

Libel

Libel is any publication that injures the reputation of another. This can occur in print, writing, pictures, or signs. All that is required for publication is that you transmit the material to at least one other person. When putting together your website, you must keep in mind that it is visible to millions of people all over the planet, and that if you libel a person or company, you may have to pay damages. Many countries do not have the freedom of speech that we do, and a statement that is not libel in the United States may be libelous elsewhere. If you are concerned about this, alter the content of your site or check with an attorney about libel laws in the country you think might take action against you.

Copyright Infringement

It is so easy to copy and borrow information on the Internet that it is easy to infringe copyrights without even knowing it. A *copyright* exists for a work as soon as the creator creates it. There is no need to register the copyright or to put a copyright notice on it. Therefore, practically everything on the Internet belongs to someone.

Some people freely give their works away. For example, many people have created Web artwork (*gifs* and *animated gifs*) that they freely allow people to copy. There are numerous sites that provide hundreds or thousands of free gifs that you can add to your Web pages. Some require you to acknowledge the source and some do not. You should always be sure that the works are free for the taking before using them.

Linking and Framing   One way to violate copyright laws is to improperly link other sites to yours, either directly or with framing. *Linking* is when you provide a link that takes the user to the linked site. *Framing* occurs when you set up your site so that when you link to another site, your site is still viewable as a frame around the linked-to site.

While many sites are glad to be linked to others, some, especially providers of valuable information, object. Courts have ruled that linking and framing can be a copyright violation. One rule that has developed is that it is usually okay to link to the first page of a site, but not to link to some valuable information deeper within the site. The rationale for this is that the owner of the site wants visitors to go through the various levels of their site (viewing all the ads) before getting the information. By linking directly to the information, you are giving away their product without the ads.

The problem with linking to the first page of a site is that it may be a tedious or difficult task to find the needed page from there. Many sites are poorly designed and make it nearly impossible to find anything.

If you wish to link to another page, the best solution is to ask permission. Email the Webmaster or other person in charge of the site, if an email address is given, and explain what you want to do. If they grant permission, be sure to print out a copy of their email for your records.

Privacy   Since the Internet is such an easy way to share information, there are many concerns that it will cause a loss of individual privacy. The two main concerns arise when you post information that others consider private, and when you gather information from customers and use it in a way that violates their privacy.

While public actions of politicians and celebrities are fair game, details about their private lives are sometimes protected by law, and details about persons who are not public figures are often protected. The laws in each state are different, and what might be allowable in one state could be illegal in another. If your site will provide any personal information about individuals, you should discuss the possibility of liability with an attorney.

Several well-known companies have been in the news lately for violations of their customers' privacy. They either shared what the customer was buying or downloading, or looked for additional information on the customer's computer. To let customers know that you do not violate certain standards of privacy, you can subscribe to one of the privacy codes that have been created for the Internet. These allow you to put a symbol on your site guaranteeing to your customers that you follow the code.

The following are the websites of two organizations that offer this service and their fees at the time of this publication.

www.privacybot.com	$100
www.bbbonline.com	$200 to $7,000

Protecting Yourself   The easiest way to protect yourself personally from the various possible types of liability is to set up a corporation or limited liability company to own the website. This is not foolproof protection since, in some cases, you could be sued personally as well, but it is one level of protection.

COPPA   If your website is aimed at children under the age of 13, or if it attracts children of that age, then you are subject to the federal *Children Online Privacy Protection Act of 1998* (COPPA). This law requires such websites to:

- ✪ give notice on the site of what information is being collected;

- ✪ obtain verifiable parental consent to collect the information;

- ✪ allow the parent to review the information collected;

- ✪ allow the parent to delete the child's information or to refuse to allow the use of the information;

- ✪ limit the information collected to only that necessary to participate on the site; and,

- ✪ protect the security and confidentiality of the information.

Illinois Law   In order to help prevent identity theft, the Illinois General Assembly enacted the *Personal Information Protection Act*. (815 ILCS 530.) The law applies to any entity that collects or handles personal information that is not known to the public at large. Examples of nonpublic personal information include:

- Social Security numbers;

- driver's license numbers; and,

- credit card numbers.

The Act states that, if there is a security breach in the entity's system of holding computerized personal data, thus compromising the confidentiality of the personal information, the entity is required to notify any Illinois resident to whom the information pertains. Notice generally must be either in writing or electronic.

HIRING A WEBSITE DESIGNER

If you hire someone to design your website, you should make sure of what rights you are buying. Under copyright law, when you hire someone to create a work, you do not get all rights to that work unless you clearly spell that out in a written agreement.

For example, if your designer creates an artistic design to go on your website, you may have to pay extra if you want to use the same design on your business cards or letterhead. Depending on how the agreement is worded, you may even have to pay a yearly fee for the rights.

If you spend a lot of money promoting your business, and a logo or design becomes important to your image, you would not want to have to pay royalties for the life of your business to someone who spent an hour or two putting together a design. Whenever you purchase a creative work from someone, be sure to get a written statement of what rights you are buying. If you are not receiving all rights for all uses for all time, you should think twice about the purchase.

If the designer also is involved with hosting your site, you should be sure you have the right to take the design with you if you move to another host. You should get a backup of your site on a CD in case it is ever lost or you need to move it to another site.

FINANCIAL TRANSACTIONS

The existing services for sending money over the Internet, such as PayPal, usually offer more risk and higher fees than traditional credit card processing. Under their service agreements, you usually must agree that they can freeze your account at any time and can take money out of your bank account at any time. Some do not offer an appeal process. Before signing up for any of these services, you should read their service agreement carefully and check the Internet for other peoples' experiences with them. For example, for PayPal you can check **www.nopaypal.com**.

For now, the easiest way to exchange money on the Internet is through traditional credit cards. Because of concerns that email can be abducted in transit and read by others, most companies use a secure site in which customers are guaranteed that their card data is encrypted before being sent.

When setting up your website, you should ask the provider if you can be set up with a secure site for transmitting credit card data. If they cannot provide it, you will need to contract with another software provider. Use one of the major search engines listed on page 74 to look for companies that provide credit card services to businesses on the Internet.

As a practical matter, there is very little to worry about when sending credit card data by email. If you do not have a secure site, another option is to allow purchasers to fax or phone in their credit card data. However, keep in mind that this extra step will lose some business unless your products are unique and your buyers are very motivated.

The least effective option is to provide an order form on the site that can be printed out and mailed in with a check. Again, your customers must be really motivated or they will lose interest after finding out this extra work is involved.

FTC RULES

Because the Internet is an instrument of interstate commerce, it is a legitimate subject for federal regulation. The Federal Trade Commission (FTC) first said that all of its consumer protection rules applied to the Internet, but lately it has been adding specific rules and issuing publications. The following publications are available from the FTC website at **www.ftc.gov/bcp/menu-internet.htm** or by mail from:

Consumer Response Center
Federal Trade Commission
600 Pennsylvania, NW
Room H-130
Washington, DC 20580

- *Advertising and Marketing on the Internet: The Rules of the Road*

- *Appliance Labeling Rule Homepage*

- *BBB-Online: Code of Online Business Practices*

- *Big Print. Little Print. What's the Deal? How to Disclose the Details*

- *Businessperson's Guide to the Mail and Telephone Order Merchandise Rule*

- *CAN-SPAM Act: Requirements for Commercial Emailers*

- *Complying with the Telemarketing Sales Rule*

- *Disclosing Energy Efficiency Information: A Guide for Online Sellers of Appliances*

- *Dot Com Disclosures: Information About Online Advertising*

- *Electronic Commerce: Selling Internationally. A Guide for Business*

- *How to Comply With The Children's Online Privacy Protection Rule*

- *Frequently Asked Questions About the Children's Online Privacy Protection Rule*

- *Internet Auctions: A Guide for Buyer and Sellers*

- *"Remove Me" Responses and Responsibilities: Email Marketers Must Honor "Unsubscribe" Claims*

- *Securing Your Server—Shut the Door on Spam*

- *Security Check: Reducing Risks to Your Computer Systems*

- *Selling on the Internet: Prompt Delivery Rules*

- *TooLate.Com: The Lowdown on Late Internet Shipments*

- *Website Woes: Avoiding Web Service Scams*

- *What's Dot and What's Not: Domain Name Registration Scams*

- *You, Your Privacy Policy & COPPA*

FRAUD

Because the Internet is somewhat anonymous, it is a tempting place for those with fraudulent schemes to look for victims. As a business consumer, you should exercise caution when dealing with unknown or anonymous parties on the Internet.

The U.S. Department of Justice, the FBI, and the National White Collar Crime Center jointly launched the Internet Crime Complaint Center (ICCC). If you suspect that you are the victim of fraud online, whether as a consumer or a business, you can report incidents to the ICCC on their website, **www.ic3.gov**. The ICCC is currently staffed by FBI agents and representatives of the National White Collar Crime Center, and will work with state and local law enforcement officials to prevent, investigate, and prosecute high-tech and economic crime online.

Health and Safety Laws

As a reaction to the terrible work conditions prevalent in the factories and mills of the nineteenth century industrial age, Congress and the states developed many laws intended to protect the health and safety of the nation's workers. These laws are difficult to understand and often seem to be very unfair to employers. Therefore, this is an area that you need to pay particular attention to as a new business. Failure to do so can result in terrible consequences for you.

FEDERAL LAWS

The federal government's laws regarding health and safety of workers are far-reaching and very important to consider in running your business, especially if you are a manufacturer or in the oil and gas, food production, or agriculture industries.

OSHA The point of the *Occupational Safety and Health Administration* (OSHA) is to place the duty on the employer to keep the workplace free from recognized hazards that are likely to cause death or serious bodily injury to workers. The regulations are not as cumbersome for small businesses as for larger enterprises. If you have ten or fewer employees or if you are in certain types of businesses, you do not have to keep a record of illnesses, injuries, and exposure to hazardous substances of employees. If you have eleven or more employees, OSHA's rules will apply. One important rule to know is that within forty-eight hours of an on-the-job death of an employee or injury of five or more employees on the job, the area director of OSHA must be contacted. For more information, write or call OSHA at:

OSHA Regional Office
230 South Dearborn Street
Room 3244
Chicago, IL 60604
312-353-2220
Fax: 312-353-7774
www.osha.gov

You can obtain copies of OSHA publications, such as *OSHA Handbook for Small Business* (OSHA 2209) and *OSHA Publications and Audiovisual Programs Catalog* (OSHA 2019), from its website. They also have a poster that is required to be posted in the workplace by all employers (OSHA 3165). All these publications are available at **www.osha.gov/pls/publications/pubindex.list**.

Hazard Communication Standard

The *Hazard Communication Standard* requires that employees be made aware of the hazards in the workplace. (Title 29, Code of Federal Regulations (C.F.R.), Section (Sec.) 1910.1200.) It is especially applicable to those working with chemicals, but this can even include offices that use copy machines. Businesses using hazardous chemicals must have a comprehensive program for informing employees of the hazards and for protecting them from contamination.

For more information, you can contact OSHA at the previously mentioned addresses, phone numbers, or websites. They can supply a copy of the regulation and a booklet called *OSHA 3084*, which explains the law.

EPA

The *Worker Protection Standard for Agricultural Pesticides* requires safety training, decontamination sites, and posters. The Environmental Protection Agency (EPA) will provide information on compliance with this law. It can be reached at 888-663-2155 or through its website at **www.epa.gov/agriculture/htc.html**.

FDA   The *Pure Food and Drug Act of 1906* prohibits the misbranding or adulteration of food and drugs. It also created the Food and Drug Administration (FDA), which has promulgated many regulations and which must give permission before a new drug can be introduced into the market. If you will be dealing with any food or drugs, keep abreast of FDA policies. Its website is **www.fda.gov**. Its small business site is **www.fda.gov/ora/fed_state/small_business/sb_guide/default.htm** and its local small business representative can be reached at:

FDA, Central Region
20 North Michigan Avenue
Suite 510
Chicago, IL 60602
312-353-9400

Hazardous Materials Transportation   There are regulations that control the shipping and packing of hazardous materials. For more information, contact:

U.S. Department of Transportation
Office of Pipeline and Hazardous Materials
Safety Administration
400 Seventh Street, SW
Washington, DC 20590
202-366-8553
http://hazmat.dot.gov

CPSC   The *Consumer Product Safety Commission* (CPSC) has a set of rules that covers the safety of products. The commission feels that because its rules cover products rather than people or companies, they apply to everyone producing such products. However, federal laws do not apply to small businesses that do not affect interstate commerce. Whether a small business would fall under a CPSC rule would depend on the size and nature of that business.

The CPSC rules are contained in the Code of Federal Regulations, Title 16, in the following parts. These can be found at most law libraries, some public libraries, and on the Internet at **www.access. gpo.gov/nara/cfr/cfr-table-search.html**. The CPSC's site is **www.cpsc.gov**.

PRODUCT	PART
Antennas, CB and TV	1402
Architectural Glazing Material	1201
Articles Hazardous to Children Under 3	1501
Baby Cribs—Full Size	1508
Baby Cribs—Non-Full Size	1509
Bicycle Helmets	1203
Bicycles	1512
Carpets and Rugs	1630, 1631
Cellulose Insulation	1209, 1404
Cigarette Lighters	1210
Citizens Band Base Station Antennas	1204
Coal and Wood Burning Appliances	1406
Consumer Products Containing Chlorofluorocarbons	1401
Electrically Operated Toys	1505
Emberizing Materials Containing Asbestos (banned)	1305
Extremely Flammable Contact Adhesives (banned)	1302
Fireworks	1507
Garage Door Openers	1211
Hazardous Lawn Darts (banned)	1306
Hazardous Substances	1500
Human Subjects	1028
Lawn Mowers—Walk-Behind	1205
Lead-Containing Paint (banned)	1303
Matchbooks	1202
Mattresses	1632
Pacifiers	1511
Patching Compounds Containing Asbestos (banned)	1304
Poisons	1700
Rattles	1510
Self-Pressurized Consumer Products	1401
Sleepwear-Childrens	1615, 1616
Swimming Pool Slides	1207
Toys, Electrical	1505
Unstable Refuse Bins (banned)	1301

Additional Regulations

Every day there are proposals for new laws and regulations. It would be impossible to include every conceivable one in this book. To be up to date on the laws that affect your type of business, join a trade association for your industry and subscribe to newsletters that cover your industry. Attending industry conventions is a good way to learn more and to discover new ways to increase your profits.

ILLINOIS LAWS

The federal laws discussed previously are by far the most important with regard to the health and safety of your employees and customers. However, note that Illinois does have laws regarding smoking in certain places.

Smoking   The Illinois *Clean Indoor Air Act* (410 ILCS 80), passed in 1990, contains the following rules regarding smoking in public places and at public meetings.

Public places means any enclosed indoor area used by the public or serving as a place of work, including but not limited to, hospitals, restaurants, retail stores, offices, commercial establishments, elevators, indoor theatres, libraries, art museums, concert halls, public conveyances, educational facilities, nursing homes, auditoriums, arenas, and meeting rooms. As of May 2006, smoking is also prohibited in student dormitories. There are also excluded locations, including bowling establishments; places whose primary business is the sale of alcoholic beverages for consumption on the premises; rooms rented for the purpose of living quarters, sleeping, or housekeeping accommodations from a hotel; and, private, enclosed offices occupied exclusively by smokers, even though such offices may be visited by nonsmokers.

No person may smoke in a public place except in designated smoking areas and in private social functions where the seating is controlled by the sponsor.

Smoking areas of reasonable size may be designated. Smoke in adjacent nonsmoking areas must be minimized, but no physical modification of the area is required.

No more than half the rooms in a health care facility may be designated as smoking areas. No more than half the square footage of an enclosed area used for common purposes in a public place may be designated for smoking except restaurants, which cannot have more than 65% of their dining room seats located in a designated smoking area.

Designated smoking areas must be conspicuously posted with letters of reasonable size that can be easily read. *NO SMOKING EXCEPT IN DESIGNATED AREAS* signs may also be posted when appropriate.

Employers of smoking and nonsmoking employees are required to institute and post policies regarding designation of smoking and non-smoking areas.

Employment and Labor Laws

Congress and the states have heavily regulated the actions that employers can take with regard to hiring and firing, improper employment practices, and discrimination. Because the penalties for violations of these regulations can be severe, educate yourself on the proper actions to take and consult a labor and employment lawyer, if necessary, prior to making important employee decisions.

HIRING AND FIRING LAWS

For small businesses, there are not many rules regarding who you may hire or fire. The ancient law that an employee can be fired at any time (or may quit at any time) still prevails for small businesses. However, in certain situations, and as you grow, you will come under a number of laws that affect your hiring and firing practices.

One of the most important things to consider when hiring someone is that if you fire him or her, he or she may be entitled to unemployment compensation. If so, your unemployment compensation tax rate will go up, which can cost you a lot of money. Therefore, you should only hire people you are sure you will keep, and you should avoid situations in which your former employees can make claims against your company.

One way this can be done is by hiring only part-time employees. The drawback to this is that you may not be able to attract the best employees. When hiring dishwashers or busboys, this may not be an issue, but when hiring someone to develop a software product, you want to be sure he or she does not leave halfway through the development.

A better solution is to screen applicants first and only hire those who you feel certain will work out. Of course, this is easier said than done. Some people interview well but then turn out to be incompetent at the job.

The best record to look for is someone who has stayed a long time at each of his or her previous jobs. Next best is someone who has not stayed as long (for good reasons) but has always been employed. The worst type of hire would be someone who is or has been collecting unemployment compensation.

The reason those who have collected compensation are a bad risk is that if they collect in the future—even if it is not your fault—your employment of them could make you chargeable for their claim. For example, you hire someone who has been on unemployment compensation and he or she works out well for a year, but then he or she quits to take another job and is fired after a few weeks. In this situation, you would be chargeable for most of the unemployment claim, because his or her last five quarters of work are analyzed. Look for a steady job history.

The competence of an employee is often more important than his or her experience. An employee with years of typing experience may be fast, but may also be unable to figure out how to use your new computer, whereas a competent employee can learn the equipment quickly and eventually gain speed. Of course, common sense is important in all situations.

The bottom line is that you cannot know if an employee will be able to fill your needs from a résumé and interview. Once you have found someone who you think will work out, offer him or her a job with a ninety-day probationary period. If you are not completely satisfied with him or her after the ninety days, offer to extend the probationary period for an additional ninety days rather than end the relationship immediately. Of course, all of this should be in writing.

Background Checks   Checking references is important, but beware that a former boss may be a good friend or even a relative. It has always been considered acceptable to exaggerate on résumés, but in recent years some applicants have been found to be completely fabricating sections of their education and experience.

Polygraph Tests   Under the federal *Employee Polygraph Protection Act*, you cannot require an employee or prospective employee to take a polygraph test unless you are in the armored car, security alarm system, guard, or pharmaceutical business.

Drug Tests   Under the *Americans with Disabilities Act* (ADA), drug testing can only be required of applicants who have been offered jobs conditioned upon passing the drug test. Unlike some states, Illinois does not have drug-testing laws that regulate the private sector. Therefore, you are free to implement a reasonable drug-testing program on applicants or employees.

FIRING

In most cases, unless you have a contract with an employee for a set time period, you can fire him or her at any time. This is only fair, since the employee can quit at any time. This type of employment is called *at will*. You should make it clear when offering a job to someone that, upon acceptance, he or she will be an at-will employee. The exceptions to this are if you fired someone based on illegal discrimination, for filing some sort of health or safety complaint, or for refusing your sexual advances.

NEW HIRE REPORTING

In order to track down parents who do not pay child support, the federal *Personal Responsibility and Work Opportunity Reconciliation Act of 1996* (PRWORA) provides that information on new hires must be reported by employers to their state government.

Within twenty days of hiring a new employee, an employer must provide the state with information about the employee, including his or her name, Social Security number, and address. This information can be submitted in several ways, including mail, fax, or magnetic tape, or over the Internet. There is a special form that can be used for this reporting. However, an employer can also use the **EMPLOYEE'S WITHHOLDING ALLOWANCE CERTIFICATE (IRS FORM W-4)** for this purpose. A copy of the **IRS FORM W-4** is included in Appendix D. (see form 7, p.253.) Since this form must be filled out for all employees anyway, it would be pointless to use a separate form for the new hire reporting.

EMPLOYMENT AGREEMENTS

To avoid any misunderstandings with employees, you should use an employment agreement or an employee handbook. These can spell out in detail the policies of your company and the rights of your employees. They can protect your trade secrets and spell out clearly that employment can be terminated at any time by either party.

While it may be difficult or awkward to ask an existing employee to sign such an agreement, an applicant hoping you will hire him or her will usually sign whatever is necessary to obtain the job. However, because of the unequal bargaining position, do not use an agreement that would make you look bad if the matter ever went to court.

If having an employee sign an agreement is too awkward, you can usually obtain the same rights by putting the company policies in an employee manual. Each existing and new employee should be given a copy, along with a letter stating that the rules apply to all employees and that by accepting or continuing employment at your company, they agree to abide by the rules. Having an employee sign a receipt for the letter and manual is proof that he or she received it.

One danger of an employment agreement or handbook is that it may be interpreted to create a long-term employment contract. To avoid this, be sure that you clearly state in the agreement or handbook that the employment is at will and can be terminated at any time by either party.

Some other things to consider in an employment agreement or handbook include:

- ✪ what the salary and other compensation will be;

- ✪ what the hours of employment will be;

- ✪ what the probationary period will be;

- ✪ that the employee cannot sign any contracts binding the employer; and,

- ✪ that the employee agrees to mediation or arbitration rather than filing a lawsuit in the event of a serious legal complaint.

INDEPENDENT CONTRACTORS

One way to avoid problems with employees and taxes at the same time is to have all of your work done through independent contractors. This can relieve you of most of the burdens of employment laws, as well as the obligation to pay Social Security and Medicare taxes for the workers.

An independent contractor is, in effect, a separate business that you pay to do a job. You pay an independent contractor just as you pay any company from which you buy products or services. At the end of the year, if the amount paid exceeds $600, you will issue a 1099 form instead of the W-2 that you issue to employees.

This may seem too good to be true, and in some situations, it is. The Internal Revenue Service (IRS) does not like independent contractor arrangements because it is too easy for the independent contractors to cheat on their taxes. To limit the use of independent contractors, the IRS has strict regulations on who may and may not be classified as an independent contractor. Also, companies who do not appear to pay enough in wages for their field of business are audited.

Using independent contractors for jobs not traditionally done by independent contractors puts you at high risk for an IRS audit. For example, you could not get away with hiring a secretary as an independent contractor. One of the most important factors considered in determining if a worker can be an independent contractor is the amount of control the company has over his or her work. If you need someone to paint your building and you agree to pay a certain price to have it done according to the painter's own methods and schedule, you can pay the painter as an independent contractor. However, if you tell the painter when and how to do the work, and provide the tools and materials, the painter will be classified as an employee.

If you just need some typing done and you take it to a typing service and pick it up when it is ready, you will be safe in treating those workers as independent contractors. However, if you need someone to come into your office to type on your machine at your schedule, you will probably be required to treat that person as an employee for tax purposes.

The IRS has a form you can use in determining if a person is an employee or an independent contractor, called **DETERMINATION OF WORKER STATUS (IRS FORM SS-8)**. It is included in Appendix C of this book, along with instructions. (see form 6, p.247.)

Independent Contractors vs. Employees

In deciding whether to make use of independent contractors or employees, you should weigh the following advantages and disadvantages.

Advantages.

- ✪ *Lower taxes.* You do not have to pay Social Security, Medicare, unemployment, or other employee taxes.

- ✪ *Less paperwork.* You do not have to handle federal withholding deposits or the monthly employer returns to the state or federal government.

- ✪ *Less insurance.* You do not have to pay workers' compensation insurance, and since the workers are not your employees, you do not have to insure against their possible liabilities.

- ✪ *More flexibility.* You can use independent contractors when you need them and not pay them when business is slow.

Disadvantages.

- ✪ *Scrutiny from the IRS.* The IRS and state tax offices are strict about when workers can qualify as independent contractors. They will audit companies whose use of independent contractors does not appear to be legitimate.

- ✪ *Penalties for improper use.* If your use of independent contractors is found to be improper, you may have to pay back taxes and penalties, and may have problems with your pension plan.

- ✪ *Potential for injury lawsuits.* While employees usually cannot sue you for their injuries (if you have covered them with workers' compensation), independent contractors can sue you if their injuries were your fault.

- ✪ *Fewer creative works rights.* If you are paying someone to produce a creative work (writing, photography, artwork), you receive fewer rights to the work of an independent contractor.

- ✪ *Less control.* You have less control over the work of an independent contractor and less flexibility in terminating him or her if you are not satisfied that the job is being done the way you require.

- ✪ *Less loyalty.* You have less loyalty from an independent contractor who works sporadically for you and possibly others than from your own full-time employees.

For some businesses, the advantages outweigh the disadvantages. For others, they do not. Consider your business plans and the consequences from each type of arrangement. Keep in mind that it will be easier to start with independent contractors and switch to employees than to hire employees and have to fire them to hire independent contractors.

TEMPORARY WORKERS

Another way to avoid the hassles of hiring employees is to get workers from a temporary agency. In this arrangement, you may pay a higher amount per hour for the work, but the agency will take care of all of the tax and insurance requirements. Since these requirements can be expensive and time-consuming, the extra cost may be well worth it.

Whether or not temporary workers will work for you depends upon the type of business you are in and the tasks you need performed. For jobs such as sales management, you would probably want someone who will stay with you long-term and develop relationships with the buyers. For order fulfillment, temporary workers might work out well.

Another advantage of temporary workers is that you can easily stop using those who do not work out well for you, but if you find one who is ideal, you may be able to hire him or her on a full-time basis.

In recent years, a new wrinkle has developed in the temporary worker area. Many large companies are using temps because it is so much cheaper than paying the benefits demanded by full-time employees. For example, Microsoft Corporation has had as many as 6,000 temporary workers, some of whom work for them for years. Some of the temporary workers recently won a lawsuit declaring that they are really employees and are entitled to the same benefits of other employees (such as pension plans).

The law is not yet settled in this area as to what arrangements will result in a temporary worker being declared an employee. That will take several more court cases, some of which have already been filed. The following are a few things you can do to protect yourself.

- ✪ Be sure that any of your benefit plans make it clear that they do not apply to workers obtained through temporary agencies.

- ✪ Do not keep the same temporary workers for longer than a year.

- ✪ Do not list temporary workers in any employee directories or hold them out to the public as your employees.

- ✪ Do not allow temporary workers to use your business cards or stationery.

DISCRIMINATION LAWS

There are numerous federal laws forbidding discrimination based upon race, sex, pregnancy, color, religion, national origin, age, or disability. The laws apply to hiring and firing, and to employment practices such as salaries, promotions, and benefits. Most of these laws only apply to an employer who has fifteen or more employees for twenty weeks of a calendar year or has federal contracts or subcontracts. Therefore, you most likely will not be required to comply with the law immediately upon opening your business. However, there are similar state laws that may apply to your business.

One exception is the *Equal Pay Act*. It applies to employers with two or more employees and requires that women be paid the same as men in the same type of job.

Employers with fifteen or more employees are required to display a poster regarding discrimination. This poster is available from the Equal Employment Opportunity Commission at **www.eeoc.gov/ posterform.html**. Orders of more than ten copies of the poster can be obtained by contacting the EEOC.

Equal Employment Opportunity Commission Clearinghouse
8280 Greensboro Drive
Suite 300
McLean, VA 22102
800-669-3362

Employers with one hundred or more employees are required to file an annual compliance survey, called an EEO-1 report, with the EEOC.

Discriminatory Interview Questions

When hiring employees, some questions are illegal or inadvisable to ask. The following subjects should not be included on your employment application or in your interviews, unless the information is somehow directly tied to the duties of the job.

✪ Do not ask about an applicant's citizenship or place of birth. After hiring an employee, you must ask about his or her right to work in this country.

- ✪ Do not ask a female applicant her maiden name. You can ask if she has been known by any other name, in order to do a background check.

- ✪ Do not ask if applicants have children, plan to have them, or have child care. You can ask if an applicant will be able to work the required hours.

- ✪ Do not ask if the applicant has religious objections for working Saturday or Sunday. You can mention if the job requires such hours and ask whether the applicant can meet this job requirement.

- ✪ Do not ask an applicant's age. You can ask if an applicant is 18 or over, or for a liquor-related job, if he or she is 21 or over.

- ✪ Do not ask an applicant's weight.

- ✪ Do not ask if an applicant has AIDS or is HIV-positive.

- ✪ Do not ask if the applicant has filed a workers' compensation claim.

- ✪ Do not ask about the applicant's previous health problems.

- ✪ Do not ask if the applicant is married or whether his or her spouse would object to the job, hours, or duties.

- ✪ Do not ask if the applicant owns a home, furniture, or car, as it is considered racially discriminatory.

- ✪ Do not ask if the applicant has ever been arrested. You can ask if the applicant has ever been convicted of a crime.

ADA   Under the *Americans with Disabilities Act* (ADA), employers who do not make *reasonable accommodations* for disabled employees will face fines of up to $110,000, as well as other civil penalties and civil damage awards.

The ADA currently applies to employers with fifteen or more employees. Employers who need more than fifteen employees might want to consider independent contractors to avoid problems with this law, particularly if the number of employees is only slightly larger than fifteen.

To find out how this law affects your business, review the publications available from the federal government to assist businesses with ADA compliance. The *Title III Technical Assistance Manual* and the *ADA Guide for Small Businesses* are available from the official ADA website at **www.usdoj.gov/crt/ada/publicat.htm** or by calling the ADA information line at 800-514-0301.

Tax benefits. There are two types of tax credits to help small businesses with the burden of these laws.

- ✪ Businesses can deduct up to $15,000 a year for making their premises accessible to the disabled and can depreciate the rest. (Internal Revenue Code (IRC) Section 190.)

- ✪ Small businesses (under $1,000,000 in revenue and under thirty employees) can get a tax credit each year for 50% of the cost of making their premises accessible to the disabled, but this only applies to the amount between $250 and $10,250. (IRC Section 44.)

Until 2006, small businesses were able to get a credit of up to 40% of the first $6,000 of wages paid to certain new employees who qualify. See IRS Publications 334 and 954, and **Pre-Screening Notice and Certification Request for the Work Opportunity and Welfare-to-Work Credits (IRS Form 8850)** and its instructions. (see form 14, p.281.) Although these credits have expired at the time of publication, Congress is considering whether to reinstate them. Be aware of these credits in the event they are revived.

Illinois Laws   Illinois has its own laws regarding discrimination in employment practices, although they are not much different from federal laws. The Illinois *Human Rights Act* (775 ILCS 5) prohibits discrimination or classification based upon race, color, religion, disability, sex, national origin, age (over forty), handicap, marital status, or unfavorable discharge from military service. This law applies to employers with fifteen or more employees. An employer who violates this law can be sued and required to pay back pay, damages, and punitive damages. For more information, contact the Department of Human Rights at **www.state.il.us/dhr** or at the following address.

Department of Human Rights (DHR)
222 South College
Floor 1
Springfield, IL 62704
217-785-5100
312-814-6200

The *Equal Wage Act* (820 ILCS 110) is Illinois' counterpart to the federal law providing for equal pay for the same job to both sexes. This statute applies only to employers engaged in manufacturing with six or more employees.

SEXUAL HARASSMENT

In today's employment climate, all employers must pay attention to state and federal laws regarding sexual harassment in the workplace.

Federal Law   In the 1980s, the Equal Employment Opportunity Commission (EEOC) interpreted *Title VII* of the *Civil Rights Act of 1964* to forbid sexual harassment. After that, the courts took over and reviewed all types of conduct in the workplace. The numerous lawsuits that followed revealed a definite trend toward expanding the definition of sexual harassment and favoring employees.

The EEOC has held the following in sexual harassment cases.

✪   The victim and the harasser may be a woman or a man.

✪   The victim does not have to be of the opposite sex of the harasser.

✪   The harasser can be the victim's supervisor, an agent of the employer, a supervisor in another area, a coworker, or a non-employee.

- The victim does not have to be the person harassed, but could be anyone affected by the offensive conduct.

- Unlawful sexual harassment may occur without economic injury to or discharge of the victim.

- The harasser's conduct must be unwelcome.

- An employer can be held liable for sexual harassment of an employee by a supervisor, even if the employer was unaware of the supervisor's conduct.

Some of the actions that have been considered harassment are:

- displaying sexually explicit posters in the workplace;

- requiring female employees to wear revealing uniforms;

- rating of sexual attractiveness of female employees as they passed male employees' desks;

- continued sexual jokes and innuendos;

- demands for sexual favors from subordinates;

- unwelcomed sexual propositions or flirtation;

- unwelcomed physical contact;

- whistling or leering at members of the opposite sex; and,

- reassignment to a less desirable position in retaliation for complaints of sexual harassment.

The law in the area of sexual harassment is still developing, so it is difficult to make clear rules of conduct. (*Burlington Northern v. White,* No. 05-259.)

Some things a business can do to protect against claims of sexual harassment include the following.

- ✪ Distribute a written policy against all kinds of sexual harassment to all employees.

- ✪ Encourage employees to report all incidents of sexual harassment.

- ✪ Ensure there is no retaliation against those who complain.

- ✪ Make clear that your policy is *zero tolerance*.

- ✪ Explain that sexual harassment includes both requests for sexual favors and a work environment that some employees may consider hostile.

- ✪ Allow employees to report harassment to someone other than their immediate supervisor, in case that person is involved in the harassment.

- ✪ Promise as much confidentiality as possible to complainants.

Illinois Law   Although the federal civil rights laws only apply to businesses with fifteen or more employees, it is possible for an employee to sue a smaller employer for sexual harassment in state civil court. However, this is difficult and expensive, and would only be worthwhile if there were substantial damages.

WAGE AND HOUR LAWS

The federal *Fair Labor Standards Act* (FLSA) applies to all employers who are engaged in *interstate commerce* or in the production of goods for interstate commerce (anything that will cross the state line), and all employees of hospitals, schools, residential facilities for the disabled or aged, or public agencies. It also applies to all employees of enterprises that gross $500,000 or more per year.

While many small businesses might not think they are engaged in interstate commerce, the laws have been interpreted so broadly that nearly any use of the mails, interstate telephone service, or other interstate services, however minor, is enough to bring a business under the law.

Minimum Wage

The federal wage and hour laws are contained in the Fair Labor Standards Act. The current minimum wage is $5.15. In certain circumstances a wage of $4.25 may be paid to employees under 20 years of age for a ninety-day training period.

For employees who regularly receive more than $30 a month in tips, the minimum wage is $2.13 per hour. However, if the employee's tips do not bring him or her up to the full $5.15 minimum wage, then the employer must make up the difference.

Illinois Law

In 2005, the state minimum wage increased to $6.50. Workers under the age of 18 may be paid up to $.50 less per hour. Employers with fewer than four employees (not counting the employer's close relatives) are not subject to the minimum wage rate. The minimum wage is set to increase to $7.50 per hour beginning July 1, 2007. In addition, the state minimum wage will increase by an additional $.25 cents in each of the following three years to $7.75 on July 1, 2008, $8.00 on July 1, 2009, and $8.25 on July 1, 2010. For more information, contact:

Department of Labor
1 West Old State Capitol Plaza
Room 300
Springfield, IL 62701
217-782-6206
www.state.il.us/agency/idol

Exempt Employees

While nearly all businesses are covered, certain employees are exempt from the FLSA. Exempt employees include employees that are considered executives, administrative, managerial, professionals, computer professionals, and outside salespeople.

Whether or not one of these exceptions applies to a particular employee is a complicated legal question. Thousands of court cases have been decided on this issue, but they have given no clear answers. In one case a person could be determined to be exempt because of his or her duties, but in another, a person with the same duties could be found not exempt.

One thing that is clear is that the determination is made on the employee's function and not just the job title. You cannot make a secretary exempt by calling him or her a manager if most of his or her duties are clerical. For more information, contact:

U.S. Department of Labor
Wage and Hour Division
200 Constitution Avenue, NW
Room S-3325
Washington, DC 20210
866-4USA-DOL
www.dol.gov/esa

Chicago District Office
230 South Dearborn Street
Room 412
Chicago, IL 60604
866-487-9243

Springfield District Office
509 West Capitol Avenue
Suite 205
Springfield, IL 62704

Overtime   On the Internet you can obtain information on the Department of Labor's *First Step Employment Law Advisor* at **www.dol.gov/elaws/ firststep**.

The general rule is that employees who work more than forty hours a week must be paid time-and-a-half for hours worked over forty. However, there are many exemptions to this general rule based on salary and position. These exceptions were completely revised in 2004, and an explanation of the changes is available at **www.dol.gov/esa**. For answers to questions about the law, call the U.S. Department of Labor at 866-487-9243.

PENSION AND BENEFIT LAWS

There are no laws requiring small businesses to provide any types of special benefits to employees. Such benefits are given to attract and keep good employees. The main concern with pension plans is that if you do start one, it must comply with federal tax laws.

Holidays

There are no federal or Illinois laws that require that employees be given holidays off. You can require them to work Thanksgiving and Christmas, and dock their pay or fire them for failing to show, but of course, you will not have much luck keeping employees with such a policy.

Most companies give full-time employees a certain number of paid holidays, such as New Year's Day (January 1), Memorial Day (last Monday in May), Fourth of July, Labor Day (first Monday in September), Thanksgiving (fourth Thursday in November), and Christmas (December 25). Some employers include other holidays, such as Martin Luther King, Jr.'s birthday (January 15), President's Day, and Columbus Day. If one of the holidays falls on a Saturday or Sunday, many employers give the preceding Friday or following Monday off.

Sick Days

There is no federal or Illinois law mandating that an employee be paid for time he or she is home sick. The situation seems to be that the larger the company, the more paid sick leave is allowed. Part-time workers rarely get sick leave, and small business sick leave is usually limited because a small business cannot afford to pay for time that employees do not work.

Some small companies have an official policy of no paid sick leave, but when an important employee misses a day because he or she is clearly sick, it is paid.

Breaks

There are no federal or Illinois laws requiring coffee breaks or lunch breaks. However, it is common sense that employees will be more productive if they have reasonable breaks.

Pension Plans

Few small new businesses can afford to provide pension plans for their employees. The first concern of a small business is usually how the owner can shelter income in a pension plan without having to set up a pension plan for an employee. Under most pension plans, this is not allowed.

IRA. Anyone with $4,000 of earnings can put up to that amount in an Individual Retirement Account (IRA). Individuals age 50 or older before 2007 can contribute up to $5,000 to a traditional IRA in 2006. Unless the person (or his or her spouse) is covered by a company pension plan and has income over a certain amount, the amount put into the account is fully tax-deductible.

ROTH IRA. Contributions to a Roth IRA are not tax-deductible, but when the money is taken out, it is not taxable. People who expect to still have taxable income when they withdraw from their IRA can benefit from these plans.

SEP IRA, SAR-SEP IRA, SIMPLE IRA. With these types of retirement accounts, a person can put a much greater amount into a retirement plan and deduct it from his or her taxable income. Employees must also be covered by such plans, but because certain employees are exempt, it is sometimes possible to use these for the owners alone. The best source for more information is a mutual fund company (such as Vanguard, Fidelity, Dreyfus, etc.) or a local bank. Either can set up the plan and provide you with all of the rules. These have an advantage over qualified plans because they do not have the high annual fees. The Internal Revenue Service Publication 560, Retirement Plans for Small Business, contains useful information on these accounts. This publication can be found online at **www.irs.gov/pub/irs-pdf/p560.pdf**.

Qualified retirement plans. Qualified retirement plans are 401(k) plans, Keogh plans, and corporate retirement plans. These are covered by the *Employee Retirement Income Security Act* (ERISA), which is a complicated law meant to protect employee pension plans in situations where the plan goes bankrupt. Many banks and mutual funds have created canned plans, which can be used instead of drafting a new one from scratch. Still, the fees for administering them are steep. Check with a bank or mutual fund for details.

FAMILY AND MEDICAL LEAVE LAW

Congress passed the *Family and Medical Leave Act of 1993* (FMLA), which requires an employee to be given up to twelve weeks of unpaid leave when:

❂ the employee or employee's spouse has a child;

❂ the employee adopts a child or takes in a foster child;

❂ the employee needs to care for an ill spouse, child, or parent; or,

❂ the employee becomes seriously ill.

The law only applies to employers with fifty or more employees. Also, the most highly paid 10% of an employer's salaried employees can be denied this leave because of the disruption to business their loss could cause. Only employees who have been employed over the previous twelve months and have been employed for at least 1,250 hours in those twelve months are eligible for benefits under the Act.

Illinois Law   Illinois statutes require that employers must give each employee up to eight hours off to attend a child's school activities or conferences that cannot be held during other hours. (820 ILCS 147/15.) The employee must first use up all other vacation and other time off, and must give the employer seven days' notice, unless it is an emergency. Time off under this statute does not need to be paid leave.

CHILD LABOR LAWS

The Fair Labor Standards Act also contains rules regarding the hiring of children. The basic rules state that children under 16 years old may not be hired, except in a few jobs (such as acting and newspaper delivery). Also, those under age 18 may not be hired for dangerous jobs. Children may not work more than three hours a day (eighteen hours a week) in a school week or more than eight hours a day (forty hours a week) in a nonschool week. If you plan to hire children, you should check the Fair Labor Standards Act, which is in Chapter 8, Title 29, United States Code (29 USC Chapter 8), as well as the related regulations found in Title 29 of the Code of Federal Regulations (29 C.F.R.).

IMMIGRATION LAWS

There are strict penalties for any business that hires aliens who are not eligible to work. You must verify both the identity and the employment eligibility of anyone you hire by using the **EMPLOYMENT ELIGIBILITY VERIFICATION (FORM I-9)**. (see form 4, p.235.) Both you and the employee must fill out the form, and you must check an employee's identification cards or papers. Fines for hiring illegal aliens range from $250 to $2,000 for the first offense and up to $10,000 for the third offense. Failure to maintain the proper paperwork may result in a fine of up to $1,000. The law does not apply to independent contractors with whom you may contract, and it does not penalize you if the employee used fake identification.

There are also penalties that apply to employers of four or more persons for discriminating against eligible applicants because they appear foreign or because of their national origin or citizenship status.

Appendix D has a list of acceptable documentation, a blank form, and instructions. (see form 4, p.235.) The blank form can also be downloaded at **www.uscis.gov/graphics/formsfee/forms/i-9.htm**.

For more information, call 800-357-2099. For the *Handbook for Employers and Instructions for Completing Form I-9, check the United States Citizenship and Immigration Services* (USCIS) website at **www.uscis.gov**.

Foreign Employees

If you wish to hire employees who are foreign citizens and are not able to provide the proper documentation, they must first obtain a work visa from USCIS.

Work visas for citizens of other countries are not easy to get. Millions of people around the globe would like to come to the U.S. to work, but the laws are designed to keep most of them out to protect the jobs of American citizens.

Whether or not a person can get a work visa depends on whether there is a shortage of U.S. workers available to fill the job. For jobs requiring few or no skills, it is practically impossible to get a visa. For highly skilled jobs, such as nurses and physical therapists, and for those of exceptional ability, such as Nobel Prize winners and Olympic medalists, obtaining a visa is fairly easy.

There are several types of visas, and different rules for different countries. For example, NAFTA has made it easier for some types of workers to enter the U.S. from Canada and Mexico. For some positions, the shortage of workers is assumed by the USCIS. For others, a business must first advertise a position available in the United States. Only after no qualified persons apply can it hire someone from another country.

The visa system is complicated and subject to regular change. If you wish to hire a foreign worker, you should consult with an immigration specialist or a book on the subject.

HIRING OFF THE BOOKS

Because of the taxes, insurance, and red tape involved with hiring employees, some new businesses hire people *off the books*. The employers pay them in cash and never admit they are employees. While the cash paid in wages would not be tax deductible, they consider this a smaller cost than compliance. Some even use off the books receipts to cover it.

Except when your spouse or child is giving you some temporary help, this is a terrible idea. Hiring people off the books can result in civil fines, loss of insurance coverage, and even criminal penalties. When engaged in dangerous work, like roofing or using power tools, you are risking millions of dollars in potential damages if a worker is seriously injured or killed.

It may be more costly and time-consuming to comply with the employment laws, but if you are focused on long-term growth with less risk, it is the wiser way to go.

FEDERAL CONTRACTS

Companies that do work for the federal government are subject to several laws.

The *Davis-Bacon Act* requires contractors engaged in U.S. government construction projects to pay wages and benefits that are equal to or better than the prevailing wages in the area.

The *McNamara-O'Hara Service Contract Act* sets wages and other labor standards for contractors furnishing services to agencies of the U.S. government.

The *Walsh-Healey Public Contracts Act* requires the Department of Labor to settle disputes regarding manufacturers supplying products to the U.S. government.

MISCELLANEOUS LAWS

In addition to the broad categories of laws affecting businesses, there are several other federal and state laws that you should be familiar with.

Federal Law   Federal law regulates affirmative action, layoffs, unions, and informational posters.

Affirmative action. In most cases, the federal government does not yet tell employers who they must hire, especially small new businesses. The only situation in which a small business would need to comply with affirmative action requirements would be if it accepted federal contracts or subcontracts. These requirements could include the hiring of minorities or Vietnam veterans.

Layoffs. Companies with one hundred or more full-time employees at one location are subject to the *Worker Adjustment and Retraining Notification Act.* (29 USC Chapter 23.) This law requires a sixty-day notification prior to certain layoffs, and has other strict provisions.

Unions. The *National Labor Relations Act of 1935* (29 USC Section 151 et seq.) gives employees the right to organize or join a union. There are things employers can do to protect themselves, but you should consult a labor attorney or a book on the subject before taking action that might be illegal and could result in fines.

Poster laws. Certain posters must be displayed to inform employees of their rights. Not all businesses are required to display all posters. The following list provides guidance in determining the poster requirements for your business.

- ✪ All employers subject to minimum wage provisions must display the wage and hour poster available from:

U.S. Department of Labor
200 Constitution Avenue, NW
Washington, DC 20210
866-4-USWAGE
www.dol.gov/esa/regs/compliance/posters/flsa.htm

- ✪ Employers with fifteen or more employees for twenty weeks of the year and employers with federal contracts or subcontracts of $10,000 or more must display the sex, race, religion, ethnic, age, equal pay, and disability discrimination poster (see page 116), available from:

EEOC Clearinghouse
1801 L Street, NW
Washington, DC 20507
202-663-4900

- ✪ The poster also specifically prohibits discrimination against Vietnam Era veterans in the case of employers with federal contracts or subcontracts of $100,000 or more.

- ✪ Employers with government contracts subject to the *Service Contract Act* or the *Public Contracts Act* must display a notice to employees working on government contracts, which is available from:

Employment Standards Administration
U.S. Department of Labor
200 Constitution Avenue, NW
Washington, DC 20210
866-487-9243
www.dol.gov/esa/regs/compliance/posters/pdf/govbw.pdf

✪ Employers who employ fifty or more employees in twenty or more work weeks and who are engaged in commerce or in any industry or activity affecting commerce are required to post a notice explaining employees' rights under the federal Family and Medical Leave Act. The poster is available from the Employment Standards Division, or online at **www.dol.gov/ esa/regs/compliance/posters/pdf/fmlaen.pdf**.

Illinois Law   Illinois law regulates termination due to wage assignments, AIDS testing, access to records, payment by mail, health and physical fitness requirements, sexual orientation, or a family member called to active duty in the military.

Termination of employee due to wage assignments or wage deduction orders. It is illegal in Illinois to fire or suspend an employee because of wage assignments. The quantity of these wage assignments is unimportant. However, it is legal to fire an employee if he or she is subject to two or more wage deduction orders based on more than one debt.

AIDS testing. No employer may require an employee to undergo an AIDS test unless the test subject gives written consent. (410 ILCS 305/4.) No employer may disclose the identity of the subject of an AIDS test or disclose the test results, except to the test subject or legally authorized representative. (410 ILCS 305/9.)

Records access. There are restrictions concerning the type of records an employer may keep on an employee. An employee has the right to inspect his or her own personnel records, excluding items such as letters of reference, test documents, or staff planning materials. (820 ILCS 40.)

Payment by mail. An employer must pay wages to an absent employee by mail if the employee so requests in writing.

Health and physical fitness requirements. Employers may require job applicants to submit to a pre-employment physical or a psychological examination to determine his or her capability to adequately perform the job requirements. One limitation on the use of such tests is that an employer may not use such tests to deny employment to an applicant on the basis of future risk of injury. The results of these tests must be made available if requested by an applicant. (Ill. Admin. Code Title 56, Section 2500.60(b).)

Discrimination based on sexual orientation. Effective January 1, 2006, the Illinois General Assembly amended the Illinois Human Rights Act to include sexual orientation as a protected class. Sexual orientation includes heterosexuality, homosexuality, bisexuality, and gender identity. Discrimination in employment is prohibited by the Human Rights Act, 775 ILCS 5/2.

Family Military Leave Act. In 2005, the General Assembly enacted the Illinois Family Military Leave Act. The Act requires employers of fifteen or more employees to allow unpaid leave to spouses and parents of members of the military who are called to active duty for more than thirty days.

Required poster. The Illinois Department of Labor requires employers to display the poster entitled *Notice to Employers and Employees.* Request the poster at:

Illinois Department of Labor
Fair Labor Standards Division
160 North LaSalle Street
Suite C-1300
Chicago, IL 60601
312-793-2800
www.state.il.us/agency/idol/Posters/poster.htm

Equal Employment Opportunity is

THE LAW

Employers Holding Federal Contracts or Subcontracts

Applicants to and employees of companies with a Federal government contract or subcontract are protected under the following Federal authorities:

RACE, COLOR, RELIGION, SEX, NATIONAL ORIGIN

Executive Order 11246, as amended, prohibits job discrimination on the basis of race, color, religion, sex or national origin, and requires affirmative action to ensure equality of opportunity in all aspects of employment.

INDIVIDUALS WITH DISABILITIES

Section 503 of the Rehabilitation Act of 1973, as amended, prohibits job discrimination because of disability and requires affirmative action to employ and advance in employment qualified individuals with disabilities who, with reasonable accommodation, can perform the essential functions of a job.

VIETNAM ERA, SPECIAL DISABLED, RECENTLY SEPARATED, AND OTHER PROTECTED VETERANS

38 U.S.C. 4212 of the Vietnam Era Veterans' Readjustment Assistance Act of 1974, as amended, prohibits job discrimination and requires affirmative action to employ and advance in employment qualified Vietnam era veterans, qualified special disabled veterans, recently separated veterans, and other protected veterans.

Any person who believes a contractor has violated its nondiscrimination or affirmative action obligations under the authorities above should contact immediately:

The Office of Federal Contract Compliance Programs (OFCCP), Employment Standards Administration, U.S. Department of Labor, 200 Constitution Avenue, N.W., Washington, D.C. 20210 or call (202) 693-0101, or an OFCCP regional or district office, listed in most telephone directories under U.S. Government, Department of Labor.

Private Employment, State and Local Governments, Educational Institutions

Applicants to and employees of most private employers, state and local governments, educational institutions, employment agencies and labor organizations are protected under the following Federal laws:

RACE, COLOR, RELIGION, SEX, NATIONAL ORIGIN

Title VII of the Civil Rights Act of 1964, as amended, prohibits discrimination in hiring, promotion, discharge, pay, fringe benefits, job training, classification, referral, and other aspects of employment, on the basis of race, color, religion, sex or national origin.

DISABILITY

The Americans with Disabilities Act of 1990, as amended, protects qualified applicants and employees with disabilities from discrimination in hiring, promotion, discharge, pay, job training, fringe benefits, classification, referral, and other aspects of employment on the basis of disability. The law also requires that covered entities provide qualified applicants and employees with disabilities with reasonable accommodations that do not impose undue hardship.

AGE

The Age Discrimination in Employment Act of 1967, as amended, protects applicants and employees 40 years of age or older from discrimination on the basis of age in hiring, promotion, discharge, compensation, terms, conditions or privileges of employment.

SEX (WAGES)

In addition to sex discrimination prohibited by Title VII of the Civil Rights Act of 1964, as amended (see above), the Equal Pay Act of 1963, as amended, prohibits sex discrimination in payment of wages to women and men performing substantially equal work in the same establishment.

Retaliation against a person who files a charge of discrimination, participates in an investigation, or opposes an unlawful employment practice is prohibited by all of these Federal laws.

If you believe that you have been discriminated against under any of the above laws, you should contact immediately:

The U.S. Equal Employment Opportunity Commission (EEOC), 1801 L Street, N.W., Washington, D.C. 20507 or an EEOC field office by calling toll free (800) 669-4000. For individuals with hearing impairments, EEOC's toll free TDD number is (800) 669-6820.

Programs or Activities Receiving Federal Financial Assistance

RACE, COLOR, RELIGION, NATIONAL ORIGIN, SEX

In addition to the protection of Title VII of the Civil Rights Act of 1964, as amended, Title VI of the Civil Rights Act prohibits discrimination on the basis of race, color or national origin in programs or activities receiving Federal financial assistance. Employment discrimination is covered by Title VI if the primary objective of the financial assistance is provision of employment, or where employment discrimination causes or may cause discrimination in providing services under such programs. Title IX of the Education Amendments of 1972 prohibits employment discrimination on the basis of sex in educational programs or activities which receive Federal assistance.

INDIVIDUALS WITH DISABILITIES

Sections 501, 504 and 505 of the Rehabilitation Act of 1973, as amended, prohibits employment discrimination on the basis of disability in any program or activity which receives Federal financial assistance in the federal government. Discrimination is prohibited in all aspects of employment against persons with disabilities who, with reasonable accommodation, can perform the essential functions of a job.

If you believe you have been discriminated against in a program of any institution which receives Federal assistance, you should contact immediately the Federal agency providing such assistance.

Publication OFCCP 1420
Revised 2004

Advertising and Promotion Laws

Because of the unscrupulous and deceptive advertising techniques and multitude of con artists trying to steal from innocent consumers, numerous federal and state statutes have been enacted that make it unlawful to use improper advertising and promotional techniques in soliciting business.

ADVERTISING LAWS AND RULES

The federal government regulates advertising through the *Federal Trade Commission* (FTC). The rules are contained in the Code of Federal Regulations (C.F.R.). You can find these rules in most law libraries and many public libraries. If you plan any advertising that you think may be questionable, you might want to check the rules. As you read the rules discussed, you will probably think of many violations you see every day.

Federal rules do not apply to every business. Small businesses that operate only within the state and do not use the postal service may be exempt. However, many of the federal rules have been adopted into law by the state of Illinois. Therefore, a violation could be prosecuted by the state rather than the federal government.

Some of the important rules are summarized below. If you wish, obtain copies of the Code of Federal Regulations from your library.

Deceptive Pricing

When prices are being compared, it is required that actual and not inflated prices are used. For example, if an object would usually be sold for $7, you should not first offer it for $10 and then start offering it at 30% off. It is considered misleading to suggest that a discount from list price is a bargain if the item is seldomly sold at list price. If most surrounding stores sell an item for $7 it is considered misleading to say it has a retail value of $10, even if there are some stores elsewhere selling it at that price. (16 C.F.R. Ch. I, Part 233.)

Bait Advertising

Bait advertising is placing an ad when you do not really want the respondents to buy the product offered, but to switch to another item. (16 C.F.R. Ch. I, Part 238.)

Use of Free, Half-Off, etc.

Use of words such as *free*, *1¢ sale*, and the like must not be misleading. This means that the regular price must not include a markup to cover the free item. The seller must expect to sell the product without the free item at some time in the future. (16 C.F.R. Ch. I, Part 251.)

Substantiation of Claims

The FTC requires that advertisers be able to substantiate their claims. (16 C.F.R. Sec 3.40; 48 F.R. Page 10471.) Some information on this policy is contained at **www.ftc.gov/bcp/guides/ad3subst.htm**.

Endorsements

Rules forbid endorsements that are misleading. An example is a quote from a film review that is used in such a way as to change the substance of the review. It is not necessary to use the exact words of the person endorsing the product as long as the opinion is not distorted. If a product is changed, an endorsement that does not apply to the new version cannot be used. For some items, such as drugs, claims cannot be used without scientific proof. Endorsements by organizations cannot be used unless one is sure that the membership holds the same opinion. (16 C.F.R. Ch. I, Part 255.)

Unfairness

Any advertising practices that can be deemed to be unfair are forbidden by the FTC. (15 USC Sec. 45.) An explanation of this policy is located at **www.ftc.gov/bcp/policystmt/ad-unfair.htm**.

Negative Option Plans

When a seller uses a sales system in which the buyer must notify the seller if he or she does not want the goods, the seller must provide the buyer with a form to decline the sale and at least ten days in which to decline. Bonus merchandise must be shipped promptly and the seller must promptly terminate the plans of any buyer who so requests after completion of the contract. (16 C.F.R. Ch. I, Part 425.)

Laser Eye Surgery

Under the laws governing deceptive advertising, the FTC and the FDA are regulating the advertising of laser eye surgery. Anyone involved in this area should obtain a copy of these rules. They are located on the Internet at **www.ftc.gov/bcp/guides/eyecare2.htm**. (15 USC Sections 45, 52–57.)

Food and Dietary Supplements

Under the *Nutritional Labeling Education Act*, the FTC and the Federal Drug Administration (FDA) regulate the packaging and advertising of food and dietary products. Anyone involved in this area should obtain a copy of these rules. (21 USC Sec. 343.) A guide to this Act can be found online at **www.fda.gov/ora/inspect_ref/igs/nleatxt.html**.

Jewelry and Precious Metals

The FTC has numerous rules governing the sale and advertising of jewelry and precious metals. Anyone in this business should obtain a copy of these rules. (61 F.R. Page 27212.) They are located at **www.ftc.gov/bcp/guides/jewel-gd.htm**.

Illinois Laws

Illinois has its own set of laws regulating advertising and promotion.

Misleading advertising. It is illegal to use advertising that is untrue, misleading, or deceptive. Violation of the act is a misdemeanor. (720 ILCS 295/1a.)

Free gifts. It is an unlawful practice for any person to promote or advertise any business or product by means of offering free prizes or gifts, unless all material terms and conditions relating to the offer are clearly and conspicuously disclosed at the offset of the offer. (815 ILCS 505/2P.)

Going-out-of-business sales. No person may advertise or represent to the public that any sale of goods is a going-out-of-business, creditor's, or insolvent's sale of goods, unless a license is first obtained. The license must be prominently displayed. Violation is subject to a misdemeanor, injunction, or both. (815 ILCS 350.)

Bait and switch. It is forbidden to advertise a product or service when there is no intention to fulfill the offer in the ad. Violators are subject to a misdemeanor, injunction, or both. (720 ILCS 295/1b.)

INTERNET SALES LAWS

There are not yet specific laws governing Internet transactions that are different from laws governing other transactions. The FTC feels that its current rules regarding deceptive advertising, substantiation, disclaimers, refunds, and related matters must be followed by Internet businesses, and that consumers are adequately protected by them. For some specific guidelines on Internet advertising, see the FTC's site at **www.ftc.gov/bcp/conline/pubs/buspubs/ruleroad.htm**.

EMAIL ADVERTISING

The Controlling the Assault of Non-Solicited Pornography And Marketing Act of 2003 (CAN-SPAM) has put numerous controls on how you can use email to solicit business for your company. It requires unsolicited commercial email messages to be labeled, and the message must include opt-out instructions and the sender's physical address. Some of the prohibited activities under the Act are:

- false or misleading information in an email;

- deceptive subject heading;

- failure to include a functioning return address;

- mailing to someone who has asked not to receive solicitations;

- failure to include a valid postal address;

- omitting an opt-out procedure;

- failure to clearly mark the email as advertising; and,

- including sexual material without adequate warnings.

Some of the provisions contain criminal penalties as well as civil fines. For more information on the CAN-SPAM Act, see **www.gigalaw.com/canspam**. For text of the Act plus other spam laws around the world, see **www.spamlaws.com**.

HOME SOLICITATION LAWS

The Federal Trade Commission has rules governing door-to-door sales. In any such sale it is a deceptive trade practice to fail to furnish a receipt explaining the sale (in the language of the presentation) and giving notice that there is a right to back out of the contract within three days, known as a *right of rescission*. The notice must be supplied in duplicate, must be in at least ten-point type, and must be captioned either "Notice of Right to Cancel" or "Notice of Cancellation." The notice must be worded as follows.

NOTICE OF CANCELLATION

_____
(Date)

YOU MAY CANCEL THIS TRANSACTION, WITHOUT ANY PENALTY OR OBLIGATION, WITHIN THREE BUSINESS DAYS FROM THE ABOVE DATE.

IF YOU CANCEL, ANY PROPERTY TRADED IN, ANY PAYMENTS MADE BY YOU UNDER THE CONTRACT OR SALE, AND ANY NEGOTIABLE INSTRUMENT EXECUTED BY YOU WILL BE RETURNED TO YOU WITHIN 10 BUSINESS DAYS FOLLOWING RECEIPT BY THE SELLER OF YOUR CANCELLATION NOTICE, AND ANY SECURITY INTEREST ARISING OUT OF THE TRANSACTION WILL BE CANCELLED.

IF YOU CANCEL, YOU MUST MAKE AVAILABLE TO THE SELLER AT YOUR RESIDENCE, IN SUBSTANTIALLY AS GOOD CONDITION AS WHEN RECEIVED, ANY GOODS DELIVERED TO YOU UNDER THIS CONTRACT OR SALE; OR YOU MAY IF YOU WISH, COMPLY WITH THE INSTRUCTIONS OF THE SELLER REGARDING THE RETURN SHIPMENT OF THE GOODS AT THE SELLER'S EXPENSE AND RISK.

IF YOU DO MAKE THE GOODS AVAILABLE TO THE SELLER AND THE SELLER DOES NOT PICK THEM UP WITHIN 20 DAYS OF THE DATE OF YOUR NOTICE OF CANCELLATION, YOU MAY RETAIN OR DISPOSE OF THE GOODS WITHOUT ANY FURTHER OBLIGATION. IF YOU FAIL TO MAKE THE GOODS AVAILABLE TO THE SELLER, OR IF YOU AGREE TO RETURN THE GOODS AND FAIL TO DO SO, THEN YOU REMAIN LIABLE FOR PERFORMANCE OF ALL OBLIGATIONS UNDER THE CONTRACT.

TO CANCEL THIS TRANSACTION, MAIL OR DELIVER A SIGNED AND DATED COPY OF THIS CANCELLATION NOTICE OR ANY OTHER WRITTEN NOTICE, OR SEND A TELEGRAM, TO _____, AT _____ NOT LATER THAN MIDNIGHT OF _____ (date).

I HEREBY CANCEL THIS TRANSACTION.

_____   _____
(Buyer's signature)   (Date)

The seller must complete the notice and orally inform the buyer of the right to cancel. He or she cannot misrepresent the right to cancel, assign the contract until the fifth business day, or include a confession of judgment in the contract. (For more specific details, see the rules contained at 16 C.F.R. Ch. I, Part 429.)

Illinois Laws   Illinois has its own laws concerning home solicitation.

Right to cancel. The buyer may cancel, in writing, any sale over $25 solicited at the buyer's home. The notice must be postmarked any time before midnight of the third business day after the sales day. (815 ILCS 505/2B.)

Written agreement. Every sale solicited at the buyer's home must be in writing and must contain a similar notice as the following.

You, the consumer, may cancel this transaction at any time prior to midnight of the third business day after the date of this transaction. See the attached notice of cancellation form for an explanation of this right.

The notice should appear in bold, ten-point type. You will need to consult the statute to obtain the additional language required for the cancellation form.

Refund. The refund must be made to the buyer within ten days of receiving the notice of cancellation. If it is not, the seller may be subject to criminal and civil penalties.

TELEPHONE SOLICITATION LAWS

Telephone solicitations are governed by the *Telephone Consumer Protection Act* (47 USC Sec. 227) and the Federal Communications Commission rules implementing the Act (47 C.F.R. Sec. 64.1200). Violators of the Act can be sued for $500 in damages by consumers and can be fined $10,000 by the FCC. Some of the requirements under the law are:

❂ calls can only be made between 8 a.m. and 9 p.m.;

❂ solicitors must keep a *do not call* list and honor requests to not call;

❂ there must be a written policy stating that the parties called are told the name of the caller, the caller's business name, and the phone number or address. They must also be informed that the call is a sales call and the nature of the goods or services;

❂ personnel must be trained in the policies; and,

❂ recorded messages cannot be used to call residences.

Do Not Call Registry

In 2003, the FCC introduced the national *Do Not Call Registry*, where individuals could register their telephone numbers and prohibit certain telephone solicitors from calling the registered numbers. Once a person registers a telephone number, it remains on the registry for five years. Telemarketing firms can receive heavy fines for violating the registry statute, with fines ranging up to $11,000 per violation. Not all telephone solicitations are barred, however. The following solicitors may still contact a person whose telephone number has been entered in the registry:

❂ calls from companies with which the registered person has a prior business relationship;

❂ calls for which the recipient has given written consent;

❂ calls that do not include advertisements; and,

❂ calls from charitable organizations.

It is illegal under the Act to send advertising faxes to anyone who has not consented to receiving such faxes or is an existing customer.

Illinois Law   The *Telephone Solicitations Act* (815 ILCS 413) applies to any telephone communication to solicit the sale of goods. Penalties for violations include:

- ✪ a judgment for three times the amount of damages;

- ✪ attorney's fees; and,

- ✪ court costs.

The law contains the following main provisions.

Identification. Any person who makes a telephone solicitation call must identity him- or herself by true first and last name, and the name of the business represented, immediately upon making contact.

Time. No calls may be made between the hours of 9 p.m. and 8 a.m.

Consent. The person who makes a telephone solicitation call must obtain the consent of the person called at the beginning of the call.

Exceptions. This law does not apply to telephone calls made by registered investment advisors or brokers.

It is illegal to send unsolicited advertising materials by fax within the state of Illinois. (720 ILCS 5/26-3.)

Illinois has passed a law providing for a *do not call* list to be published. Businesses calling persons on this list are subject to fines. (815 ILCS 413/15.)

WEIGHTS AND LABELING

All food products are required to have labels with information on the nutritional values, such as calories, fat, and protein. For most products, the label must be in the required format so that consumers can easily compare products. However, if such a format will not fit on the product label, the information may be presented in another form that is easily readable.

Federal rules require metric measurement be included on products. Metric measures do not have to be the first measurement on the container, but they must be included. Food items that are packaged as they are sold, such as delicatessen items, do not have to contain metric labels.

Illinois Laws   The Illinois *Weights and Measures Act* governs many specific aspects of weighing and packaging, especially food and agricultural products. If your product fits into one of these categories, consult this statute. (225 ILCS 470.)

DECEPTIVE PRACTICES

If a business engages in deceptive or unfair practices in a consumer transaction, the Illinois Attorney General or a state's attorney may bring court action against the business for injunctions, damages to consumers, and fines of up to $50,000. If the court finds that the practice in question was entered into with an intent to defraud, it may impose a penalty of up to $50,000 per violation. (815 ILCS 505.)

No damages can be recovered against a retailer who acted in *good faith* in repeating claims of a manufacturer or wholesaler, and did not know the claims were in violation of this law.

Payment and Collection Laws

Depending on the business you are in, you may be paid by cash, checks, credit cards, or some sort of financing arrangement, such as a promissory note or mortgage. Both state and federal laws affect the type of payments you collect. Failure to follow the laws can cost you considerably.

CASH

Cash is probably the easiest form of payment and it is subject to few restrictions. The most important one is that you keep an accurate accounting of your cash transactions and that you report all of your cash income on your tax return. Recent efforts to stop the drug trade have resulted in some serious penalties for failing to report cash transactions and for money laundering. The laws are so sweeping that even if you deal in cash in an ordinary business, you may violate the law and face huge fines and imprisonment.

The most important law to be concerned with is the one requiring the filing of the **REPORT OF CASH PAYMENTS OVER $10,000 RECEIVED IN A TRADE OR BUSINESS (IRS FORM 8300)**. (see form 13, p.275.) A transaction does not have to happen in one day. If a person brings you smaller amounts of cash that add up to $10,000 and the government can construe them as one transaction, then the form must be filed. Under this law, *cash* also includes travelers' checks and money orders, but not cashier's checks or bank checks.

CHECKS

It is important to accept checks in your business. While there is a small percentage that will be bad, most checks will be good and you will be able to accommodate more customers. To avoid having problems with checks, follow these rules.

Illinois law forbids a business from requiring a customer to provide a credit card number or expiration date in order to pay by or cash a check. (810 ILCS 5/3-505A.) However, the business can request to see a card to establish that the customer is creditworthy or for additional identification, and can record the type of credit card and issuing company. The business cannot record the number of the card. The penalty for the first violation is a fine of $500.

Bad Checks   Illinois has a fairly effective bad check collection process. If you follow the rules, you will probably be able to collect on a bad check. Some counties even have special divisions of the sheriff's department that actively help you collect on bad checks.

The first rule is that you must be able to identify the person who gave you the check. To do this, you should require identification and write down the sources of identification on the face of the check, such as his or her phone, driver's license, and Social Security numbers. Another rule is that you cannot accept post-dated checks. Also, you must send a demand to the person by certified mail, return receipt requested, that he or she pay the amount of the check plus a penalty of $25. (810 ILCS 5/3-806.) If the customer fails to pay the amount of the written check within thirty days, he or she is liable for costs and expenses, including reasonable attorneys' fees, incurred in collection proceedings. Another option is to contact the local state's attorney's office to initiate criminal prosecution.

Refunds after Cashing Check

A popular scam is for a person to purchase something by using a check, only to return the next day demanding a refund. After making the refund, the business discovers the initial payment check bounced. Do not make refunds until checks clear.

CREDIT CARDS

In our buy now, pay later society, credit cards can add greatly to your sales potential, especially with large, discretionary purchases. For MasterCard, Visa, and Discover, the fees you pay are about 2%, and this amount is easily paid for by the extra purchases that the cards allow. (American Express, however, charges 4–5%.)

A business that has an account with a financial institution that allows the business to accept credit card transactions is said to have obtained *merchant status*. For businesses that have a *retail outlet*, there is usually no problem getting merchant status. Most commercial banks can handle it. Discover can also set you up to accept their card as well as MasterCard and Visa, and they will wire the money into your bank account daily. However, for mail order businesses, especially those operating out of the home, it is much harder to get merchant status. (American Express will accept mail order companies operating out of the home. However, not as many people have their cards.)

Some companies open a small storefront (or share one) to get merchant status and then process mostly mail orders. The processors usually do not want to accept you if you will do more than 50% mail order, because credit card companies fear mail order fraud. However, if you have not had many complaints from your customers, you may be allowed to process mostly mail orders.

You might be tempted to try to run your charges through another business. This may be okay if you actually sell your products through them; however, if you run your business charges through their account, the other business may lose its merchant status. Someone who bought a book by mail from you and then has a charge on his or her statement from a florist shop will probably call the credit card company saying that he or she never bought anything from the florist shop. After too many of these complaints, the account will be closed.

FINANCING LAWS

Some businesses can make sales more easily if they finance the purchases themselves. If the business has enough capital to do this, it can earn extra profits on the financing terms. However, because of abuses, many consumer protection laws have been passed by both the federal and state governments.

Federal Law   Two important federal laws regarding financing are called the *Truth in Lending Act* and the *Fair Credit Billing Act*. These are implemented by what is called *Regulation Z* (commonly known as *Reg. Z*), issued by the Board of Governors of the Federal Reserve System. It is contained in Volume 12 of the Code of Federal Regulations, page 226.

The regulation covers all transactions in which the following four conditions are met:

1.   credit is offered;

2.   the offering of credit is regularly done;

3.   there is a finance charge for the credit or there is a written agreement with more than four payments; and,

4.   the credit is for personal, family, or household purposes.

It also covers credit card transactions in which only the first two conditions are met. It applies to leases if the consumer ends up paying the full value and keeping the item leased. It does not apply to the following transactions:

✪   transactions with businesses or agricultural purposes;

✪   transactions with organizations such as corporations or the government;

✪   transactions of over $25,000 that are not secured by the consumer's dwelling;

✪   credit involving public utilities;

- ✪ credit involving securities or commodities;

- ✪ home fuel budget plans; and,

- ✪ student loan programs.

The way for a small business to avoid Reg. Z violations is to avoid transactions that meet the conditions or to make sure all transactions fall under the exceptions. This is easy for many businesses. Instead of extending credit to customers, accept credit cards and let the credit card company extend the credit. However, if your customers usually do not have credit cards or if you are in a business that often extends credit (such as used car sales), consult a lawyer knowledgeable about Reg. Z.

Illinois Laws   Illinois also has laws regarding financing arrangements. The law specifies what size type must be used in printed contracts, what notices must be included in them, and many other details. Anyone engaged in installment sales in Illinois should carefully review the latest versions of the following statutes:

- ✪ *Consumer Installment Loan Act* (205 ILCS 670);

- ✪ *Motor Vehicle Retail Installment Sales Act* (815 ILCS 375);

- ✪ *Rental-Purchase Agreement Act* (815 ILCS 655); and,

- ✪ *Retail Installment Sales Act* (815 ILCS 405).

In addition to these Acts, Illinois law forbids discrimination based upon sex, religion, age, disability, marital status, or race in the areas of loaning money and granting credit. (775 ILCS 5/4-102.) Discrimination in transactions regarding or the financing of residential real estate based upon race, color, national origin, sex, handicap, familial status, or religion is forbidden. (775 ILCS 5/3-102.)

USURY

Usury is the charging of an illegally high rate of interest. In Illinois, the maximum rate of interest you may charge is 20%. In some cases, the maximum rate is 9%. (815 ILCS 205/4, 4a.) If there is no written agreement as to the rate of interest, the rate is set by law.

The penalty for charging above the legal rate is that the borrower may recover twice the total of all interest and charges, plus attorney's fees and court costs.

Anyone charging or receiving interest at a rate of over 20% is guilty of a felony.

COLLECTIONS

The federal *Fair Debt Collection Practices Act of 1977* bans the use of deception, harassment, and other unreasonable acts in the collection of debts. It has strict requirements whenever someone is collecting a debt for someone else. If you are in the collection business, you must obtain a copy of this law.

The Federal Trade Commission has issued some rules that prohibit deceptive representations, such as:

✪   pretending to be in the motion picture industry, the government, or a credit bureau;

✪   using questionnaires that do not say their purpose is collecting a debt; or,

✪   any combination of these.

Illinois Laws   The Illinois *Collection Agency Act* applies to debts owed by persons (not corporations) for transactions that were for personal, family, or household purposes. (225 ILCS 425.) The law forbids:

- ✪ simulating a law enforcement officer or government agency;

- ✪ using or threatening force or violence;

- ✪ threatening to disclose the debt to others without explaining that the dispute over the debt will also be disclosed;

- ✪ contacting or threatening to contact a debtor's employer prior to obtaining a final judgment after the debt went to collection (unless the debtor gave permission in writing or agreed in writing as to the debt);

- ✪ disclosing information affecting the debtor's reputation to persons outside the debtor's family who do not have a legitimate business need for the information;

- ✪ disclosing false information affecting the debtor's reputation;

- ✪ disclosing information about a disputed debt without disclosing the dispute;

- ✪ willfully harassing the debtor or his or her family;

- ✪ using profane, obscene, vulgar, or willfully abusive language with the debtor or his or her family;

- ✪ attempting to collect a debt that is not legitimate;

- ✪ claiming a legal right, knowing that this right does not exist;

- ✪ using communication that looks like it is from a court, government, or attorney if it is not;

- ✪ pretending to be an attorney by using an attorney's stationery or forms;

- ✪ orally pretending to be an attorney or associated with an attorney;

- ✪ advertising or threatening to advertise the sale of a claim, unless under court order or as assignee;

- ✪ publishing or posting a deadbeat list;

- ✪ refusing to identify one's self or employer when requested by a debtor;

- ✪ mailing any communication to a debtor that contains embarrassing words on the outside of the envelope; and,

- ✪ communicating with a debtor between 9 p.m. and 8 a.m. without prior consent of the debtor.

Violation of any of these actions is subject to a fine of not more than $5,000 for a first offense, and not more than $10,000 for a subsequent offense. The Division of Consumer Services also investigates debtors' complaints of violations of this law. The agency may issue warnings, reprimands, revocation of licensing, and fines. The state's attorney may seek criminal penalties and injunctions for certain violations.

Business Relations Law

At both the federal and state levels, there exist many laws regarding how businesses relate to one another. Some of the more important ones are discussed in this chapter.

THE UNIFORM COMMERCIAL CODE

The *Uniform Commercial Code* (UCC) is a set of laws regulating numerous aspects of business. A national group drafted this set of uniform laws to avoid having a patchwork of different laws around the fifty states. Although some states modified some sections of the laws, the code is basically the same in most of the states. In Illinois, the UCC is contained in 810 ILCS 5/2. Each chapter is concerned with a different aspect of commercial relations, such as sales, warranties, bank deposits, commercial paper, and bulk transfers.

Businesses that wish to know their rights in all types of transactions should obtain a copy of the UCC. It is especially useful in transactions between merchants. However, the meaning is not always clear from a reading of the statutes.

COMMERCIAL DISCRIMINATION

The *Robinson-Patman Act of 1936* prohibits businesses from injuring competition by offering the same goods at different prices to different buyers. This means that the large chain stores should not be getting a better price than your small shop. It also requires that promotional allowances must be made on proportionally the same terms to all buyers.

As a small business, you may be a victim of a Robinson-Patman Act violation, but fighting a much larger company in court would probably be too expensive for you. Your best bet, if an actual violation has occurred, would be to see if you could get the government to prosecute it. For more information on what constitutes a violation, see the Federal Trade Commission and the Department of Justice's joint site at **www.ftc.gov/bc/compguide/index.htm**.

Illinois Law Unlike some states, Illinois has not enacted a separate state version of the Robinson-Patman Act.

RESTRAINING TRADE

One of the earliest federal laws affecting business is the *Sherman Antitrust Act of 1890*. The purpose of this law was to protect competition in the marketplace by prohibiting monopolies.

Examples of some prohibited actions are:

- agreements between competitors to sell at the same prices;

- agreements between competitors on how much will be sold or produced;

- agreements between competitors to divide up a market;

- refusing to sell one product without a second product; and,

- exchanging information among competitors that results in similarity of prices.

As a new business, you probably will not be in a position to violate the Act, but you should be aware of it in case a larger competitor tries to put you out of business.

Illinois Law   Under the Illinois *Antitrust Act*, it is unlawful to have any contract, combination, or conspiracy to restrain trade. (740 ILCS 10.) It is also unlawful to monopolize, attempt to monopolize, or combine or conspire with any other person to monopolize, any part of trade or commerce. The penalty for any violation is up to $100,000 for a person, and up to $1,000,000 for a company. A person whose business is hurt by a violation can seek an injunction to prohibit violations. In a suit against a violator, he or she may collect triple damages, plus costs and attorney's fees.

COMMERCIAL BRIBERY

A person commits commercial bribery in Illinois when he or she confers any benefit upon any employee, without the consent of the employer, with intent to influence the employee's conduct in relation to his or her employer's affairs. Violations result in a fine of up to $5,000. (720 ILCS 5/29A-1.)

INTELLECTUAL PROPERTY PROTECTION

As a business owner, you should know enough about intellectual property laws to protect your own creations and to keep from violating the rights of others. Intellectual property is the product of human creativity, such as writings, designs, inventions, melodies, and processes. Intellectual property is something that can be stolen without being physically taken. For example, if you write a book, someone can steal the words from your book without stealing a physical copy of it.

As the Internet grows, intellectual property is becoming more valuable. Smart business owners will take the actions necessary to protect their company's intellectual property. Additionally, business owners should know intellectual property laws to make certain they do not violate the rights of others. Even an unknowing violation of the law can result in stiff fines and penalties.

The following paragraphs explain the types of intellectual property and the ways to protect them.

Patent

A *patent* is protection given to new and useful inventions, discoveries, and designs. To be entitled to a patent, a work must be completely new and unobvious. The first inventor who files for a patent gets it. Once an invention is patented, no one else can make use of that invention, even if they discover it independently. In general, a new patent lasts for twenty years from the date of filing the patent application with the *United States Patent and Trademark Office* (PTO). Patents cannot be renewed. The patent application must clearly explain how to make the invention, so when the patent expires, others will be able to freely make and use the invention. Patents are registered with the United States Patent and Trademark Office. Patentable items include mechanical devices or new drug formulas.

Copyright

A *copyright* is protection given to original works of authorship, such as written works, musical works, visual works, performance works, or computer software programs. A copyright exists from the moment of creation, but one cannot register a copyright until it has been fixed in tangible form. Also, titles, names, or slogans cannot be copyrighted. A copyright currently gives the author and his or her heirs exclusive right to the work for the life of the author plus seventy years. Copyrights first registered before 1978 last for ninety-five years. This was previously seventy-five years, but was extended twenty years to match the European system. Copyrights on works that are created on or after January 1, 1978 apply automatically from the time of creation, and generally last until seventy years after the author's death. Copyrights are registered with the Register of Copyrights at the Library of Congress. The fee to register a copyright increased to $45 on July 1, 2006. Examples of works that are copyrightable include books, paintings, songs, poems, plays, drawings, and films. Contact the U.S. Copyright Office at:

Library of Congress
101 Independence Avenue, SE
Washington, DC 20559
202-707-3000
www.copyright.gov

Trademark   A *trademark* is protection given to a name or symbol that is used to distinguish one person's goods or services from those of others. It can consist of letters, numbers, packaging, labeling, musical notes, colors, or a combination of these. If a trademark is used on services as opposed to goods, it is called a *service mark*. A trademark lasts indefinitely if it is used continuously and renewed properly. Trademarks are registered with the United States Patent and Trademark Office and with individual states. (This is explained further in Chapter 3.) Examples of trademarks include the Chrysler name on automobiles, the red border on TIME magazine, and the shape of the Coca-Cola bottle.

Trade Secrets   A *trade secret* is information or a process that provides a commercial advantage that is protected by keeping it a secret. Examples of trade secrets may be a list of successful distributors, the formula for Coca-Cola, or some unique source code in a computer program. Trade secrets are not registered anywhere, but they are protected by the fact that they are not disclosed. They are protected only for as long as they are kept secret. If you independently discover the formula for Coca-Cola tomorrow, you can freely market it. (You still cannot use the trademark Coca-Cola on your product to market it.)

Illinois law. Illinois has passed the *Uniform Trade Secrets Act*, which protects trade secrets from appropriation by other businesses. (765 ILCS 1065/1.) It provides for injunctions, damages, and attorney's fees for violation of the act.

There are numerous other Illinois laws dealing with trade secrets. If you have some concerns about trade secrets in your business, you should check the index to Illinois statutes under trade secrets.

Protecting Your Idea   Some things are just not protectable, such as ideas, systems, and discoveries that are not allowed any protection under law. If you have a great idea, such as selling packets of hangover medicine in bars, you cannot stop others from doing the same thing. If you invent a new medicine, you can patent it; if you pick a distinctive name for it, you can register the name as a trademark; and, if you create a unique picture or instructions for the package, you can copyright it. However, you cannot stop others from using your basic business idea of marketing hangover medicine in bars.

Notice the subtle differences among the protective systems available. If you invent something two days after someone else does and that person has patented it, you cannot even use it for yourself. However, if you write the same poem as someone else and neither of you copied the other, both of you can copyright the poem. If you patent something, you can have the exclusive rights to it for the term of the patent, but you must disclose how others can recreate it after the patent expires. However, if you keep it a trade secret, you have exclusive rights as long as no one learns the secret.

The law of intellectual property is in a time of transition. Every year new changes are made in the laws and new forms of creativity win protection. For more information, consult a new edition of a book on these types of property.

Endless Laws

The state of Illinois and the federal government have numerous laws and rules that apply to every aspect of every type of business. There are laws governing such things as fence posts, hosiery, rabbit raising, refund policies, frozen desserts, and advertising. Every business is affected by one or another of these endless laws.

Some activities are covered by both state and federal laws. In such cases, you must obey the stricter of the rules. In addition, more than one agency of the state or federal government may have rules governing your business. Each of these may have the power to investigate violations and impose fines or other penalties.

Penalties for violations of these laws can range from a warning to a criminal fine and even jail time. In some cases, employees can sue for damages. Since ignorance of the law is no excuse, it is your duty to learn what laws apply to your business.

Few people in business know the laws that apply to their businesses. If you take the time to learn them, you can become an expert in your field and avoid problems with regulators. You can also fight back if one of your competitors uses an illegal method to compete with you.

The laws and rules that affect most businesses are explained in this section. Following the explanation is a list of more specialized laws. You should read through this list and see which ones may apply to your business. Then, go to your public library or law library and read them. Some may not apply to your aspect of the business. If any of them do apply, you should make copies to keep on hand.

FEDERAL LAWS

The federal laws that are most likely to affect small businesses are rules of the Federal Trade Commission (FTC). The FTC has some rules that affect many businesses; the rules about labeling, warranties, and mail order sales are just some examples. Other rules affect only certain industries.

If you sell goods by mail, you should send for the FTC's booklet, *A Business Guide to the Federal Trade Commission's Mail or Telephone Order Merchandise Rule*. It is also available online at **www.ftc.gov/ bcp/conline/pubs/buspubs/mailorder.htm**. You should ask for their latest information on the subject if you are going to be involved in an industry such as those listed below, or using warranties or your own labeling. The address is:

Federal Trade Commission
600 Pennsylvania Avenue, NW
Washington, DC 20580
202-326-2222

The rules of the FTC are contained in the Code of Federal Regulations (C.F.R.) in Title 16.

Some other federal laws that affect businesses are as follows:

- ✪ *Alcohol Administration Act*

- ✪ *Child Protection and Toy Safety Act*

- ✪ *Clean Water Act*

- ✪ *Comprehensive Smokeless Tobacco Health Education Act*

- ✪ *Consumer Credit Protection Act*

- ✪ *Consumer Product Safety Act*

- ✪ *Energy Policy and Conservation Act*

- ✪ *Environmental Pesticide Control Act of 1972*

- ✪ *Fair Credit Reporting Act*

- ✪ *Fair Packaging and Labeling Act*

- ✪ *Flammable Fabrics Act*

- ✪ *Food, Drug, and Cosmetic Act*

- ✪ *Food Safety Enforcement Enhancement Act of 1997*

- ✪ *Fur Products Labeling Act*

- ✪ *Hazardous Substances Act*

- ✪ *Hobby Protection Act*

- ✪ *Insecticide, Fungicide, and Rodenticide Act*

- ✪ *Magnuson-Moss Warranty Act*

- ✪ *Nutrition Labeling and Education Act of 1990*

- ✪ *Poison Prevention Packaging Act of 1970*

- ✪ *Solid Waste Disposal Act*

- ✪ *Textile Fiber Products Identification Act*

- ✪ *Toxic Substance Control Act*

- ✪ *Wool Products Labeling Act*

Homeland Security Concerns

The recent formation of the U.S. Department of Homeland Security (DHS) has caused a variety of new issues to arise that affect business. New laws designed to protect national interests have been and will continue to be enacted that will directly impact how businesses are operated. The DHS also has a need for products and services that will ensure national security. This, in turn, will provide many opportunities for companies engaged in businesses that can deliver those goods and services. For more information about DHS opportunities, contact the Department at:

U.S. Department of Homeland Security
Washington, DC 20528
www.dhs.gov/dhspublic

Sarbanes-Oxley Act

In the wake of crises at Enron as well as other publicly traded companies several years ago, Congress enacted the *Sarbanes-Oxley Act* in 2002. The purpose of this legislation is to, as Congress stated, "protect investors by improving the accuracy and reliability of corporate disclosures made pursuant to the securities law." The Act applies to all publicly traded companies, no matter how small. Among other things, the Act requires that:

- corporate officers certify that they have reviewed the company's financial reports and that no false or misleading information is contained therein;

- changes in the financial standing or operations of the company be disclosed;

- the company makes no loans to insiders; and,

- compliance with the Act is achieved by certain set deadlines.

The text of the Sarbanes-Oxley Act can be found online at **www.sec.gov/about/laws/soa2002.pdf**.

Punishment for violations of the Act includes multimillion dollar fines and prison time, so it is extremely important that the Sarbanes-Oxley requirements are followed. Firms offering assistance with compliance to companies is becoming big business in and of itself. It may pay off for you to consider hiring an expert to guide your business through the compliance process.

ILLINOIS LAWS

Illinois has numerous laws regulating specific types of businesses or certain activities of businesses. The following is a list of the laws that are most likely to affect small businesses. Citations refer to a version of Illinois laws called the Illinois Compiled Statutes.

INDUSTRY	LAW
Adoption Agencies	750 ILCS 50/4.1
Adult Congregate Living Facilities	210 ILCS 35
Adult Foster Care	210 ILCS 135/3
Air-Conditioning	65 ILCS 5/11-32-1, 720 ILCS 220
Alarm Contractors	225 ILCS 447
Ambulance Services	210 ILCS 50
Animals	510 ILCS 5
Bail Bondsmen	725 ILCS 5/103-9
Banking	810 ILCS 5/4
Bed and Breakfast Establishments	50 ILCS 820
Boiler Safety	430 ILCS 75
Boxing and Fighting	225 ILCS 105
Brake Fluid	625 ILCS 5/12-302
Business Records	805 ILCS 410
Cemeteries	65 ILCS 5/11-49-1
Charitable Solicitation	225 ILCS 460
Child Day Care	225 ILCS 10/3
Collections	225 ILCS 425
Condominiums	765 ILCS 605
Construction	225 ILCS 335
Consumer Finance	205 ILCS 660
Cosmetics	410 ILCS 620
Credit Cards	720 ILCS 250
Credit Services Organizations	815 ILCS 605
Dairies	410 ILCS 635
Dance Studios	815 ILCS 610
Dating Referral Services	815 ILCS 615

Drugs	30 ILCS 580,
	410 ILCS 620,
	720 ILCS 570
Elevators	430 ILCS 80,
	410 ILCS 30
Energy Conservation Standards	20 ILCS 1115
Explosives	225 ILCS 210
Fences	765 ILCS 130
Fertilizers	505 ILCS 80
Fiduciaries	205 ILCS 620
Fireworks	425 ILCS 30
Food	410 ILCS 620
Franchises	815 ILCS 705
Fruits and Vegetables	505 ILCS 70
Fuels	430 ILCS 30
Gambling and Lotteries	720 ILCS 5/28
Gas, Liquefied Petroleum	430 ILCS 5
Glass	430 ILCS 60
Hazardous Substances	430 ILCS 35,
	415 ILCS 5
Health Care	20 ILCS 3960,
	305 ILCS 5/5
Health Clubs	815 ILCS 645
Home Health Agencies	210 ILCS 55
Honey	410 ILCS 620/11
Horse Sales, Shows, Exhibitions	510 ILCS 65
Hospices	210 ILCS 60
Hotels	740 ILCS 90
Household Products	720 ILCS 5/16C-1
Identification Cards	15 ILCS 335
Insurance and Service Plans	215 ILCS 5
Invention Development	815 ILCS 620/101
Job Referral Services	815 ILCS 630
Land Sales	765 ILCS 86
Lasers and Non-ionizing Radiation	420 ILCS 56
Lead Acid Batteries	415 ILCS 5/22
Legal Services	705 ILCS 210
Linen Suppliers	765 ILCS 1045
Liquor	235 ILCS 5
Livestock	510 ILCS 5

POSTER LAWS

Illinois requires that employers post certain notices in the workplace. Some of these notices have been previously discussed (for example, posters relating to discrimination, wage and hour laws, workers' compensation, etc.). These may be obtained from the Illinois Department of Employment Security at 800-247-4984 or **www.ides.state.il.us/employer/pubs/fastfax.asp#posters**.

chapter 17

Bookkeeping and Accounting

It is beyond the scope of this book to explain all the intricacies of setting up a business's bookkeeping and accounting systems. However, if you do not set up an understandable bookkeeping system, your business will undoubtedly fail.

Without accurate records of where your income is coming from and where it is going, you will be unable to increase your profits, lower your expenses, obtain needed financing, or make the right decisions in all areas of your business. The time to decide how you will handle your bookkeeping is when you open your business, not a year later when it is tax time.

INITIAL BOOKKEEPING

If you do not understand business taxation, you should pick up a good book on the subject, as well as the Internal Revenue Service (IRS) tax guide for your type of business (proprietorship, partnership, or corporation). The IRS tax book for small businesses is Publication 334, *Tax Guide for Small Businesses*. There are also instruction booklets for each type of business's form: Schedule C for proprietorships, U.S. income tax return Form 1120 or 1120S for C corporations and S corporations, and Form 1065 for partnerships and businesses that are taxed like partnerships (LLCs and LLPs).

Keep in mind that the IRS does not give you the best advice for saving on taxes and does not give you the other side of contested issues. For that, you need a private tax guide or advisor.

The most important thing to do is to set up your bookkeeping so that you can easily fill out your monthly, quarterly, and annual tax returns. The best way to do this is to get copies of the returns, note the totals that you will need to supply, and set up your bookkeeping system to group those totals.

For example, for a sole proprietorship, you will use Schedule C to report business income and expenses to the IRS at the end of the year. Use the categories on that form to sort your expenses. To make your job especially easy, every time you pay a bill, put the category number on the check.

ACCOUNTANTS

Most likely, your new business will not be able to afford hiring an accountant to handle your books, but that is fine. Doing them yourself will force you to learn about business accounting and taxation. The worst way to run a business is to know nothing about the tax laws and turn everything over to an accountant at the end of the year to find out what is due.

You should know the basics of tax law before making basic decisions such as whether to buy or rent equipment or premises. You should understand accounting so you can time your financial affairs appropriately. If your business needs to buy supplies, inventory, or equipment, and provides goods or services throughout the year, you need to at least have a basic understanding of the system you are working within.

Once you can afford an accountant, weigh the cost against your time and the risk that you will make an error. Even if you think you know enough to do your own corporate tax return, you might take it to an accountant one year to see if you have been missing any deductions that you did not know about. You might decide that the money saved is worth the cost of the accountant's services.

COMPUTER PROGRAMS

Today, every business should keep its books by computer. There are inexpensive programs, such as Quicken, that can instantly provide you with reports of your income and expenses and the right figures to plug into your tax returns. Most programs offer a tax program each year that will take all of your information and print it out on the current year's tax forms.

TAX TIPS

The following are a few tax tips that may help businesses save money.

- Usually, when you buy equipment for a business, you must amortize the cost over several years. That is, you do not deduct the entire cost when you buy it, but take, say, 25% of the cost off your taxes each year for four years. (The time is determined by the theoretical usefulness of the item.) However, small businesses are allowed to write off the entire cost of a limited amount of items under Internal Revenue Code, Section 179. If you have income to shelter, use it.

- Owners of S corporations do not have to pay Social Security or Medicare taxes on the part of their profits that is not considered salary. As long as you pay yourself a reasonable salary, other money you take out is not subject to these taxes.

- Do not neglect to deposit withholding taxes for your own salary or profits. Besides resulting in a large sum to come up with at once in April, there are penalties that must be paid for failure to do so.

- Be sure to keep track of, and remit, your employees' withholding. You will be personally liable for them even if your business is a corporation.

- ✪ If you keep track of your use of your car for business, you can deduct mileage (see IRS guidelines for the amount, as it can change each year). If you use your car for business a considerable amount of the time, you may be able to depreciate it.

- ✪ If your business is a corporation and if you designate the stock as "Section 1244 stock," then if the business fails you are able to get a much better deduction for the loss, which will be considered an ordinary (rather than a capital) loss.

- ✪ By setting up a retirement plan, you can exempt up to 20% of your salary from income tax. However, do not use money you might need later. There are penalties for taking it out of the retirement plan.

- ✪ When you buy things that will be resold or made into products that will be resold (i.e., you are buying from a wholesaler), you do not have to pay sales tax on those purchases.

Paying Federal Taxes

The federal government levies many different types of taxes on individuals and businesses. It is very important that you consult an accountant or attorney to properly comply with and take advantage of the incredibly complex federal tax code and regulations. The following discusses several of the most important federal taxes that will most likely affect your new business.

INCOME TAX

The following section describes the manner in which each type of business pays taxes.

Proprietorship

A proprietor reports profits and expenses on Schedule C attached to the usual Form 1040 and pays tax on all of the net income of the business. Each quarter, Form 1040ES (estimated tax) must be filed, along with payment of one-quarter of the amount of income tax and Social Security tax estimated to be due for the year. Publication 334, *Tax Guide for Small Business*, is available online at **www.irs.gov**.

Partnership

The partnership files a return showing the income and expenses, but pays no tax. Each partner is given a form showing his or her share of the profits or losses and reports these on Schedule E of Form 1040. Each quarter, Form 1040ES must be filed by each partner, along with payment of one-quarter of the amount of income tax and Social Security tax estimated to be due for the year.

C Corporation

A regular corporation is a separate taxpayer and pays tax on its profits after deducting all expenses, including officers' salaries. If dividends are distributed, they are paid out of after-tax dollars, and the shareholders pay tax a second time when they receive the dividends. If a corporation needs to accumulate money for investment, it may be able to do so at lower tax rates than the shareholders pay. But if all profits will be distributed to shareholders, the double taxation may be excessive unless all income is paid as salaries. A C corporation files Form 1120.

S Corporation

A small corporation has the option of being taxed like a partnership. If Form 2553 (*Election by a Small Business Corporation*) is filed by the corporation and accepted by the Internal Revenue Service, the S corporation will only file an informational return listing profits and expenses. Each shareholder will be taxed on a proportional share of the profits (or be able to deduct a proportional share of the losses). Unless a corporation will make a large profit that will not be distributed, S status is usually best in the beginning. An S corporation files Form 1120S and distributes Form K-1 (*Shareholder's Share of Income, Credits, Deductions, etc.*) to each shareholder. If any money is taken out by a shareholder that is not listed as wages subject to withholding, the shareholder will usually have to file Form 1040ES each quarter, along with payment of the estimated withholding on the withdrawals.

Limited Liability Companies and Partnerships

Limited liability companies and limited liability partnerships are allowed to elect to be taxed either as a partnership or a corporation by the IRS. To make this election, file Form 8832, *Entity Classification Election*, with the IRS.

Tax Workshops and Booklets

The IRS conducts workshops to inform businesses about the tax laws. (Do not expect an in-depth study of the loopholes.) For more information, call the IRS toll-free at 800-829-4933 or write to the IRS at the following addresses.

Internal Revenue Service
230 South Dearborn Street
Chicago, IL 60604
312-566-4912

Internal Revenue Service
3101 Constitution Drive
Springfield, IL 62704
217-862-6015

The IRS also offers online workshops for small businesses at **www.irs.gov/businesses/small/index.html**.

WITHHOLDING, SOCIAL SECURITY, AND MEDICARE TAXES

If you need basic information on business tax returns, the IRS publishes a rather large booklet that answers most questions and is available free of charge. Call or write the IRS and ask for Publication No. 334. If you have any questions, look up their toll-free number in the phone book under United States Government/Internal Revenue Service. If you want more creative answers and tax saving information, find a good accountant. However, to get started, you will need the following.

Employer Identification Number

If you are a sole proprietor with no employees, you can use your Social Security number for your business. If you are a corporation, a partnership, or a proprietorship with employees, you must obtain an *employer identification number*. This is done by filing the **APPLICATION FOR EMPLOYER IDENTIFICATION NUMBER (IRS FORM SS-4)**. (see form 5, p.239.) It usually takes a week or two to receive. You will need this number to open bank accounts for the business, so you should file this form as soon as you decide to go into business. A sample, filled-in form and instructions are in Appendix C. (see p.199.)

Employee's Withholding Allowance Certificate

You must have each employee fill out a **FORM W-4** to calculate the amount of federal taxes to be deducted, and to obtain his or her Social Security number. (see form 7, p.253.) The number of allowances on this form is used with IRS Publication 15, *Circular E, Employer's Tax Guide*, to figure out the exact deductions. A sample, filled-in form is included in Appendix C. (see p.207.)

Federal Tax Deposit Coupons

After taking withholdings from employees' wages, you must deposit them at a bank that is authorized to accept such funds. Your required schedule for making deposits is explained in Publication 15 and depends upon the amount of taxes withheld from employees' wages. The deposit is made using the coupons in the Form 8109 booklet, which the IRS will provide.

Estimated Tax Payment Voucher

Sole proprietors and partners usually take draws from their businesses without the formality of withholding. However, they are still required to make deposits of income and FICA taxes each quarter. If more than $500 is due in April on a person's 1040 form, not enough money was withheld each quarter. In this situation, a penalty is assessed, unless the person falls under an exception. The quarterly withholding is submitted on Form 1040ES on April 15th, June 15th, September 15th, and January 15th each year. If these days fall on a weekend, the due date is the following Monday. The worksheet with Form 1040ES can be used to determine the amount to pay.

NOTE: *One exception to the rule is that if you withhold the same amount as last year's tax bill, you do not have to pay a penalty. This is usually much easier than filling out the 1040ES worksheet.*

Employer's Quarterly Tax Return

Each quarter, you must file Form 941 to report your federal withholding and FICA taxes. If you owe more than $2,500 at the end of a quarter, you are required to make a deposit to an authorized financial institution. Most banks are authorized to accept deposits. Consult the instructions for Form 941. In some cases, electronic deposit of taxes may be required.

However, starting in 2006, certain employers need only file one annual return, *IRS Form 944*. This change was meant to make life easier for owners of small businesses. In order to qualify for Form 944 filing, your liability for FICA and other withheld income taxes must be less than $1,000 per year. If you want to determine your eligibility for Form 944 filing, contact the IRS at 800-829-0115.

Wage and Tax Statement

At the end of each year, you are required to issue a W-2 form to each employee. This form shows the amount of wages paid to the employee during the year, as well as the amounts withheld for taxes, Social Security, Medicare, and other purposes.

Miscellaneous   If you pay at least $600 to a person (not a corporation) who is not an employee (such as an independent contractor), you are required to file a Form 1099-Misc for that person. Along with the 1099s, you must file a Form 1096, which is a summary sheet.

Many people are not aware of this law and fail to file these forms, but the forms are required for such things as services, royalties, rents, awards, and prizes that you pay to individuals (but not corporations). The rules for this are quite complicated, so you should either obtain Instruction 1099 from the IRS or consult your accountant.

Earned Income Credit   People who are not liable to pay income tax may have the right to a check from the government because of the *Earned Income Credit*. You are required to notify your employees of this in one of the following ways:

- ✪ a W-2 form with the notice on the back;

- ✪ a substitute for the W-2 form with the notice on it;

- ✪ a copy of Notice 797; or,

- ✪ a written statement with the wording from Notice 797.

A Notice 797 can be obtained by calling 800-829-3676, or via the Internet at **www.irs.gov**.

EXCISE TAX

Excise taxes are taxes on certain activities or items. A few remain, but most federal excise taxes have been eliminated since World War II.

Some of the things that are subject to federal excise taxes are tobacco and alcohol, gasoline, tires and inner tubes, some trucks and trailers, firearms, ammunition, bows, arrows, fishing equipment, the use of highway vehicles of over 55,000 pounds, aircraft, wagering, telephone and teletype services, coal, hazardous wastes, and vaccines. If you are involved with any of these, obtain IRS Publication No. 510, *Information on Excise Taxes*.

UNEMPLOYMENT COMPENSATION TAXES

You must pay federal unemployment taxes (FUTA) if you paid wages of $1,500 in any quarter or if you had at least one employee for twenty calendar weeks. Temporary and part-time employees are included for purposes of FUTA. The federal tax amount is 6.2% of the first $7,000 of wages paid each employee. However, in some cases that rate may be reduced by as much as 5.4% for employers who receive a tax credit for paying into a state unemployment fund.

If the FUTA tax is more than $100 at the end of a quarter, then the tax must be deposited quarterly; otherwise, it may be paid yearly with Form 940 or Form 940EZ. This is your annual report of federal unemployment taxes. You will receive an original form from the IRS.

Electronic Federal Tax Payment System

The Internal Revenue Service has initiated a program, called the *Electronic Federal Tax Payment System* (EFTPS), by which business owners can pay taxes online. For many businesses, this will be a more convenient and cost effective way of making deposits than using the federal tax deposit coupons. Businesses that have deposited a total of more than $200,000 in taxes in a calendar year are *required* to use EFTPS starting the second year following the year the $200,000 threshold is reached. Enrollment in EFTPS is free of charge, and can be done by contacting EFTPS at 800-555-4477 or 800-316-6541, or online at **www.eftps.gov**.

Paying Illinois Taxes

In addition to the federal taxes an Illinois business must pay, the state of Illinois imposes several of its own.

SALES AND USE TAX

If you will be selling or renting goods or services at retail, you must collect Illinois sales and use tax. Some services, such as doctors' and lawyers' fees and newspaper advertising, are not taxed. If you have any doubt, check with the Illinois Department of Revenue.

First, you must obtain a an Illinois Business Tax (IBT) number by filling out form **REG-1** (formerly NUC-1). A sample filled-in copy of the form is in Appendix C. (see p.209.) For more details about the tax, contact the Department of Revenue at their main number, 800-356-6302, or get their forms online at **www.revenue.state.il.us/taxforms**. Or, simply register electronically via the Illinois Business Gateway website at **www.revenue.state.il.us/app/ibri**.

Their address is:

Illinois Department of Revenue
P.O. Box 19034
Springfield, IL 62794

In general, the sales and use tax returns are due for each month on the 20th of the following month. However, depending on taxpayer liability, the Department may require only a quarterly or annual filing. You are allowed to deduct 1.75% of the tax, or $5 per calendar year, whichever is greater, as your reimbursement for collecting the tax. In some cases, if your sales are very limited, you may be allowed to file returns quarterly. According to the Department of Revenue Law, 20 ILCS 2505, a taxpayer who owes $200,000 or more in tax per year is required to remit payment by electronic transfer.

Once you file your **APPLICATION FOR SALES AND USE TAX REGISTRATION** and receive your Certificate of Registration and Illinois Business Tax number, you will have to start filing monthly returns (use Illinois Use Tax Return (ST-44)) whether you have any sales or not. (see form 11, p.271.) If you do not expect to have any sales for the first few months while you are setting up your business, you probably should wait before sending in the registration. Otherwise, you may forget to file the returns and end up paying the penalties.

If you have any sales before you get your monthly tax return forms, you should calculate the tax and submit it anyway. Otherwise, you will be charged a penalty, even if it was not your fault that you did not have the forms.

One reason to get a tax number early is to exempt your purchases from tax. When you buy a product that you will resell, or use as part of a product that you will sell, you are exempt from paying tax on it. To get the exemption, you need to submit an **ILLINOIS CERTIFICATE OF RESALE (CRT-61)** to the seller. (see form 12, p.273.) This form must contain your sales and use tax registration number.

If you will only be selling items wholesale or out of state, you might think that you do not need a tax number or to submit returns. However, you will need to be registered to obtain the tax number to exempt your purchases.

After you obtain your tax number, you will be required to collect sales tax on all sales that are not exempt. Note that Illinois retailers are obligated to collect sales tax if the goods are delivered to an Illinois address.

If you sell to someone who claims to be exempt from sales and use taxes, because they plan to resell merchandise they have purchased from you, you must have them complete the **CERTIFICATE OF RESALE**. (see form 12, p.273.)

INCOME TAX

If you have employees, you will have to withhold Illinois income tax from their salaries and remit it to the state Department of Revenue. Tax on the business's profits will also need to be paid, either by the business (if taxed as a corporation) or by the owners (if set up as a pass-through entity). When you file **FORM REG-1**, you will receive forms and instructions for the Illinois income tax.

Be aware that some municipalities and counties impose their own taxes in addition to the state and federal taxes previously discussed. You should contact your local revenue department to determine if additional taxes apply to your business activities.

If you have incorporated your business, the corporation will have to pay the income taxes for which it is liable, in addition to withholding taxes for its employees. Corporate tax returns are due annually. In the case of Illinois income tax, the return is filed on Form IL-1120, Illinois Corporation Income and Replacement Tax Return.

EXCISE TAX

Illinois imposes taxes on the following businesses, among others:

- wholesale tobacco dealers and tobacco vending machine operators;

- alcohol manufacturers and distributors;

- motor fuel dealers;

- telecommunications; and,

- charitable games.

For more information and registration forms, contact the Department of Revenue at 800-356-6302.

Selling to Tax-Exempt Purchasers   You are required to collect sales and use taxes for all sales you make, unless you have documentation on file proving that a purchase was exempt from the tax. A person can fill out a form for a particular sale or they can fill out one form to be used for all their interactions with you. The latter is called a blanket **Certificate of Resale**. (see form 12, p.273.)

UNEMPLOYMENT COMPENSATION TAXES

You are not liable to pay unemployment compensation (often referred to as unemployment insurance (UI)) taxes until you have had an employee work a part of a day in any twenty calendar weeks or paid $1,500 in wages in a quarter. However, once you reach that point, you are liable for all back taxes. The minimum UI tax rate for employers in 2006 is 1%, while the maximum is 8.2%. The tax is paid on the first $11,500 of wages of each employee in 2006.

When you have had an employee work for twenty weeks, you should send in an Illinois Department of Employment Security (IDES) **Form UI-1 Report to Determine Liability under the Unemployment Insurance Act**. (see form 9, p.259.) A sample, filled-in form is in Appendix C. Quarterly returns may be filed by mail, or via the new Illinois Tax Net e-filing system. Information can be found at **https://taxnet.ides.state.il.us**.

Some businesses try to keep taxes low by having all their work done by independent contractors instead of employees. One thing to be aware of is if a business has no employees for several quarters, the Illinois unemployment tax rate increases. A payment of a small wage to someone each quarter may avoid this problem.

For more information on unemployment compensation, consult the IDES Guide to the *Illinois U.I. Act*. Contact:

Department of Employment Security
850 East Madison Street
Springfield, IL 62702
217-782-2790
www.ides.state.il.us

For more information on Illinois taxes, contact:

Department of Revenue
101 West Jefferson
Springfield, IL 62794
800-732-8866
www.revenue.state.il.us

Out-of-State Taxes

As an Illinois business, if you operate your business outside of the borders of the state of Illinois, you not only have to comply with Illinois and federal tax laws, but also with the laws of the states and other countries in which you do business. This can prove to be very complicated.

STATE SALES TAXES

In 1992, the United States Supreme Court struck a blow for the rights of small businesses by ruling that state tax authorities cannot force them to collect sales taxes on interstate mail orders. (*Quill Corporation v. North Dakota.*) Unfortunately, the court left open the possibility that Congress could allow interstate taxation of mail order sales, and since then several bills have been introduced that would do so.

At present, companies are only required to collect sales taxes for states in which they *do business*. Exactly what business is enough to trigger taxation is a legal question, and some states try to define it as broadly as possible.

If you have an office in a state, clearly you are doing business there, and any goods shipped to consumers in the state are subject to sales taxes. If you have a full-time employee working in the state much of the year, many states will consider you to be doing business there. In some states, attending a two-day trade show is enough business to trigger taxation for the entire year for every order shipped to the state. One loophole that often works is to be represented at shows by persons who are not your employees.

Because the laws are different in each state, you will have to do some research on a state-by-state basis to find out how much business you can do in a state without being subject to their taxation. You can request a state's rules from its department of revenue, but keep in mind that what a department of revenue wants the law to be is not always what the courts will rule that it is.

BUSINESS TAXES

Sometimes your business will be subject to the income or other business taxes of other sates. For example, California charges every company doing business in the state an annual fee and charges income tax on a portion of the company's worldwide income. Doing a small amount of business in the state is clearly not worth getting mired in California taxation.

For this reason, some trade shows have been moved from the state and this has resulted in a review of the tax policies and some *safe-harbor* guidelines to advise companies on what they can do without becoming subject to taxation.

Write to the department of revenue of any state with which you have business contacts to see what might trigger your taxation.

INTERNET TAXES

State revenue departments are excited about the prospect of taxing commerce on the Internet. Theories have already been proposed that websites available to state residents mean a company is doing business in a state. Congress has passed a moratorium on taxation of Internet access, which extends until November 2007 as of the time of this publication.

CANADIAN TAXES

The Canadian government expects American companies that sell goods by mail order to Canadians to collect the Canadian Goods and Services Tax (GST) for them and file returns with Revenue Canada, their tax department. Those who receive an occasional unsolicited order are not expected to register and Canadian customers who order things from the U.S. pay the GST. However, companies that carry on business in Canada are expected to be registered for purposes of the GST if their worldwide income is $30,000 (Canadian) or more per year. In some cases, a company may be required to post a bond and to pay for the cost of Canadian auditors visiting its premises and auditing its books. For these reasons, you may notice that some companies decline to accept orders from Canada.

The End...and the Beginning

If you have read through this whole book, you know more about the rules and laws for operating an Illinois business than most people in business today. However, after learning about all the governmental regulations, you may become discouraged. You are probably wondering how you can keep track of all the laws and how you will have any time left to make money after complying with the laws. It is not that bad. People are starting businesses every day and they are making lots of money.

Congratulations on deciding to start a business in Illinois!

Glossary

A

acceptance. Agreeing to the terms of an offer and creating a contract.

affirmative action. Hiring an employee to achieve a balance in the workplace and avoid existing or continuing discrimination based on minority status.

alien. A person who is not a citizen of the country.

articles of incorporation. The document that sets forth the organization of a corporation.

B

bait advertising. Offering a product for sale with the intention of selling another product.

bulk sales. Selling substantially all of a company's inventory.

C

C corporation. A corporation that pays taxes on its profits.

collections. The gathering of money owed to a business.

common law. Laws that are determined in court cases rather than statutes.

consideration. The exchange of value or promises in a contract.

contract. An agreement between two or more parties.

copyright. Legal protection given to original works of authorship.

corporation. An artificial person that is set up to conduct a business owned by shareholders and run by officers and directors.

D

deceptive pricing. Pricing goods or services in a manner intended to deceive the customers.

discrimination. The choosing among various options based on their characteristics.

domain name. The address of a website.

E

employee. Person who works for another, under that person's control and direction.

endorsements. Positive statements about goods or services.

excise tax. A tax paid on the sale or consumption of goods or services.

express warranty. A specific guarantee of a product or service.

F

fictitious name. A name used by a business that is not its personal or legal name.

G

general partnership. A business that is owned by two or more persons.

goods. Items of personal property.

guarantee/guaranty. A promise of quality of a good or service.

I

implied warranty. A guarantee of a product or service that is not specifically made, but can be implied from the circumstances of the sale.

independent contractor. Person who works for another as a separate business, not as an employee.

injunction. An order by a court barring a defendant from committing a particular act.

intangible property. Personal property that does not have physical presence, such as the ownership interest in a corporation.

intellectual property. Legal rights to the products of the mind, such as writings, musical compositions, formulas, and designs.

L

liability. The legal responsibility to pay for an injury.

limited liability company. An entity recognized as a legal person that is set up to conduct a business owned and run by members.

limited liability partnership. An entity recognized as a legal person that is set up to conduct a business owned and run by members that is set up for professionals such as attorneys or doctors.

limited partnership. A business that is owned by two or more persons of which one or more is liable for the debts of the business and one or more has no liability for the debts.

limited warranty. A guarantee covering certain aspects of a good or service.

M

merchant. A person who is in business.

merchant's firm offer. An offer by a business made under specific terms.

N

nonprofit corporation. An entity recognized as a legal person that is set up to run an operation in which none of the profits are distributed to controlling members.

O

occupational license. A government-issued permit to transact business.

offer. A proposal to enter into a contract.

overtime. Hours worked in excess of forty hours in one week or eight hours in one day.

P

partnership. A business formed by two or more persons.

patent. Protection given to inventions, discoveries, and designs.

personal property. Any type of property other than land and the structures attached to it.

pierce the corporate veil. When a court ignores the structure of a corporation and holds its owners responsible for its debts or liabilities.

proprietorship. A business that is owned by one person.

prospectus. A summary of a business venture, used to provide information to prospective investors.

R

real property. Land and the structures attached to it.

resident alien. A person who is not a citizen of the country, but who may legally reside and work there.

S

S corporation. A corporation in which the profits are taxed to the shareholders.

sale on approval. Selling an item with the agreement that it may be brought back and the sale cancelled.

sale or return. An agreement whereby goods are to be purchased or returned to the vendor.

securities. Interests in a business such as stocks or bonds.

service mark. An advertisement symbol or logo used to identify a service.

sexual harassment. Activity that causes an employee to feel or be sexually threatened.

shares. Units of stock in a corporation.

statute of frauds. Law that requires certain contracts to be in writing.

stock. Ownership interests in a corporation.

sublease. An agreement to rent premises from an existing tenant.

T

tangible property. Physical personal property such as desks and tables.

trade secret. Commercially valuable information or process that is protected by being kept a secret.

trademark. A name or symbol used to identify the source of goods or services.

U

unemployment compensation. Payments to a former employee who was terminated from a job for a reason not based on his or her fault.

usury. Charging an interest rate higher than that allowed by law.

W

withholding. Money taken out of an employee's salary and remitted to the government.

workers' compensation. Insurance program to cover injuries or deaths of employees.

Government Resources

This appendix lists some governmental resources for a new business and some useful website addresses.

Assumed Names (Cook County)
Cook County Building
118 North Clark—Lower Level
Chicago, IL 60602
312-603-0906
www.cookctyclerk.com

Business Tax Number

Illinois Department of Revenue
Income Tax Division
101 West Jefferson
Springfield, IL 62702
800-732-8866
217-782-3336

Illinois Department of Revenue
100 West Randolph
Concourse Level
Chicago, IL 60601
312-814-5232

Federal Websites
www.ada.gov
(Information and guidance for the Americans with Disabilities Act)

www.business.gov
    (Government resources for businesses)
www.dol.gov/compliance/guide
    (Department of Labor Employment Law Guide)
www.firstgov.gov
    (Internet portal for the federal government)
www.ftc.gov/ftc/business.htm
    (Advertising guidelines)
www.irs.gov
    (IRS forms)
www.sba.gov
    (Small Business Administration)
www.uscis.gov
    (Immigration—employee form I-9)

First-Stop Business Information Center of Illinois
Provides general information on business assistance programs and services and information on related state agencies.
    800-252-2923
    www.commerce.state.il.us

General Business License (Chicago)
   Chicago Department of Revenue
   City Hall
   121 North LaSalle Street
   Room 107
   Chicago, IL 60602
   312-747-4747

General Government Information
   Federal: 800-333-4636
   Illinois: 312-793-3500
                     800-642-3112
   Cook County: 312-603-5500
   Chicago: 312-744-5844

Illinois Attorney General
   Chicago Main Office   Springfield Main Office
   100 West Randolph Street   500 South Second Street
   Chicago, IL 60601   Springfield, IL 62706
   312-814-3000   217-782-1090
   www.ag.state.il.us

Incorporation

Secretary of State	**Secretary of State**
Department of	Department of
Business Services	Business Services
501 South Second Street	69 West Washington
Suite 328	Suite 1240
Springfield, IL 62756	Chicago, IL 60602
217-782-6961	312-793-3380

Miscellaneous Websites

www.govspot.com
   (Links to state, federal, and foreign government sites)

State of Illinois Websites

www.business.illinois.gov
   (State of Illinois Business Portal)
www.commerce.state.il.us
   (Business information center)
www.dpr.state.il.us
   (Department of Professional Regulation)
www.ides.state.il.us
   (Unemployment insurance)
www.ienconnect.com
   (Illinois Entrepreneurship Network)
www.revenue.state.il.us
   (Department of Revenue)
www.sos.state.il.us
   (Business registration)
www.state.il.us/agency/iic
   (Workers' compensation)

Trademark Inquiries

Secretary of State's Office
Department of Business Services—Trademarks
501 South Second Street
Springfield, IL 62756
217-782-6961

Business Start-Up Checklist and Tax Timetable

The following start-up checklist and tax timetable may be photocopied or removed from this book and used immediately.

BUSINESS START-UP CHECKLIST

❏ Make your plan
  ❏ Obtain and read all relevant publications on your type of business
  ❏ Obtain and read all laws and regulations affecting your business
  ❏ Calculate whether your plan will produce a profit
  ❏ Plan your sources of capital
  ❏ Plan your sources of goods or services
  ❏ Plan your marketing efforts
❏ Choose your business name
  ❏ Check other business names and trademarks
  ❏ Register your name, trademark, etc.
❏ Choose the business form
  ❏ Prepare and file organizational papers
  ❏ Prepare and file fictitious name if necessary
❏ Choose the location
  ❏ Check competitors
  ❏ Check zoning
❏ Obtain necessary licenses
  ❏ City   ❏ State
  ❏ County   ❏ Federal
❏ Choose a bank
  ❏ Checking
  ❏ Credit card processing
  ❏ Loans
❏ Obtain necessary insurance
  ❏ Workers' Comp   ❏ Automobile
  ❏ Liability   ❏ Health
  ❏ Hazard   ❏ Life/disability
❏ File necessary federal tax registrations
❏ File necessary state tax registrations
❏ Set up a bookkeeping system
❏ Plan your hiring
  ❏ Obtain required posters
  ❏ Obtain or prepare employment application
  ❏ Obtain new hire tax forms
  ❏ Prepare employment policies
  ❏ Determine compliance with health and safety laws
❏ Plan your opening
  ❏ Obtain all necessary equipment and supplies
  ❏ Obtain all necessary inventory
  ❏ Do all necessary marketing and publicity
  ❏ Obtain all necessary forms and agreements
  ❏ Prepare you company policies on refunds, exchanges, returns

TAX TIMETABLE

	Illinois				Federal			
	Sales **	Unem-ployment	IL-W-4 Withholding	Income Tax	Est. Payment	Annual Return	Form 941*	Misc.
JAN.		31st	31st (IL-941)		15th		31st	31st 940
FEB.			28th (IL-W-3)					28th W-2, W-3 1099
MAR.				Corporate 15th***		15th Corp. & Partnership		31st (W-2,W-3, 1099 filed elec-tronically)
APR.		30th	30th (IL-941)	Individual 15th	15th	15th Personal	30th	
MAY								
JUN.					15th			
JUL.		31st	31st (IL-941)				31st	
AUG.								
SEP.					15th			
OCT.		31st	31st (IL-941)				31st	
NOV.								
DEC.								

* In addition to Form 941, deposits must be made regularly if withholding exceeds $1,000 in any month. Certain small employers are able to file Form 944 annually, rather than Form 941.
** Sales tax returns (Form ST-556) are due by the 20th day following the delivery date. General Retailers file Form ST-1, Sales and Use Tax Return, according to the Department of Revenue determination of the taxpayers' average monthly sales tax liability.
***Form 1120, U.S. Corporation Income Tax Return, and Form IL-1120, Illinois Corporation Tax Return, are due by the 15th day of the third month following the close of the taxable year.

Sample, Filled-In Forms

The following forms are *selected* filled-in forms for demonstration purposes. The form numbers in this appendix correspond to the form numbers in Appendix D. If there is no blank for a particular form, it is because you must obtain it from a government agency. If you need instructions for these forms as you follow how they are filled out, they can be found in Appendix D or in those pages in the chapters that discuss those forms.

FORM **BCA 2.10** (rev. Dec. 2003)
ARTICLES OF INCORPORATION
Business Corporation Act

Jesse White, Secretary of State
Department of Business Services
Springfield, IL 62756
Telephone (217) 782-9522
            (217) 782-6961
http://www.cyberdriveillinois.com

Remit payment in the form of a cashier's
check, certified check, money order
or an Illinois attorney's or CPA's check
payable to the Secretary of State.
SEE NOTE 1 TO DETERMINE FEES!

Filing Fee: $150.00 Franchise Tax $_____ Total $_____ File #_____ Approved:
———————————Submit in duplicate———————Type or Print clearly in black ink—————Do not write above this line——————————

1. CORPORATE NAME: _____ Doe Company _____

    _____
    (The corporate name must contain the word "corporation", "company," "incorporated," "limited" or an abbreviation thereof.)

2. Initial Registered Agent: __John_____ __M.__ ___Doe_____
                                First Name   Middle Initial   Last name

    Initial Registered Office: __4444 Deer Street_____
                               Number   Street   Suite #   (A P.O. BOX ALONE IS NOT ACCEPTABLE)
                               __Chicago_____ IL ___60603_____ __Cook_____
                               City   ZIP Code   County

3. Purpose or purposes for which the corporation is organized:
    (If not sufficient space to cover this point, add one or more sheets of this size.)

    The transaction of any or all lawful businesses for which corporations may be incorporated under the Illinois Business
    Corporation Act.

4. Paragraph 1: Authorized Shares, Issued Shares and Consideration Received:

Class	Number of Shares Authorized	Number of Shares Proposed to be Issued	Consideration to be Received Therefor
	10,000	3000	$ 10/share

TOTAL = $ 30,000

Paragraph 2: The preferences, qualifications, limitations, restrictions and special or relative rights in respect of the shares
of each class are:
(If not sufficient space to cover this point, add one or more sheets of this size.)

C-162.24   (over)

5. *OPTIONAL:* (a) Number of directors constituting the initial board of directors of the corporation:_____ .

   (b) Names and addresses of the persons who are to serve as directors until the first annual meeting of shareholders or until their successors are elected and qualify:

Name	Address	City, State, ZIP

6. *OPTIONAL:* (a) It is estimated that the value of all property to be owned by the corporation for the following year wherever located will be: $_____

   (b) It is estimated that the value of the property to be located within the State of Illinois during the following year will be: $_____

   (c) It is estimated that the gross amount of business that will be transacted by the corporation during the following year will be: $_____

   (d) It is estimated that the gross amount of business that will be transacted from places of business in the State of Illinois during the following year will be: $_____

7. *OPTIONAL:* *OTHER PROVISIONS*

   Attach a separate sheet of this size for any other provision to be included in the Articles of Incorporation, e.g., authorizing preemptive rights, denying cumulative voting, regulating internal affairs, voting majority requirements, fixing a duration other than perpetual, etc.

8. **NAME(S) & ADDRESS(ES) OF INCORPORATOR(S)**

The undersigned incorporator(s) hereby declare(s), under penalties of perjury, that the statements made in the foregoing Articles of Incorporation are true.

Dated _____ January 29 _____ , __2007__
        (Month & Day)   Year

Signature and Name		**Address**		
1. *John Doe*		1. 101 Fawn Pkwy.		
Signature		Street		
John Doe		Chicago,	IL	60603
(Type or Print Name)		City/Town	State	ZIP Code
2. *John Doe*		2. 101 Fawn Pkwy.		
Signature		Street		
John Doe		Chicago,	IL	60603
(Type or Print Name)		City/Town	State	ZIP Code
3. *John Doe*		3. 101 Fawn Pkwy.		
Signature		Street		
John Doe		Chicago,	IL	60603
(Type or Print Name)		City/Town	State	ZIP Code

(Signatures must be in **BLACK INK** on original document. Carbon copy, photocopy or rubber stamp signatures may only be used on conformed copies.)

NOTE: If a corporation acts as incorporator, the name of the corporation and the state of incorporation shall be shown and the execution shall be by a duly authorized corporate officer. Type or print officer's name and title beneath signature.

Note 1: Fee Schedule

The initial franchise tax is assessed at the rate of 15/100 of 1 percent ($1.50 per $1,000) on the paid-in capital represented in this State. (Minimum initial franchise tax is $25)

The filing fee is $150

The **minimum total due** (franchise tax + filing fee) is $175.

Note 2: Return to:

Doe Company
(Firm name)

John Doe
(Attention)

4444 Deer Street
(Mailing Address)

Chicago, IL 60603
(City, State, ZIP Code)

Form **BCA-4.15/4.20**

(Rev. Jan. 2003)

Jesse White
Secretary of State
Department of Business Services
Springfield, IL 62756
Telephone (217) 782-9520
www.cyberdriveillinois.com

Remit payment in check or money
order, payable to "Secretary of State".

APPLICATION TO ADOPT, CHANGE OR CANCEL, AN ASSUMED CORPORATE NAME

File #

SUBMIT IN DUPLICATE

This space for use by
Secretary of State

Date

Filing Fee
(See Note Below)
Approved:

1. CORPORATE NAME: _____Doe Company_____

2. State or Country of Incorporation:____Illinois_____

3. Date incorporated *(if an Illinois corporation)* or date authorized to transact business in Illinois *(if a foreign corporation)*: _____May 25_____, ____2007__ .
    (Month & Day)   (Year)

    (Complete No. 4 and No. 5 if adopting or changing an assumed corporate name.)

4. The corporation intends to adopt and to transact business under the assumed corporate name of:

    _____Doe Construction_____

5. The right to use the assumed corporate name shall be effective from the date this application is filed by the Secretary of State until____May 1_____, __2008__, the first day of the corporation's anniversary
    (Month & Day)   (Year)
    month in the next year which is evenly divisible by five.

    (Complete No. 6 if changing or cancelling an assumed corporate name.)

6. The corporation intends to cease transacting business under the assumed corporate name of:

    _____

7. The undersigned corporation has caused this statement to be signed by a duly authorized officer who affirms, under penalties of perjury, that the facts stated herein are true.

    Dated _____June 1_____ , ___2007___   _____Doe Company_____
              (Month & Day)   (Year)   (Exact Name of Corporation)

    _____*John Doe*_____
    (Any Authorized Officer's Signature)

    _____John Doe_____
    (Type or Print Name and Title)

NOTE: The filing fee to adopt an assumed corporate name is $150 if the current year ends with either 0 or 5, $120 if the current year ends with either 1 or 6, $90 if the current year ends with either 2 or 7, $60 if the current year ends with either 3 or 8, $30 if the current year ends with either 4 or 9.
        The fee for cancelling an assumed corporate name is $5.00.
        The fee to change an assumed name is $25.00.

C-148.15

This page is intentionally left blank.

State of Illinois
Trademark or Servicemark
Application

This space for use by Secretary of State

Complete and return with $10 fee and three specimens to:

**Secretary of State
Department of Business Services
Trademark Division
3rd Floor, Howlett Building
Springfield, IL 62756**

**217-524-0400
www.cyberdriveillinois.com**

Must be typewritten or legibly printed in black ink.

This application must be accompanied by three specimens of the mark and a $10 filing fee payable to the Secretary of State. Please paperclip specimens to the application. DO NOT GLUE OR STAPLE.

Send a separate check for each application. This will prevent the return of multiple applications for correction.

Items 1–4 refer to Registrant

1. Name of Registrant (Owner of the Mark) __Sidney Bones__

2. Mailing Address _____ 6789 Graves Ave. _____
   Street
   _____ Chicago, IL 60601 _____
   City, State, ZIP Code

3. Is Registrant a (check one)
   - ☐ Corporation ☐ Union ☐ General Partnership ☐ Limited Liability Partnership (LLP)
   - ☒ Individual ☐ Association ☐ Limited Partnership (LP) ☐ Limited Liability Company (LLC)
   - ☐ Other (specify) _____

4. a) If a Corporation, LP, LLP or LLC, in what state is it organized? _____
   b) If an LP or LLP, what is the name of one of the general partners? _____

---

5. Name of mark _____ Sid's Bones _____
   Does the mark involve a design or logo? ☐ Yes ☐ No
   If yes, briefly describe major features of design _____

6. Describe the specific goods or services in connection with which mark is used (provided by the mark)

   novelty items

---

7. Class No. __28__ (One classification number only; classes are listed on the back. The Secretary of State will fill in the answer if no answer is given and has the right to change the classification if that furnished by the applicant is not correct. Each classification requires a separate application, set of three specimens and fee.)

8. a) If a **Trademark**, check how the mark is used (check as many as apply). Mark is applied:
    - ❏ directly to the goods
    - ❏ on documents, wrappers or articles delivered in connection with the service rendered
    - ❏ in another fashion, please specify_____

    OR

    b) If a **Servicemark**, check how the mark is used (check as many as apply). Mark is displayed:
    - ❏ in advertisements of the service
    - ❏ on documents, wrappers or articles delivered in connection with the service rendered
    - ❏ in another fashion, please specify _____

9. Date of the first use of mark by applicant or predecessor. Mark must be used in Illinois prior to registration. (If first use of mark was in Illinois, use same date in both A and B.)

    a) Anywhere ____January 29, 2007____   b) In Illinois ____January 29, 2007____
                        Month, Day, Year   Month, Day, Year

10. If either of the above first uses was by a predecessor of the applicant, state which use or uses were by a predecessor and identify predecessor _____

The applicant hereby appoints the Secretary of State of Illinois as agent for service of process in an action relating only to the registration, which may be issued pursuant to this application, if the renewal registrant be, or shall become, a non-resident individual, or foreign partnership, limited liability company, association, or corporation not licensed to do business in the State, or cannot be found in this State.

The undersigned hereby declares, under penalty of perjury, that the statements made in the foregoing application are true, and that to his/her knowledge no other person has registered the mark, either federally or in this State, or has the right to use the mark either in the identical form thereof or in such near resemblance thereto as to be likely, when applied to the goods or services of such other person, to cause confusion or to cause mistake, or to deceive.

X _*Sidney Bones*_____   Sidney Bones_____
        Signature of Applicant   Type or Print Name of Applicant

___Owner_____   312-555-1234_____
        Official Capacity   Contact Phone Number

The following general classes of goods and services are established for convenience of administration of this Act, not to limit or extend the applicant's or registrant's rights. A single application for registration of a mark may include any or all goods or services upon which the mark is actually being used and which are comprised in a single class. In no event shall a single application include goods or services upon which the mark is being used and which fall within different classes.

Classification of Goods for Trademarks

1 Chemicals	12 Vehicles	23 Yarns and threads
2 Paints	13 Firearms	24 Fabrics
3 Cosmetics and cleaning preparations	14 Jewelry	25 Clothing
4 Lubricants and fuels	15 Musical instruments	26 Fancy goods
5 Pharmaceuticals	16 Paper goods and printed matter	27 Floor coverings
6 Metal goods	17 Rubber goods	28 Toys and sporting goods
7 Machinery	18 Leather goods	29 Meals and processed foods
8 Hand tools	19 Non-metallic building materials	30 Staple foods
9 Electrical and scientific apparatus	20 Furniture and articles not otherwise classified	31 Natural agricultural products
10 Medical apparatus	21 Housewares and glass	32 Light beverages
11 Environmental control apparatus	22 Cordage and fibers	33 Wine and spirits
		34 Smoker's articles

Classification of Services for Servicemarks

35 Advertising and business	39 Transportation and storage	43 Restaurants, hotels, motels and boarding
36 Insurance and financial	40 Treatment of materials	44 Medical, veterinary, beauty care and forestry
37 Building construction and repair	41 Education and entertainment	45 Personal, social and security
38 Telecommunications	42 Scientific technological or legal	

Department of Homeland Security
U.S. Citizenship and Immigration Services

OMB No. 1615-0047; Expires 03/31/07

Employment Eligibility Verification

INSTRUCTIONS
PLEASE READ ALL INSTRUCTIONS CAREFULLY BEFORE COMPLETING THIS FORM.

Anti-Discrimination Notice. It is illegal to discriminate against any individual (other than an alien not authorized to work in the U.S.) in hiring, discharging, or recruiting or referring for a fee because of that individual's national origin or citizenship status. It is illegal to discriminate against work eligible individuals. Employers **CANNOT** specify which document(s) they will accept from an employee. The refusal to hire an individual because of a future expiration date may also constitute illegal discrimination.

Section 1- Employee.
All employees, citizens and noncitizens, hired after November 6, 1986, must complete Section 1 of this form at the time of hire, which is the actual beginning of employment. **The employer is responsible for ensuring that Section 1 is timely and properly completed.**

Preparer/Translator Certification. The Preparer/Translator Certification must be completed if Section 1 is prepared by a person other than the employee. A preparer/translator may be used only when the employee is unable to complete Section 1 on his/her own. However, the employee must still sign Section 1 personally.

Section 2 - Employer.
For the purpose of completing this form, the term "employer" includes those recruiters and referrers for a fee who are agricultural associations, agricultural employers or farm labor contractors.

Employers must complete Section 2 by examining evidence of identity and employment eligibility within three (3) business days of the date employment begins. If employees are authorized to work, but are unable to present the required document(s) within three business days, they must present a receipt for the application of the document(s) within three business days and the actual document(s) within ninety (90) days. However, if employers hire individuals for a duration of less than three business days, Section 2 must be completed at the time employment begins. **Employers must record: 1)** document title; **2)** issuing authority; **3)** document number, **4)** expiration date, if any; and **5)** the date employment begins. Employers must sign and date the certification. Employees must present original documents. Employers may, but are not required to, photocopy the document(s) presented. These photocopies may only be used for the verification process and must be retained with the I-9. **However, employers are still responsible for completing the I-9.**

Section 3 - Updating and Reverification.
Employers must complete Section 3 when updating and/or reverifying the I-9. Employers must reverify employment eligibility of their employees on or before the expiration date recorded in Section 1. Employers **CANNOT** specify which document(s) they will accept from an employee.

- If an employee's name has changed at the time this form is being updated/reverified, complete Block A.

- If an employee is rehired within three (3) years of the date this form was originally completed and the employee is still eligible to be employed on the same basis as previously indicated on this form (updating), complete Block B and the signature block.

- If an employee is rehired within three (3) years of the date this form was originally completed and the employee's work authorization has expired **or** if a current employee's work authorization is about to expire (reverification), complete Block B and:

- examine any document that reflects that the employee is authorized to work in the U.S. (see List A **or** C),

- record the document title, document number and expiration date (if any) in Block C, and

- complete the signature block.

Photocopying and Retaining Form I-9. A blank I-9 may be reproduced, provided both sides are copied. The Instructions must be available to all employees completing this form. Employers must retain completed I-9s for three (3) years after the date of hire or one (1) year after the date employment ends, whichever is later.

For more detailed information, you may refer to the Department of Homeland Security (DHS) Handbook for Employers, (Form M-274). You may obtain the handbook at your local U.S. Citizenship and Immigration Services (USCIS) office.

Privacy Act Notice. The authority for collecting this information is the Immigration Reform and Control Act of 1986, Pub. L. 99-603 (8 USC 1324a).

This information is for employers to verify the eligibility of individuals for employment to preclude the unlawful hiring, or recruiting or referring for a fee, of aliens who are not authorized to work in the United States.

This information will be used by employers as a record of their basis for determining eligibility of an employee to work in the United States. The form will be kept by the employer and made available for inspection by officials of the U.S. Immigration and Customs Enforcement, Department of Labor and Office of Special Counsel for Immigration Related Unfair Employment Practices.

Submission of the information required in this form is voluntary. However, an individual may not begin employment unless this form is completed, since employers are subject to civil or criminal penalties if they do not comply with the Immigration Reform and Control Act of 1986.

Reporting Burden. We try to create forms and instructions that are accurate, can be easily understood and which impose the least possible burden on you to provide us with information. Often this is difficult because some immigration laws are very complex. Accordingly, the reporting burden for this collection of information is computed as follows: **1)** learning about this form, 5 minutes; **2)** completing the form, 5 minutes; and **3)** assembling and filing (recordkeeping) the form, 5 minutes, for an average of 15 minutes per response. If you have comments regarding the accuracy of this burden estimate, or suggestions for making this form simpler, you can write to U.S. Citizenship and Immigration Services, Regulatory Management Division, 111 Massachuetts Avenue, N.W., Washington, DC 20529. OMB No. 1615-0047.

NOTE: This is the 1991 edition of the Form I-9 that has been rebranded with a current printing date to reflect the recent transition from the INS to DHS and its components.

EMPLOYERS MUST RETAIN COMPLETED FORM I-9
PLEASE DO NOT MAIL COMPLETED FORM I-9 TO ICE OR USCIS

Form I-9 (Rev. 05/31/05)Y

Department of Homeland Security
U.S. Citizenship and Immigration Services

OMB No. 1615-0047; Expires 03/31/07

Employment Eligibility Verification

Please read instructions carefully before completing this form. The instructions must be available during completion of this form. ANTI-DISCRIMINATION NOTICE: It is illegal to discriminate against work eligible individuals. Employers CANNOT specify which document(s) they will accept from an employee. The refusal to hire an individual because of a future expiration date may also constitute illegal discrimination.

Section 1. Employee Information and Verification. To be completed and signed by employee at the time employment begins.

Print Name: Last	First	Middle Initial	Maiden Name
Reddenbacher	Mary	J.	Hassenfus

Address (Street Name and Number)	Apt. #	Date of Birth (month/day/year)
1234 Liberty Lane		1/26/79

City	State	Zip Code	Social Security #
Chicago	IL	60606	123-45-6788

I am aware that federal law provides for imprisonment and/or fines for false statements or use of false documents in connection with the completion of this form.

I attest, under penalty of perjury, that I am (check one of the following):

[X] A citizen or national of the United States
[ ] A Lawful Permanent Resident (Alien #) A _____
[ ] An alien authorized to work until _____
(Alien # or Admission #) _____

Employee's Signature	Date (month/day/year)
Mary Reddenbacher	1/29/07

Preparer and/or Translator Certification. (To be completed and signed if Section 1 is prepared by a person other than the employee.) I attest, under penalty of perjury, that I have assisted in the completion of this form and that to the best of my knowledge the information is true and correct.

Preparer's/Translator's Signature	Print Name

Address (Street Name and Number, City, State, Zip Code)	Date (month/day/year)

Section 2. Employer Review and Verification. To be completed and signed by employer. Examine one document from List A OR examine one document from List B and one from List C, as listed on the reverse of this form, and record the title, number and expiration date, if any, of the document(s).

List A	OR	List B	AND	List C
Document title: Passport				
Issuing authority: Passport Agency Chicago				
Document #: 123456789				
Expiration Date (if any): 10/5/09				
Document #:				
Expiration Date (if any):				

CERTIFICATION - I attest, under penalty of perjury, that I have examined the document(s) presented by the above-named employee, that the above-listed document(s) appear to be genuine and to relate to the employee named, that the employee began employment on (month/day/year) 1/29/07 **and that to the best of my knowledge the employee is eligible to work in the United States. (State employment agencies may omit the date the employee began employment.)**

Signature of Employer or Authorized Representative	Print Name	Title
Sidney Bones	Sidney Bones	Owner

Business or Organization Name	Address (Street Name and Number, City, State, Zip Code)	Date (month/day/year)
Sid's Bones, 6789 Graves Avenue, Chicago IL 60601		1/29/07

Section 3. Updating and Reverification. To be completed and signed by employer.

A. New Name (if applicable)	B. Date of Rehire (month/day/year) (if applicable)

C. If employee's previous grant of work authorization has expired, provide the information below for the document that establishes current employment eligibility.

Document Title:	Document #:	Expiration Date (if any):

I attest, under penalty of perjury, that to the best of my knowledge, this employee is eligible to work in the United States, and if the employee presented document(s), the document(s) I have examined appear to be genuine and to relate to the individual.

Signature of Employer or Authorized Representative	Date (month/day/year)

NOTE: This is the 1991 edition of the Form I-9 that has been rebranded with a current printing date to reflect the recent transition from the INS to DHS and its components.

Form I-9 (Rev. 05/31/05)Y Page 2

LISTS OF ACCEPTABLE DOCUMENTS

LIST A		LIST B		LIST C
Documents that Establish Both Identity and Employment Eligibility	**OR**	**Documents that Establish Identity**	**AND**	**Documents that Establish Employment Eligibility**

LIST A

Documents that Establish Both Identity and Employment Eligibility

1. U.S. Passport (unexpired or expired)

2. Certificate of U.S. Citizenship (*Form N-560 or N-561*)

3. Certificate of Naturalization (*Form N-550 or N-570*)

4. Unexpired foreign passport, with *I-551 stamp or* attached *Form I-94* indicating unexpired employment authorization

5. Permanent Resident Card or Alien Registration Receipt Card with photograph (*Form I-151 or I-551*)

6. Unexpired Temporary Resident Card (*Form I-688*)

7. Unexpired Employment Authorization Card (*Form I-688A*)

8. Unexpired Reentry Permit (*Form I-327*)

9. Unexpired Refugee Travel Document (*Form I-571*)

10. Unexpired Employment Authorization Document issued by DHS that contains a photograph (*Form I-688B*)

LIST B

Documents that Establish Identity

1. Driver's license or ID card issued by a state or outlying possession of the United States provided it contains a photograph or information such as name, date of birth, gender, height, eye color and address

2. ID card issued by federal, state or local government agencies or entities, provided it contains a photograph or information such as name, date of birth, gender, height, eye color and address

3. School ID card with a photograph

4. Voter's registration card

5. U.S. Military card or draft record

6. Military dependent's ID card

7. U.S. Coast Guard Merchant Mariner Card

8. Native American tribal document

9. Driver's license issued by a Canadian government authority

For persons under age 18 who are unable to present a document listed above:

10. School record or report card

11. Clinic, doctor or hospital record

12. Day-care or nursery school record

LIST C

Documents that Establish Employment Eligibility

1. U.S. social security card issued by the Social Security Administration (*other than a card stating it is not valid for employment*)

2. Certification of Birth Abroad issued by the Department of State (*Form FS-545 or Form DS-1350*)

3. Original or certified copy of a birth certificate issued by a state, county, municipal authority or outlying possession of the United States bearing an official seal

4. Native American tribal document

5. U.S. Citizen ID Card (*Form I-197*)

6. ID Card for use of Resident Citizen in the United States (*Form I-179*)

7. Unexpired employment authorization document issued by DHS (*other than those listed under List A*)

Illustrations of many of these documents appear in Part 8 of the Handbook for Employers (M-274)

This page is intentionally left blank.

Form SS-4
(Rev. February 2006)
Department of the Treasury
Internal Revenue Service

Application for Employer Identification Number

(For use by employers, corporations, partnerships, trusts, estates, churches, government agencies, Indian tribal entities, certain individuals, and others.)

► See separate instructions for each line.   ► Keep a copy for your records.

OMB No. 1545-0003

EIN

Type or print clearly.

1 Legal name of entity (or individual) for whom the EIN is being requested
Sidney Bones

2 Trade name of business (if different from name on line 1)
Bones Enterprises

3 Executor, administrator, trustee, "care of" name

4a Mailing address (room, apt., suite no. and street, or P.O. box)
6789 Graves Avenue

4b City, state, and ZIP code
Chicago, IL 60601

5a Street address (if different) (Do not enter a P.O. box.)

5b City, state, and ZIP code

6 County and state where principal business is located
Cook, IL

7a Name of principal officer, general partner, grantor, owner, or trustor
Sidney Bones

7b SSN, ITIN, or EIN
123-45-6789

8a Type of entity (check only one box)
- ☒ Sole proprietor (SSN) 123 45 6789
- ☐ Partnership
- ☐ Corporation (enter form number to be filed) ► _____
- ☐ Personal service corporation
- ☐ Church or church-controlled organization
- ☐ Other nonprofit organization (specify) ► _____
- ☐ Other (specify) ►
- ☐ Estate (SSN of decedent) _____
- ☐ Plan administrator (SSN) _____
- ☐ Trust (SSN of grantor) _____
- ☐ National Guard   ☐ State/local government
- ☐ Farmers' cooperative ☐ Federal government/military
- ☐ REMIC   ☐ Indian tribal governments/enterprises

Group Exemption Number (GEN) ► _____

8b If a corporation, name the state or foreign country (if applicable) where incorporated
State _____   Foreign country _____

9 Reason for applying (check only one box)
- ☒ Started new business (specify type) ► _____
  novelty store
- ☐ Hired employees (Check the box and see line 12.)
- ☐ Compliance with IRS withholding regulations
- ☐ Other (specify) ►
- ☐ Banking purpose (specify purpose) ► _____
- ☐ Changed type of organization (specify new type) ► _____
- ☐ Purchased going business
- ☐ Created a trust (specify type) ► _____
- ☐ Created a pension plan (specify type) ► _____

10 Date business started or acquired (month, day, year). See instructions.
1-29-06

11 Closing month of accounting year
December

12 First date wages or annuities were paid (month, day, year). **Note.** If applicant is a withholding agent, enter date income will first be paid to nonresident alien. (month, day, year) ► 2-13-06

13 Highest number of employees expected in the next 12 months (enter -0- if none).

Do you expect to have $1,000 or less in employment tax liability for the calendar year? ☐ **Yes** ☐ **No.** (If you expect to pay $4,000 or less in wages, you can mark yes.)

Agricultural	Household	Other

14 Check **one** box that best describes the principal activity of your business.
- ☐ Construction   ☐ Rental & leasing   ☐ Transportation & warehousing
- ☐ Real estate   ☐ Manufacturing   ☐ Finance & insurance
- ☐ Health care & social assistance   ☐ Wholesale-agent/broker
- ☐ Accommodation & food service   ☐ Wholesale-other   ☒ Retail
- ☐ Other (specify)

15 Indicate principal line of merchandise sold, specific construction work done, products produced, or services provided.
novelty stores

16a Has the applicant ever applied for an employer identification number for this or any other business? . . . . ☐ Yes   ☒ No
Note. If "Yes," please complete lines 16b and 16c.

16b If you checked "Yes" on line 16a, give applicant's legal name and trade name shown on prior application if different from line 1 or 2 above.
Legal name ►   Trade name ►

16c Approximate date when, and city and state where, the application was filed. Enter previous employer identification number if known.
Approximate date when filed (mo., day, year) | City and state where filed | Previous EIN

Third Party Designee

Complete this section **only** if you want to authorize the named individual to receive the entity's EIN and answer questions about the completion of this form.

Designee's name

Designee's telephone number (include area code)
(   )

Address and ZIP code

Designee's fax number (include area code)
(   )

Under penalties of perjury, I declare that I have examined this application, and to the best of my knowledge and belief, it is true, correct, and complete.

Name and title (type or print clearly) ► Sidney Bones, owner

Applicant's telephone number (include area code)
(312) 555-1234

Signature ► *Sidney Bones*   Date ► 1/29/07

Applicant's fax number (include area code)
(   )

For Privacy Act and Paperwork Reduction Act Notice, see separate instructions.   Cat. No. 16055N   Form **SS-4** (Rev. 2-2006)

Do I Need an EIN?

File Form SS-4 if the applicant entity does not already have an EIN but is required to show an EIN on any return, statement, or other document.[1] See also the separate instructions for each line on Form SS-4.

IF the applicant...	AND...	THEN...
Started a new business	Does not currently have (nor expect to have) employees	Complete lines 1, 2, 4a–8a, 8b (if applicable), and 9–16c.
Hired (or will hire) employees, including household employees	Does not already have an EIN	Complete lines 1, 2, 4a–6, 7a–b (if applicable), 8a, 8b (if applicable), and 9–16c.
Opened a bank account	Needs an EIN for banking purposes only	Complete lines 1–5b, 7a–b (if applicable), 8a, 9, and 16a–c.
Changed type of organization	Either the legal character of the organization or its ownership changed (for example, you incorporate a sole proprietorship or form a partnership)[2]	Complete lines 1–16c (as applicable).
Purchased a going business[3]	Does not already have an EIN	Complete lines 1–16c (as applicable).
Created a trust	The trust is other than a grantor trust or an IRA trust[4]	Complete lines 1–16c (as applicable).
Created a pension plan as a plan administrator[5]	Needs an EIN for reporting purposes	Complete lines 1, 3, 4a–b, 8a, 9, and 16a–c.
Is a foreign person needing an EIN to comply with IRS withholding regulations	Needs an EIN to complete a Form W-8 (other than Form W-8ECI), avoid withholding on portfolio assets, or claim tax treaty benefits[6]	Complete lines 1–5b, 7a–b (SSN or ITIN optional), 8a–9, and 16a–c.
Is administering an estate	Needs an EIN to report estate income on Form 1041	Complete lines 1, 2, 3, 4a–6, 8a, 9-11, 12-15 (if applicable), and 16a–c.
Is a withholding agent for taxes on non-wage income paid to an alien (i.e., individual, corporation, or partnership, etc.)	Is an agent, broker, fiduciary, manager, tenant, or spouse who is required to file Form 1042, Annual Withholding Tax Return for U.S. Source Income of Foreign Persons	Complete lines 1, 2, 3 (if applicable), 4a–5b, 7a–b (if applicable), 8a, 9, and 16a–c.
Is a state or local agency	Serves as a tax reporting agent for public assistance recipients under Rev. Proc. 80-4, 1980-1 C.B. 581[7]	Complete lines 1, 2, 4a–5b, 8a, 9, and 16a–c.
Is a single-member LLC	Needs an EIN to file Form 8832, Entity Classification Election, for filing employment tax returns, **or** for state reporting purposes[8]	Complete lines 1–16c (as applicable).
Is an S corporation	Needs an EIN to file Form 2553, Election by a Small Business Corporation[9]	Complete lines 1–16c (as applicable).

[1] For example, a sole proprietorship or self-employed farmer who establishes a qualified retirement plan, or is required to file excise, employment, alcohol, tobacco, or firearms returns, must have an EIN. A partnership, corporation, REMIC (real estate mortgage investment conduit), nonprofit organization (church, club, etc.), or farmers' cooperative must use an EIN for any tax-related purpose even if the entity does not have employees.

[2] However, do not apply for a new EIN if the existing entity only (a) changed its business name, (b) elected on Form 8832 to change the way it is taxed (or is covered by the default rules), or (c) terminated its partnership status because at least 50% of the total interests in partnership capital and profits were sold or exchanged within a 12-month period. The EIN of the terminated partnership should continue to be used. See Regulations section 301.6109-1(d)(2)(iii).

[3] Do not use the EIN of the prior business unless you became the "owner" of a corporation by acquiring its stock.

[4] However, grantor trusts that do not file using Optional Method 1 and IRA trusts that are required to file Form 990-T, Exempt Organization Business Income Tax Return, must have an EIN. For more information on grantor trusts, see the Instructions for Form 1041.

[5] A plan administrator is the person or group of persons specified as the administrator by the instrument under which the plan is operated.

[6] Entities applying to be a Qualified Intermediary (QI) need a QI-EIN even if they already have an EIN. See Rev. Proc. 2000-12.

[7] See also Household employer on page 3. **Note.** State or local agencies may need an EIN for other reasons, for example, hired employees.

[8] Most LLCs do not need to file Form 8832. See Limited liability company (LLC) on page 4 for details on completing Form SS-4 for an LLC.

[9] An existing corporation that is electing or revoking S corporation status should use its previously-assigned EIN.

Instructions for Form SS-4

Department of the Treasury
Internal Revenue Service

(Rev. February 2006)

Application for Employer Identification Number

Section references are to the Internal Revenue Code unless otherwise noted.

General Instructions

Use these instructions to complete Form SS-4, Application for Employer Identification Number. Also see *Do I Need an EIN?* on page 2 of Form SS-4.

Purpose of Form

Use Form SS-4 to apply for an employer identification number (EIN). An EIN is a nine-digit number (for example, 12-3456789) assigned to sole proprietors, corporations, partnerships, estates, trusts, and other entities for tax filing and reporting purposes. The information you provide on this form will establish your business tax account.

 An EIN is for use in connection with your business activities only. Do not use your EIN in place of your social security number (SSN).

Reminders

Apply online. Generally, you can apply for and receive an EIN online using the Internet. See *How To Apply* below.

File only one Form SS-4. Generally, a sole proprietor should file only one Form SS-4 and needs only one EIN, regardless of the number of businesses operated as a sole proprietorship or trade names under which a business operates. However, if the proprietorship incorporates or enters into a partnership, a new EIN is required. Also, each corporation in an affiliated group must have its own EIN.

EIN applied for, but not received. If you do not have an EIN by the time a return is due, write "Applied For" and the date you applied in the space shown for the number. Do not show your SSN as an EIN on returns.

If you do not have an EIN by the time a tax deposit is due, send your payment to the Internal Revenue Service Center for your filing area as shown in the instructions for the form that you are filing. Make your check or money order payable to the "United States Treasury" and show your name (as shown on Form SS-4), address, type of tax, period covered, and date you applied for an EIN.

Federal tax deposits. New employers that have a federal tax obligation will be pre-enrolled in the Electronic Federal Tax Payment System (EFTPS). EFTPS allows you to make all of your federal tax payments online at *www.eftps.gov* or by telephone. Shortly after we have assigned you your EIN, you will receive instructions by mail for activating your EFTPS enrollment. You will also receive an EFTPS Personal Identification Number (PIN) that you will use to make your payments, as well as instructions for obtaining an Internet password you will need to make payments online.

If you are not required to make deposits by EFTPS, you can use Form 8109, Federal Tax Deposit (FTD) Coupon, to make deposits at an authorized depositary. If

you would like to receive Form 8109, call 1-800-829-4933. Allow 5 to 6 weeks for delivery. For more information on federal tax deposits, see Pub. 15 (Circular E).

How To Apply

You can apply for an EIN online, by telephone, by fax, or by mail depending on how soon you need to use the EIN. Use only one method for each entity so you do not receive more than one EIN for an entity.

Online. Generally, you can receive your EIN by Internet and use it immediately to file a return or make a payment. Go to the IRS website at *www.irs.gov/businesses* and click on Employer ID Numbers.

Applicants that may not apply online. The online application process is not yet available to:
- Applicants with foreign addresses (including Puerto Rico),
- Limited Liability Companies (LLCs) that have not yet determined their entity classification for federal tax purposes (see *Limited liability company (LLC)* on page 4),
- Real Estate Investment Conduits (REMICs),
- State and local governments,
- Federal Government/Military, and
- Indian Tribal Governments/Enterprises.

Telephone. You can receive your EIN by telephone and use it immediately to file a return or make a payment. Call the IRS at 1-800-829-4933. (International applicants must call 215-516-6999.) The hours of operation are 7:00 a.m. to 10:00 p.m. local time (Pacific time for Alaska and Hawaii). The person making the call must be authorized to sign the form or be an authorized designee. See *Signature* and *Third Party Designee* on page 6. Also see the *TIP* below.

If you are applying by telephone, it will be helpful to complete Form SS-4 before contacting the IRS. An IRS representative will use the information from the Form SS-4 to establish your account and assign you an EIN. Write the number you are given on the upper right corner of the form and sign and date it. Keep this copy for your records.

If requested by an IRS representative, mail or fax (facsimile) the signed Form SS-4 (including any Third Party Designee authorization) within 24 hours to the IRS address provided by the IRS representative.

 *Taxpayer representatives can apply for an EIN on behalf of their client and request that the EIN be faxed to their client on the same day. **Note.** By using this procedure, you are authorizing the IRS to fax the EIN without a cover sheet.*

Fax. Under the Fax-TIN program, you can receive your EIN by fax within 4 business days. Complete and fax Form SS-4 to the IRS using the Fax-TIN number listed on page 2 for your state. A long-distance charge to callers outside of the local calling area will apply. Fax-TIN

Cat. No. 62736F

numbers can only be used to apply for an EIN. The numbers may change without notice. Fax-TIN is available 24 hours a day, 7 days a week.

Be sure to provide your fax number so the IRS can fax the EIN back to you.

Note. By using this procedure, you are authorizing the IRS to fax the EIN without a cover sheet.

Mail. Complete Form SS-4 at least 4 to 5 weeks before you will need an EIN. Sign and date the application and mail it to the service center address for your state. You will receive your EIN in the mail in approximately 4 weeks. See also *Third Party Designee* on page 6.

Call 1-800-829-4933 to verify a number or to ask about the status of an application by mail.

Where to Fax or File

If your principal business, office or agency, or legal residence in the case of an individual, is located in:	Fax or file with the "Internal Revenue Service Center" at:
Connecticut, Delaware, District of Columbia, Florida, Georgia, Maine, Maryland, Massachusetts, New Hampshire, New Jersey, New York, North Carolina, Ohio, Pennsylvania, Rhode Island, South Carolina, Vermont, Virginia, West Virginia	Attn: EIN Operation Holtsville, NY 11742 Fax-TIN: 631-447-8960
Illinois, Indiana, Kentucky, Michigan	Attn: EIN Operation Cincinnati, OH 45999 Fax-TIN: 859-669-5760
Alabama, Alaska, Arizona, Arkansas, California, Colorado, Hawaii, Idaho, Iowa, Kansas, Louisiana, Minnesota, Mississippi, Missouri, Montana, Nebraska, Nevada, New Mexico, North Dakota, Oklahoma, Oregon, South Dakota, Tennessee, Texas, Utah, Washington, Wisconsin, Wyoming	Attn: EIN Operation Philadelphia, PA 19255 Fax-TIN: 859-669-5760
If you have no legal residence, principal place of business, or principal office or agency in any state:	Attn: EIN Operation Philadelphia, PA 19255 Fax-TIN: 215-516-1040

How To Get Forms and Publications

Phone. Call 1-800-TAX-FORM (1-800-829-3676) to order forms, instructions, and publications. You should receive your order or notification of its status within 10 workdays.

Internet. You can access the IRS website 24 hours a day, 7 days a week at *www.irs.gov* to download forms, instructions, and publications.

CD-ROM. For small businesses, return preparers, or others who may frequently need tax forms or publications, a CD-ROM containing over 2,000 tax products (including many prior year forms) can be purchased from the National Technical Information Service (NTIS).

To order Pub. 1796, IRS Tax Products CD, call 1-877-CDFORMS (1-877-233-6767) toll free or connect to *www.irs.gov/cdorders*.

Tax Help for Your Business

IRS-sponsored Small Business Workshops provide information about your federal and state tax obligations. For information about workshops in your area, call 1-800-829-4933.

Related Forms and Publications

The following forms and instructions may be useful to filers of Form SS-4.
- Form 990-T, Exempt Organization Business Income Tax Return.
- Instructions for Form 990-T.
- Schedule C (Form 1040), Profit or Loss From Business.
- Schedule F (Form 1040), Profit or Loss From Farming.
- Instructions for Form 1041 and Schedules A, B, D, G, I, J, and K-1, U.S. Income Tax Return for Estates and Trusts.
- Form 1042, Annual Withholding Tax Return for U.S. Source Income of Foreign Persons.
- Instructions for Form 1065, U.S. Return of Partnership Income.
- Instructions for Form 1066, U.S. Real Estate Mortgage Investment Conduit (REMIC) Income Tax Return.
- Instructions for Forms 1120 and 1120-A.
- Form 2553, Election by a Small Business Corporation.
- Form 2848, Power of Attorney and Declaration of Representative.
- Form 8821, Tax Information Authorization.
- Form 8832, Entity Classification Election.

For more information about filing Form SS-4 and related issues, see:
- Pub. 51 (Circular A), Agricultural Employer's Tax Guide;
- Pub. 15 (Circular E), Employer's Tax Guide;
- Pub. 538, Accounting Periods and Methods;
- Pub. 542, Corporations;
- Pub. 557, Tax-Exempt Status for Your Organization;
- Pub. 583, Starting a Business and Keeping Records;
- Pub. 966, The Secure Way to Pay Your Federal Taxes for Business and Individual Taxpayers;
- Pub. 1635, Understanding Your EIN;
- Package 1023, Application for Recognition of Exemption Under Section 501(c)(3) of the Internal Revenue Code; and
- Package 1024, Application for Recognition of Exemption Under Section 501(a).

Specific Instructions

Print or type all entries on Form SS-4. Follow the instructions for each line to expedite processing and to avoid unnecessary IRS requests for additional information. Enter "N/A" (nonapplicable) on the lines that do not apply.

Line 1 — Legal name of entity (or individual) for whom the EIN is being requested. Enter the legal name of the entity (or individual) applying for the EIN exactly as it appears on the social security card, charter, or other applicable legal document. An entry is required.

Individuals. Enter your first name, middle initial, and last name. If you are a sole proprietor, enter your individual name, not your business name. Enter your business name on line 2. Do not use abbreviations or nicknames on line 1.

Trusts. Enter the name of the trust.

Estate of a decedent. Enter the name of the estate. For an estate that has no legal name, enter the name of the decedent followed by "Estate."

Partnerships. Enter the legal name of the partnership as it appears in the partnership agreement.

Corporations. Enter the corporate name as it appears in the corporate charter or other legal document creating it.

Plan administrators. Enter the name of the plan administrator. A plan administrator who already has an EIN should use that number.

Line 2 — Trade name of business. Enter the trade name of the business if different from the legal name. The trade name is the "doing business as " (DBA) name.

 Use the full legal name shown on line 1 on all tax returns filed for the entity. (However, if you enter a trade name on line 2 and choose to use the trade name instead of the legal name, enter the trade name on all returns you file.) To prevent processing delays and errors, always use the legal name only (or the trade name only) on all tax returns.

Line 3 — Executor, administrator, trustee, "care of" name. Trusts enter the name of the trustee. Estates enter the name of the executor, administrator, or other fiduciary. If the entity applying has a designated person to receive tax information, enter that person's name as the "care of" person. Enter the individual's first name, middle initial, and last name.

Lines 4a-b — Mailing address. Enter the mailing address for the entity's correspondence. If line 3 is completed, enter the address for the executor, trustee or "care of" person. Generally, this address will be used on all tax returns.

TIP *File Form 8822, Change of Address, to report any subsequent changes to the entity's mailing address.*

Lines 5a-b — Street address. Provide the entity's physical address only if different from its mailing address shown in lines 4a-b. Do not enter a P.O. box number here.

Line 6 — County and state where principal business is located. Enter the entity's primary physical location.

Lines 7a-b — Name of principal officer, general partner, grantor, owner, or trustor. Enter the first name, middle initial, last name, and SSN of (a) the principal officer if the business is a corporation, (b) a general partner if a partnership, (c) the owner of an entity that is disregarded as separate from its owner (disregarded entities owned by a corporation enter the corporation's name and EIN), or (d) a grantor, owner, or trustor if a trust.

If the person in question is an alien individual with a previously assigned individual taxpayer identification number (ITIN), enter the ITIN in the space provided and submit a copy of an official identifying document. If necessary, complete Form W-7, Application for IRS Individual Taxpayer Identification Number, to obtain an ITIN.

You must enter an SSN, ITIN, or EIN unless the only reason you are applying for an EIN is to make an entity classification election (see Regulations sections 301.7701-1 through 301.7701-3) and you are a nonresident alien or other foreign entity with no effectively connected income from sources within the United States.

Line 8a — Type of entity. Check the box that best describes the type of entity applying for the EIN. If you are an alien individual with an ITIN previously assigned to you, enter the ITIN in place of a requested SSN.

 This is not an election for a tax classification of an entity. See Limited liability company (LLC) *on page 4.*

Other. If not specifically listed, check the "Other" box, enter the type of entity and the type of return, if any, that will be filed (for example, "Common Trust Fund, Form 1065" or "Created a Pension Plan"). Do not enter "N/A." If you are an alien individual applying for an EIN, see the *Lines 7a-b* instructions above.

● **Household employer.** If you are an individual, check the "Other" box and enter "Household Employer" and your SSN. If you are a state or local agency serving as a tax reporting agent for public assistance recipients who become household employers, check the "Other" box and enter "Household Employer Agent." If you are a trust that qualifies as a household employer, you do not need a separate EIN for reporting tax information relating to household employees; use the EIN of the trust.

● **QSub.** For a qualified subchapter S subsidiary (QSub) check the "Other" box and specify "QSub."

● **Withholding agent.** If you are a withholding agent required to file Form 1042, check the "Other" box and enter "Withholding Agent."

Sole proprietor. Check this box if you file Schedule C, C-EZ, or F (Form 1040) and have a qualified plan, or are required to file excise, employment, alcohol, tobacco, or firearms returns, or are a payer of gambling winnings. Enter your SSN (or ITIN) in the space provided. If you are a nonresident alien with no effectively connected income from sources within the United States, you do not need to enter an SSN or ITIN.

Corporation. This box is for any corporation other than a personal service corporation. If you check this box, enter the income tax form number to be filed by the entity in the space provided.

 If you entered "1120S" after the "Corporation" checkbox, the corporation must file Form 2553 no later than the 15th day of the 3rd month of the tax year the election is to take effect. Until Form 2553 has been received and approved, you will be considered a Form 1120 filer. See the Instructions for Form 2553.

Personal service corporation. Check this box if the entity is a personal service corporation. An entity is a personal service corporation for a tax year only if:
● The principal activity of the entity during the testing period (prior tax year) for the tax year is the performance of personal services substantially by employee-owners, and
● The employee-owners own at least 10% of the fair market value of the outstanding stock in the entity on the last day of the testing period.

Personal services include performance of services in such fields as health, law, accounting, or consulting. For more information about personal service corporations, see the Instructions for Forms 1120 and 1120-A and Pub. 542.

Other nonprofit organization. Check this box if the nonprofit organization is other than a church or church-controlled organization and specify the type of nonprofit organization (for example, an educational organization).

 If the organization also seeks tax-exempt status, you must file either Package 1023 or Package 1024. See Pub. 557 for more information.

If the organization is covered by a group exemption letter, enter the four-digit group exemption number (GEN). (Do not confuse the GEN with the nine-digit EIN.) If you do not know the GEN, contact the parent organization. Get Pub. 557 for more information about group exemption numbers.

If the organization is a section 527 political organization, check the box for *Other nonprofit organization* and specify "section 527 organization" in the space to the right. To be recognized as exempt from tax, a section 527 political organization must electronically file Form 8871, Political Organization Notice of Section 527 Status, within 24 hours of the date on which the organization was established. The organization may also have to file Form 8872, Political Organization Report of Contributions and Expenditures. See *www.irs.gov/polorgs* for more information.

Plan administrator. If the plan administrator is an individual, enter the plan administrator's SSN in the space provided.

REMIC. Check this box if the entity has elected to be treated as a real estate mortgage investment conduit (REMIC). See the Instructions for Form 1066 for more information.

State/local government. If you are a government employer and you are not sure of your social security and Medicare coverage options, go to *www.ncsssa.org/ssaframes.html* to obtain the contact information for your state's Social Security Administrator.

Limited liability company (LLC). An LLC is an entity organized under the laws of a state or foreign country as a limited liability company. For federal tax purposes, an LLC may be treated as a partnership or corporation or be disregarded as an entity separate from its owner.

By default, a domestic LLC with only one member is disregarded as an entity separate from its owner and must include all of its income and expenses on the owner's tax return (for example, Schedule C (Form 1040)). Also by default, a domestic LLC with two or more members is treated as a partnership. A domestic LLC may file Form 8832 to avoid either default classification and elect to be classified as an association taxable as a corporation. For more information on entity classifications (including the rules for foreign entities), see the instructions for Form 8832.

 Do not file Form 8832 if the LLC accepts the default classifications above. If the LLC is eligible to be treated as a corporation that meets certain tests and it will be electing S corporation status, it must timely file Form 2553. The LLC will be treated as a corporation as of the effective date of the S corporation election and does not need to file Form 8832. See the Instructions for Form 2553.

Complete Form SS-4 for LLCs as follows.

• A single-member domestic LLC that accepts the default classification (above) does not need an EIN and generally should not file Form SS-4. Generally, the LLC should use the name and EIN of its owner for all federal tax purposes. However, the reporting and payment of employment taxes for employees of the LLC may be made using the name and EIN of either the owner or the LLC as explained in Notice 99-6. You can find Notice 99-6 on page 12 of Internal Revenue Bulletin 1999-3 at *www.irs.gov/pub/irs-irbs/irb99-03.pdf.* (**Note.** If the LLC applicant indicates in box 13 that it has employees or expects to have employees, the owner (whether an individual or other entity) of a single-member domestic LLC will also be assigned its own EIN (if it does not already have one) even if the LLC will be filing the employment tax returns.)
• A single-member, domestic LLC that accepts the default classification (above) and wants an EIN for filing employment tax returns (see above) or non-federal purposes, such as a state requirement, must check the "Other" box and write "Disregarded Entity" or, when applicable, "Disregarded Entity — Sole Proprietorship" in the space provided.
• A multi-member, domestic LLC that accepts the default classification (above) must check the "Partnership" box.
• A domestic LLC that will be filing Form 8832 to elect corporate status must check the "Corporation" box and write in "Single-Member" or "Multi-Member" immediately below the "form number" entry line.

Line 9 — Reason for applying. Check only one box. Do not enter "N/A."

Started new business. Check this box if you are starting a new business that requires an EIN. If you check this box, enter the type of business being started. Do not apply if you already have an EIN and are only adding another place of business.

Hired employees. Check this box if the existing business is requesting an EIN because it has hired or is hiring employees and is therefore required to file employment tax returns. Do not apply if you already have an EIN and are only hiring employees. For information on employment taxes (for example, for family members), see Pub. 15 (Circular E).

 You may have to make electronic deposits of all depository taxes (such as employment tax, excise tax, and corporate income tax) using the Electronic Federal Tax Payment System (EFTPS). See Federal tax deposits *on page 1; section 11,* Depositing Taxes, *of Pub. 15 (Circular E); and Pub. 966.*

Created a pension plan. Check this box if you have created a pension plan and need an EIN for reporting purposes. Also, enter the type of plan in the space provided.

TIP *Check this box if you are applying for a trust EIN when a new pension plan is established. In addition, check the "Other" box in line 8a and write "Created a Pension Plan" in the space provided.*

Banking purpose. Check this box if you are requesting an EIN for banking purposes only, and enter the banking purpose (for example, a bowling league for depositing dues or an investment club for dividend and interest reporting).

Changed type of organization. Check this box if the business is changing its type of organization. For example, the business was a sole proprietorship and has been incorporated or has become a partnership. If you check this box, specify in the space provided (including available space immediately below) the type of change made. For example, "From Sole Proprietorship to Partnership."

Purchased going business. Check this box if you purchased an existing business. Do not use the former owner's EIN unless you became the "owner" of a corporation by acquiring its stock.

Created a trust. Check this box if you created a trust, and enter the type of trust created. For example, indicate if the trust is a nonexempt charitable trust or a split-interest trust.

Exception. Do not file this form for certain grantor-type trusts. The trustee does not need an EIN for the trust if the trustee furnishes the name and TIN of the grantor/owner and the address of the trust to all payors. However, grantor trusts that do not file using Optional Method 1 and IRA trusts that are required to file Form 990-T, Exempt Organization Business Income Tax Return, must have an EIN. For more information on grantor trusts, see the Instructions for Form 1041.

TIP *Do not check this box if you are applying for a trust EIN when a new pension plan is established. Check "Created a pension plan."*

Other. Check this box if you are requesting an EIN for any other reason; and enter the reason. For example, a newly-formed state government entity should enter "Newly-Formed State Government Entity" in the space provided.

Line 10 — Date business started or acquired. If you are starting a new business, enter the starting date of the business. If the business you acquired is already operating, enter the date you acquired the business. If you are changing the form of ownership of your business, enter the date the new ownership entity began. Trusts should enter the date the trust was funded. Estates should enter the date of death of the decedent whose name appears on line 1 or the date when the estate was legally funded.

Line 11 — Closing month of accounting year. Enter the last month of your accounting year or tax year. An accounting or tax year is usually 12 consecutive months, either a calendar year or a fiscal year (including a period of 52 or 53 weeks). A calendar year is 12 consecutive months ending on December 31. A fiscal year is either 12 consecutive months ending on the last day of any month other than December or a 52-53 week year. For more information on accounting periods, see Pub. 538.

Individuals. Your tax year generally will be a calendar year.

Partnerships. Partnerships must adopt one of the following tax years.
• The tax year of the majority of its partners.
• The tax year common to all of its principal partners.
• The tax year that results in the least aggregate deferral of income.
• In certain cases, some other tax year.

See the Instructions for Form 1065 for more information.

REMICs. REMICs must have a calendar year as their tax year.

Personal service corporations. A personal service corporation generally must adopt a calendar year unless it meets one of the following requirements.
• It can establish a business purpose for having a different tax year.
• It elects under section 444 to have a tax year other than a calendar year.

Trusts. Generally, a trust must adopt a calendar year except for the following trusts.
• Tax-exempt trusts.
• Charitable trusts.
• Grantor-owned trusts.

Line 12 — First date wages or annuities were paid. If the business has employees, enter the date on which the business began to pay wages. If the business does not plan to have employees, enter "N/A."

Withholding agent. Enter the date you began or will begin to pay income (including annuities) to a nonresident alien. This also applies to individuals who are required to file Form 1042 to report alimony paid to a nonresident alien.

Line 13 — Highest number of employees expected in the next 12 months. Complete each box by entering the number (including zero ("-0-")) of "Agricultural," "Household," or "Other" employees expected by the applicant in the next 12 months. Check the appropriate box to indicate if you expect your annual employment tax liability to be $1,000 or less. Generally, if you pay $4,000 or less in wages subject to social security and Medicare taxes and federal income tax withholding, you are likely to pay $1,000 or less in employment taxes.

For more information on employment taxes, see Pub. 15 (Circular E); or Pub. 51 (Circular A) if you have agricultural employees (farmworkers).

Lines 14 and 15. Check the one box in line 14 that best describes the principal activity of the applicant's business. Check the "Other" box (and specify the applicant's principal activity) if none of the listed boxes applies. You must check a box.

Use line 15 to describe the applicant's principal line of business in more detail. For example, if you checked the "Construction" box in line 14, enter additional detail such as "General contractor for residential buildings" in line 15. An entry is required.

Construction. Check this box if the applicant is engaged in erecting buildings or engineering projects, (for example, streets, highways, bridges, tunnels). The term "Construction" also includes special trade contractors, (for example, plumbing, HVAC, electrical, carpentry, concrete, excavation, etc. contractors).

Real estate. Check this box if the applicant is engaged in renting or leasing real estate to others; managing, selling, buying or renting real estate for others; or providing related real estate services (for example, appraisal services).

Rental and leasing. Check this box if the applicant is engaged in providing tangible goods such as autos, computers, consumer goods, or industrial machinery and equipment to customers in return for a periodic rental or lease payment.

Manufacturing. Check this box if the applicant is engaged in the mechanical, physical, or chemical transformation of materials, substances, or components into new products. The assembling of component parts of manufactured products is also considered to be manufacturing.

Transportation & warehousing. Check this box if the applicant provides transportation of passengers or cargo; warehousing or storage of goods; scenic or sight-seeing transportation; or support activities related to transportation.

Finance & insurance. Check this box if the applicant is engaged in transactions involving the creation, liquidation, or change of ownership of financial assets and/or facilitating such financial transactions; underwriting annuities/insurance policies; facilitating such underwriting by selling insurance policies; or by providing other insurance or employee-benefit related services.

Health care and social assistance. Check this box if the applicant is engaged in providing physical, medical, or psychiatric care or providing social assistance activities such as youth centers, adoption agencies, individual/family services, temporary shelters, daycare, etc.

Accommodation & food services. Check this box if the applicant is engaged in providing customers with lodging, meal preparation, snacks, or beverages for immediate consumption.

Wholesale–agent/broker. Check this box if the applicant is engaged in arranging for the purchase or sale of goods owned by others or purchasing goods on a commission basis for goods traded in the wholesale market, usually between businesses.

Wholesale–other. Check this box if the applicant is engaged in selling goods in the wholesale market generally to other businesses for resale on their own account, goods used in production, or capital or durable nonconsumer goods.

Retail. Check this box if the applicant is engaged in selling merchandise to the general public from a fixed store; by direct, mail-order, or electronic sales; or by using vending machines.

Other. Check this box if the applicant is engaged in an activity not described above. Describe the applicant's principal business activity in the space provided.

Lines 16a–c. Check the applicable box in line 16a to indicate whether or not the entity (or individual) applying for an EIN was issued one previously. Complete lines 16b and 16c only if the "Yes" box in line 16a is checked. If the applicant previously applied for more than one EIN, write "See Attached" in the empty space in line 16a and attach a separate sheet providing the line 16b and 16c information for each EIN previously requested.

Third Party Designee. Complete this section only if you want to authorize the named individual to receive the entity's EIN and answer questions about the completion of Form SS-4. The designee's authority terminates at the time the EIN is assigned and released to the designee. You must complete the signature area for the authorization to be valid.

Signature. When required, the application must be signed by (a) the individual, if the applicant is an individual, (b) the president, vice president, or other principal officer, if the applicant is a corporation, (c) a responsible and duly authorized member or officer having

knowledge of its affairs, if the applicant is a partnership, government entity, or other unincorporated organization, or (d) the fiduciary, if the applicant is a trust or an estate. Foreign applicants may have any duly-authorized person, (for example, division manager), sign Form SS-4.

Privacy Act and Paperwork Reduction Act Notice. We ask for the information on this form to carry out the Internal Revenue laws of the United States. We need it to comply with section 6109 and the regulations thereunder, which generally require the inclusion of an employer identification number (EIN) on certain returns, statements, or other documents filed with the Internal Revenue Service. If your entity is required to obtain an EIN, you are required to provide all of the information requested on this form. Information on this form may be used to determine which federal tax returns you are required to file and to provide you with related forms and publications.

We disclose this form to the Social Security Administration (SSA) for their use in determining compliance with applicable laws. We may give this information to the Department of Justice for use in civil and criminal litigation, and to the cities, states, and the District of Columbia for use in administering their tax laws. We may also disclose this information to other countries under a tax treaty, to federal and state agencies to enforce federal nontax criminal laws, and to federal law enforcement and intelligence agencies to combat terrorism.

We will be unable to issue an EIN to you unless you provide all of the requested information that applies to your entity. Providing false information could subject you to penalties.

You are not required to provide the information requested on a form that is subject to the Paperwork Reduction Act unless the form displays a valid OMB control number. Books or records relating to a form or its instructions must be retained as long as their contents may become material in the administration of any Internal Revenue law. Generally, tax returns and return information are confidential, as required by section 6103.

The time needed to complete and file this form will vary depending on individual circumstances. The estimated average time is:

Recordkeeping	8 hrs., 22 min.
Learning about the law or the form	42 min.
Preparing the form	52 min.
Copying, assembling, and sending the form to the IRS	- - - - -

If you have comments concerning the accuracy of these time estimates or suggestions for making this form simpler, we would be happy to hear from you. You can write to Internal Revenue Service, Tax Products Coordinating Committee, SE:W:CAR:MP:T:T:SP, IR-6406, 1111 Constitution Avenue, NW, Washington, DC 20224. Do not send the form to this address. Instead, see *Where to Fax or File* on page 2.

Form W-4 (2006)

Purpose. Complete Form W-4 so that your employer can withhold the correct federal income tax from your pay. Because your tax situation may change, you may want to refigure your withholding each year.

Exemption from withholding. If you are exempt, complete only lines 1, 2, 3, 4, and 7 and sign the form to validate it. Your exemption for 2006 expires February 16, 2007. See Pub. 505, Tax Withholding and Estimated Tax.

Note. You cannot claim exemption from withholding if (a) your income exceeds $850 and includes more than $300 of unearned income (for example, interest and dividends) and (b) another person can claim you as a dependent on their tax return.

Basic instructions. If you are not exempt, complete the **Personal Allowances Worksheet** below. The worksheets on page 2 adjust your withholding allowances based on itemized deductions, certain credits, adjustments to income, or two-earner/two-job situations. Complete all worksheets that apply. However, you may claim fewer (or zero) allowances.

Head of household. Generally, you may claim head of household filing status on your tax return only if you are unmarried and pay more than 50% of the costs of keeping up a home for yourself and your dependent(s) or other qualifying individuals. See line E below.

Tax credits. You can take projected tax credits into account in figuring your allowable number of withholding allowances. Credits for child or dependent care expenses and the child tax credit may be claimed using the **Personal Allowances Worksheet** below. See Pub. 919, How Do I Adjust My Tax Withholding, for information on converting your other credits into withholding allowances.

Nonwage income. If you have a large amount of nonwage income, such as interest or dividends, consider making estimated tax payments using Form 1040-ES, Estimated Tax for Individuals. Otherwise, you may owe additional tax.

Two earners/two jobs. If you have a working spouse or more than one job, figure the total number of allowances you are entitled to claim on all jobs using worksheets from only one Form W-4. Your withholding usually will be most accurate when all allowances are claimed on the Form W-4 for the highest paying job and zero allowances are claimed on the others.

Nonresident alien. If you are a nonresident alien, see the Instructions for Form 8233 before completing this Form W-4.

Check your withholding. After your Form W-4 takes effect, use Pub. 919 to see how the dollar amount you are having withheld compares to your projected total tax for 2006. See Pub. 919, especially if your earnings exceed $130,000 (Single) or $180,000 (Married).

Recent name change? If your name on line 1 differs from that shown on your social security card, call 1-800-772-1213 to initiate a name change and obtain a social security card showing your correct name.

Personal Allowances Worksheet (Keep for your records.)

A Enter "1" for **yourself** if no one else can claim you as a dependent . . . . **A** _____

B Enter "1" if:
- You are single and have only one job; or
- You are married, have only one job, and your spouse does not work; or
- Your wages from a second job or your spouse's wages (or the total of both) are $1,000 or less. **B** _____

C Enter "1" for your **spouse**. But, you may choose to enter "-0-" if you are married and have either a working spouse or more than one job. (Entering "-0-" may help you avoid having too little tax withheld.) . . . . **C** _____

D Enter number of **dependents** (other than your spouse or yourself) you will claim on your tax return . . . . **D** _____

E Enter "1" if you will file as **head of household** on your tax return (see conditions under **Head of household** above) . **E** _____

F Enter "1" if you have at least $1,500 of **child or dependent care expenses** for which you plan to claim a credit . . **F** _____
(**Note.** Do **not** include child support payments. See **Pub. 503,** Child and Dependent Care Expenses, for details.)

G **Child Tax Credit** (including additional child tax credit):
- If your total income will be less than $55,000 ($82,000 if married), enter "2" for each eligible child.
- If your total income will be between $55,000 and $84,000 ($82,000 and $119,000 if married), enter "1" for each eligible child plus "1" **additional** if you have four or more eligible children. **G** _____

H Add lines A through G and enter total here. (**Note.** This may be different from the number of exemptions you claim on your tax return.) ▶ **H** _____

For accuracy, complete all worksheets that apply.
- If you plan to **itemize or claim adjustments to income** and want to reduce your withholding, see the **Deductions and Adjustments Worksheet** on page 2.
- If you have **more than one job** or are **married and you and your spouse both work** and the combined earnings from all jobs exceed $35,000 ($25,000 if married) see the **Two-Earner/Two-Job Worksheet** on page 2 to avoid having too little tax withheld.
- If **neither** of the above situations applies, **stop here** and enter the number from line H on line 5 of Form W-4 below.

- **Cut here and give Form W-4 to your employer. Keep the top part for your records.** - - - - - - - - - - - - - - -

Form **W-4**

Department of the Treasury
Internal Revenue Service

Employee's Withholding Allowance Certificate

▶ Whether you are entitled to claim a certain number of allowances or exemption from withholding is subject to review by the IRS. Your employer may be required to send a copy of this form to the IRS.

OMB No. 1545-0074

2006

1 Type or print your first name and middle initial. **John A.**	Last name **Smith**	2 Your social security number **978 65 4231**

Home address (number and street or rural route) **567 Wharf Boulevard**	3 ☒ Single ☐ Married ☐ Married, but withhold at higher Single rate.
City or town, state, and ZIP code **Chicago, IL 60601**	**Note.** If married, but legally separated, or spouse is a nonresident alien, check the "Single" box. 4 If your last name differs from that shown on your social security card, check here. You must call 1-800-772-1213 for a new card. ▶ ☐

5 Total number of allowances you are claiming (from line **H** above **or** from the applicable worksheet on page 2) **5** **1**

6 Additional amount, if any, you want withheld from each paycheck . . . . **6** $ **0**

7 I claim exemption from withholding for 2006, and I certify that I meet **both** of the following conditions for exemption.
- Last year I had a right to a refund of **all** federal income tax withheld because I had **no** tax liability **and**
- This year I expect a refund of **all** federal income tax withheld because I expect to have **no** tax liability.
If you meet both conditions, write "Exempt" here . . . . ▶ **7**

Under penalties of perjury, I declare that I have examined this certificate and to the best of my knowledge and belief, it is true, correct, and complete.

Employee's signature
(Form is not valid unless you sign it.) ▶ *John A. Smith*   Date ▶ **6/5/06**

8 Employer's name and address (Employer: Complete lines 8 and 10 only if sending to the IRS.)	9 Office code (optional)	10 Employer identification number (EIN)

For Privacy Act and Paperwork Reduction Act Notice, see page 2.   Cat. No. 10220Q   Form **W-4** (2006)

Deductions and Adjustments Worksheet

Note. Use this worksheet *only* if you plan to itemize deductions, claim certain credits, or claim adjustments to income on your 2006 tax return.

1	Enter an estimate of your 2006 itemized deductions. These include qualifying home mortgage interest, charitable contributions, state and local taxes, medical expenses in excess of 7.5% of your income, and miscellaneous deductions. (For 2006, you may have to reduce your itemized deductions if your income is over $150,500 ($75,250 if married filing separately). See *Worksheet 3* in Pub. 919 for details.) . . .	1	$ _____
2	Enter: { $10,300 if married filing jointly or qualifying widow(er) $ 7,550 if head of household $ 5,150 if single or married filing separately }	2	$ _____
3	**Subtract** line 2 from line 1. If line 2 is greater than line 1, enter "-0-"	3	$ _____
4	Enter an estimate of your 2006 adjustments to income, including alimony, deductible IRA contributions, and student loan interest	4	$ _____
5	**Add** lines 3 and 4 and enter the total. (Include any amount for credits from *Worksheet 7* in Pub. 919) .	5	$ _____
6	Enter an estimate of your 2006 nonwage income (such as dividends or interest)	6	$ _____
7	**Subtract** line 6 from line 5. Enter the result, but not less than "-0-"	7	$ _____
8	**Divide** the amount on line 7 by $3,300 and enter the result here. Drop any fraction	8	_____
9	Enter the number from the **Personal Allowances Worksheet,** line H, page 1	9	_____
10	**Add** lines 8 and 9 and enter the total here. If you plan to use the **Two-Earner/Two-Job Worksheet,** also enter this total on line 1 below. Otherwise, **stop here** and enter this total on Form W-4, line 5, page 1 .	10	_____

Two-Earner/Two-Job Worksheet (See *Two earners/two jobs* on page 1.)

Note. Use this worksheet *only* if the instructions under line H on page 1 direct you here.

1	Enter the number from line H, page 1 (or from line 10 above if you used the **Deductions and Adjustments Worksheet**)	1	_____
2	Find the number in **Table 1** below that applies to the **LOWEST** paying job and enter it here	2	_____
3	If line 1 is **more than or equal to** line 2, subtract line 2 from line 1. Enter the result here (if zero, enter "-0-") and on Form W-4, line 5, page 1. **Do not** use the rest of this worksheet	3	_____

Note. If line 1 is *less than* line 2, enter "-0-" on Form W-4, line 5, page 1. Complete lines 4–9 below to calculate the additional withholding amount necessary to avoid a year-end tax bill.

4	Enter the number from line 2 of this worksheet	4	_____
5	Enter the number from line 1 of this worksheet	5	_____
6	**Subtract** line 5 from line 4	6	_____
7	Find the amount in **Table 2** below that applies to the **HIGHEST** paying job and enter it here	7	$ _____
8	**Multiply** line 7 by line 6 and enter the result here. This is the additional annual withholding needed . .	8	$ _____
9	Divide line 8 by the number of pay periods remaining in 2006. For example, divide by 26 if you are paid every two weeks and you complete this form in December 2005. Enter the result here and on Form W-4, line 6, page 1. This is the additional amount to be withheld from each paycheck	9	$ _____

Table 1: Two-Earner/Two-Job Worksheet

Married Filing Jointly						All Others	
If wages from **HIGHEST** paying job are—	AND, wages from **LOWEST** paying job are—	Enter on line 2 above	If wages from **HIGHEST** paying job are—	AND, wages from **LOWEST** paying job are—	Enter on line 2 above	If wages from **LOWEST** paying job are—	Enter on line 2 above
$0 - $42,000	$0 - $4,500	0	$42,001 and over	32,001 - 38,000	6	$0 - $6,000	0
	4,501 - 9,000	1		38,001 - 46,000	7	6,001 - 12,000	1
	9,001 - 18,000	2		46,001 - 55,000	8	12,001 - 19,000	2
	18,001 and over	3		55,001 - 60,000	9	19,001 - 26,000	3
				60,001 - 65,000	10	26,001 - 35,000	4
$42,001 and over	$0 - $4,500	0		65,001 - 75,000	11	35,001 - 50,000	5
	4,501 - 9,000	1		75,001 - 95,000	12	50,001 - 65,000	6
	9,001 - 18,000	2		95,001 - 105,000	13	65,001 - 80,000	7
	18,001 - 22,000	3		105,001 - 120,000	14	80,001 - 90,000	8
	22,001 - 26,000	4		120,001 and over	15	90,001 - 120,000	9
	26,001 - 32,000	5				120,001 and over	10

Table 2: Two-Earner/Two-Job Worksheet

Married Filing Jointly		All Others	
If wages from **HIGHEST** paying job are—	Enter on line 7 above	If wages from **HIGHEST** paying job are—	Enter on line 7 above
$0 - $60,000	$500	$0 - $30,000	$500
60,001 - 115,000	830	30,001 - 75,000	830
115,001 - 165,000	920	75,001 - 145,000	920
165,001 - 290,000	1,090	145,001 - 330,000	1,090
290,001 and over	1,160	330,001 and over	1,160

 Printed on recycled paper

Illinois Department of Revenue

REG-1 Illinois Business Registration Application

Station # 925

Step 1: Read this information first

You may electronically file this form at **www.ILtax.com.**
To update previously submitted information, call **217 785-3707.**

Faster and Easier

Do not check here
until you have read
all of Step 4. ☐

Step 2: Provide your identification numbers and the reason for your application

Check the best description of why you are completing this application.

___ **First-time registration of your business or organization.** Tell us your federal employer identification number (FEIN). If you have applied for but not yet received your FEIN, write **"applied for."** __ __-__ __ __ __ __ __ __

Starting date of this business in Illinois: **59 /123/ 4567**
                                                   Month Day   Year

___ **Re-applying of a previously registered business.** Tell us the Illinois Business Tax number (IBT no.) and, if applicable, the license number (Lic. no.) assigned to this business.   IBT no.:__ __ __ __-__ __ __ __   Lic. no.: _____

New starting date of this business in Illinois: **1 /29 /07**
                                                          Month Day   Year

___ **Organizational change requiring a new Federal Employer Identification number (FEIN).**

What is the effective date of this change?   ___ /___ /_____
                                               Month Day Year

Is this change the result of a merger or consolidation? ○ yes ○ no

Tell us the FEIN and Illinois Business Tax number (IBT no.) previously assigned when you registered this business.

FEIN: __ __-__ __ __ __ __ __ __   IBT no.:__ __ __ __-__ __ __ __

Tell us the new FEIN assigned to your business as a result of this change. If you have applied for and not yet received your FEIN, write **"applied for."** FEIN: __ __-__ __ __ __ __ __ __

___ **Add a tax requirement or location for a currently registered business.** Tell us the Illinois Business Tax number (IBT no.) and federal employer identification number (FEIN) currently assigned to this business.

IBT no.:__ __ __ __-__ __ __ __   FEIN. __ __-__ __ __ __ __ __ __
What is the effective date of this update or addition? ___ /___ /_____
                                                        Month Day Year

Step 3: Identify your business or organization

1 Business' or organization's legal name: **Bones Enterprises**
                                              Corporate, organization, partnership, or owner's (if sole proprietor) name

2 Doing business as (DBA) or trade name (if different from above):___ **Sid's Bones** _____

3 Address of your corporate/home office or your principal Illinois business address. The address where you can be contacted.

6789 Graves Avenue _____
Street address   Apartment or suite number

Chicago _____ **IL** _____ **60601** _____
City   State   ZIP

(312) 555- 1234 _____   _____   **(312) 555- 2468** _____   _____
Daytime phone (include area code) Extension Fax (include area code)   E-mail address

4 Did you buy this business from someone?   ○ yes ○ no
   If **yes,** write the previous business' name and IBT no.

_____   __ __ __ __-__ __ __ __
Previous business' name   Previous business' IBT#

5 Check **one** to indicate your type of business ownership (using the federal income tax classification).

   X Sole proprietorship. Is this jointly owned by both husband and wife? ○ yes ⊗ no
   ___ Corporation (other than an exempt organization)
       Tell us the Illinois Corporate File (charter) number issued by the Illinois Secretary of State:_____
       Is this a small business corporation (subchapter S)?   ○ yes ○ no If **yes,** tell us how many shareholders. _____
   ___ Partnership. Write the number of general partners._____
   ___ Trust or estate
   ___ Exempt organization
   ___ Governmental agency

(REG-1N-1/00)   Page 1 of 4

Step 4: Describe your business type or activity

1 Describe your business and provide the percentage of each activity used in your description.

<u>100</u> % <u>Novelty sales</u>

_____ % _____

2 Check all that apply to your type of business:

☒ **Withholding (employees, dividends, or certain winnings) -** You pay wages, taxable dividends, or wagering transactions in Illinois; *or,* you pay wages to Illinois residents under your state's income tax reciprocity agreement with Illinois.

☒ **Sales -** You sell merchandise. Are **all** of your sales for **resale** or otherwise exempt from sales tax?   ○ yes   ○ no
Check **any** that apply to your type of **retail** sales (if applicable).
____ Vehicles, trailers, mobile homes, watercraft, aircraft   ____ Items sold from vending machines.
____ Tires   How many machines will you have? _____
____ Beverages (soft drinks) in closed or sealed containers   ____ Solvents sold to dry cleaners
____ Motor fuel (*e.g.,* gasoline, gasohol, diesel fuel)
Do your sales include purchase orders accepted outside of Illinois and items shipped directly into Illinois? ○ yes   ⊗ no
If **"yes,"** check the best description of your business.
____ Located in Illinois, including but not limited to an office or agent.
____ **No** location in Illinois but will voluntarily collect sales tax on receipts from sales into Illinois.

☐ **Use -** You buy items for use in Illinois on which you do **not** pay the Illinois sales tax to your supplier. This includes items from your inventory bought tax-free for your own use.

☐ **Services -** You provide services (*e.g.,* repairs, printing, funeral, consulting, barber) and you are **not** a public utility.
Do you transfer or sell items (*e.g.,* parts, paper, chemicals, shampoo) with your service?   ○ yes   ○ no

☐ **Motor vehicle renting -** You are in the business of renting motor vehicles (*i.e.,* automobiles, motorcycles, certain vans/ recreational vehicles) for one year or less.

☐ **Water or sewer utility services -** You provide water or sewer utility service in Illinois.

☐ **Hotel/motel operators -** You rent, lease, or let rooms to the public for living quarters for periods of less than 30 days.

☐ **Liquor warehousing (not liquor sales) -** You warehouse or deliver alcoholic liquors for compensation.

☐ **Methane gas landfills -** You are a Qualified Solid Waste Energy Facility (QSWEF).

Below are tax responsibilities that may require additional information. We will contact you for this information. If you check any of the boxes below, please check the "Additional Requirements" box in Step 1 on the front of this application.

☐ **Natural gas -** You sell natural gas, provide natural gas services to persons in Illinois, or purchase natural gas from outside of Illinois for your own use (not for resale). Check all that apply.
How do you sell natural gas or natural gas services? ____ at retail   ____ at resale
Are you a municipal utility?   ○ yes   ○ no
Do you purchase natural gas from outside of Illinois for your own use (not for resale) and want to pay the tax directly to us?
○ yes   ○ no

☐ **Telecommunications -** You provide telecommunications services in Illinois. How do you sell your service? ____ Retail ____ Resale
Is the only service you provide a paging or wireless service?   ○ yes   ○ no

☐ **Cigarette or tobacco products -** You manufacture, wholesale, or distribute cigarettes or tobacco products.
Check all that apply to your business' activities.
Cigarette: ____ Manufacture   ____ Stamp   ____ Distribute
Tobacco products: ____ Distribute   ____ Retail (purchase from distributors and tax is **not** or will **not** be paid)

☐ **Motor fuel, aviation fuels and kerosene -** Check the activities which apply to your business.
____ Distributor - **not** from retail outlets   ____ Compressed gas sales - highway use **only**   ____ Bulk storage plants - **not** at retail outlets
____ Retail outlet **only**   ____ Manufacturing   ____ Gas/motor fuel blending   ____ Importing   ____ Exporting

☐ **Electricity services -** You deliver electricity to persons in Illinois for their own use.
How do you sell your service?   ____ Retail   ____ Resale
Check **any** that apply to your type of business:
____ Electric cooperative   ____ Municipal utility
____ Self-assessing purchaser of electricity for **nonresidential use** who elects to pay the Electricity Excise Tax directly to us.

☐ **Gaming events -** You operate gaming (*i.e.,* bingo, charitable games, pull tabs) events or are a premise provider, supplier, or manufacturer of equipment used during gaming events. Check **all** that pertains to your organization or business.
____ organization operating an event   ____ supplier or manufacturer of gaming equipment   ____ premise provider for events

(REG-1 N-1/00)

Step 5: Describe your business

1 Check **all** that apply to your Illinois business activity. __X__ Retail ___ Wholesale ___ Service ___ Manufacturing/production

2 Check **all** that apply to your type of business.

___ Advertising, business services
___ Auto supplies
___ Books, jewelry, gifts, cameras
___ Building trades, construction, contractors
___ Clothing and accessories
___ Coin-operated amusement devices
___ Communication
___ Computers/programming/design/software
___ Dental, medical services/facilities
___ Dept. store/general merchandise
___ Drinking places
___ Eating places
___ Electric
___ Electronics, TVs, music, instruments
___ Forestry, livestock, agriculture, fishing

___ Furniture, flooring, appliances
___ Gasoline, other petroleum products
___ Grocery items
___ Hardware
___ Homes - mobile/modular
___ Hotel/motel
___ Leasing/renting equipment
___ Liquor
___ Lumber, building materials
___ Machines, parts, equipment
___ Mail order, direct/vending sales
___ Medical supplies
___ Metals, rubber, plastic
___ Mining, coal, other minerals
___ Natural gas

___ Not-for-profit business/organization
___ Nursery, florists, garden supplies
___ Other manufacturing not listed: _____
__X__ Other retail not listed: **novelties**
___ Other services not listed: _____
___ Other wholesale not listed: _____
___ Paper, textiles, printing, chemicals
___ Pharmaceuticals/drug stores
___ Public administration, government
___ Real estate, insurance, finance
___ Renting vehicles
___ Sporting goods, bicycles, toys
___ Tobacco products
___ Transportation
___ Vehicles, boats, motorcycles
___ Water, sewer

Step 6: Identify your business location

Do **not** complete this step unless your location is in Illinois and your business activities include sales (including vehicle sales), use, service, hotel/motel operations, telecommunications, motor vehicle renting, electricity services, natural gas, or liquor warehousing. Write your business name, address (even if it is the same as identified in Step 3), and the date the location started doing business. **Note:** Township information is required for all Madison or St. Clair County locations in Illinois.

Location 1: Is this the same address as the address in Step 3? ⊗ yes ○ no

Check **all** that apply to this location's type of activity.

__X__ Sales, Use, Service ___ Motor vehicle renting ___ Telecommunications ___ Electricity services
___ Vehicle sales ___ Liquor warehousing ___ Hotel/motel operator ___ Natural gas

Name: _____ **Starting date:** 1 / 29 07
Doing business as (DBA) or trade name if different from the name you provided in Step 3   Month Day   Year

6789 Graves Avenue
Street address (Do **not** use PO Box), include apartment or suite number (if applicable)

Chicago,   **Illinois**   60601
City   State   ZIP

County: ___Cook___ Township: _____ (312)555 1234 Ext:___ (312) 555 2468
                                          Daytime phone (include area code)   Fax (include area code)

a Check the best **physical** description of this location: ☒ permanent ☐ one that will change (e.g., fairs, flea market)

b Check the best description of this location in regards to the city, village, or town limits listed above: ☒ inside ☐ outside

Location 2:

Check **all** that apply to this location's type of activity.

___ Sales, Use, Service ___ Motor vehicle renting ___ Telecommunications ___ Electricity services
___ Vehicle sales ___ Liquor warehousing ___ Hotel/motel operator ___ Natural gas

Name: _____ **Starting date:** ___/___/_____
Doing business as (DBA) or trade name if different from the name you provided in Step 3   Month Day   Year

_____
Street address (Do **not** use PO Box), include apartment or suite number (if applicable)

                                                                           Illinois
City   State   ZIP

County: _____ Township: _____ (___)___-_____ Ext:_____ (___)___-_____
                                          Daytime phone (include area code)   Fax (include area code)

a Check the best **physical** description of this location: ☐ permanent ☐ one that will change (e.g., fairs, flea market)

b Check the best description of this location in regards to the city, village, or town limits listed above: ☐ inside ☐ outside

Additional locations:

___ Check if you need to identify more locations. Attach a separate sheet containing all of the required information in a similar format.
Tell us your **total** number of Illinois locations. _____

Step 7: Identify your officers and owners

1 If your business is a **corporation, subchapter S corporation, or nonprofit organization,** print the legal name and SSN of each officer.

President

_____ SSN ____ - ____ - ____
Legal name (Last, first, middle initial)

Vice-President

_____ SSN ____ - ____ - ____
Legal name (Last, first, middle initial)

Secretary

_____ SSN ____ - ____ - ____
Legal name (Last, first, middle initial)

Treasurer/Comptroller

_____ SSN ____ - ____ - ____
Legal name (Last, first, middle initial)

2 Is your business a limited liability company? ◯ yes   ⊗ no
If **yes**, attach a list designating each manager and member by name and SSN or FEIN.

3 If your corporation is owned (over 50 percent) by another business, print the legal name and FEIN of the owning entity.

_____ FEIN ____ - _____
Owning entity name

4 If your business is a **sole proprietorship, trust/estate, or partnership,** provide the legal name and SSN or FEIN of each owner, trustee/executor, or general partner. **Note:** If you need to identify more, attach additional sheets with the required information in a similar format.

Sidney Bones _____ 123 - 45 - 6789
Legal name (Last, first, middle initial)   SSN

_____ SSN ____ - ____ - ____
Legal name (Last, first, middle initial)

_____ FEIN ____ - _____
Business name of your owner

Step 8: Tell us your mailing address

Complete this information **only** if you want your tax forms and correspondence mailed to an address other than the one listed in Step 3.
Note: All notices and bills (containing confidential tax information), refunds, certificates, and tax forms will be sent to this address.

_____   _____
In-care-of name. Please print.   Street address

_____   _____
City   State   ZIP

Step 9: Sign below

1 **Person responsible for filing returns and paying taxes:** If in Step 4, "Withholding," "Sales," "Use," "Service," "Motor vehicle renting," or "Hotel/motel" was checked, the person(s) that will be personally responsible for filing returns and paying the tax due **must** complete the following information. This signature is required in addition to the signature in Item 2 of this step. The same person can sign both statements. **Note:** If you need to identify more, attach sheets with the required information in a similar format.

Check tax responsibility(ies): ☐ Withholding   ☐ Sales, Use, or Services   ☐ Motor vehicle renting   ☐ Hotel/motel

Sidney Bones _____ 1 /29/ 07 Sidney Bones _____ 123 - 45 - 6789
Signature   Month Day Year Printed name (Last, first, middle initial)   SSN

3251 Ulna Lane _____ Chicago _____ IL _____ 60602 _____
Street address   City   State   ZIP

Check tax responsibility(ies): ☐ Withholding   ☐ Sales, Use, or Services   ☐ Motor vehicle renting   ☐ Hotel/motel

_____ ___/___/___ _____ ____ - ____ - ____
Signature   Month Day Year Printed name (Last, first, middle initial)   SSN

_____ _____ _____ _____
Street address   City   State   ZIP

2 **This must be completed by the person completing this application and verifying the information.** Signature stamps are **not** acceptable.
Under penalties of perjury, I state that I have examined this information and, to the best of my knowledge, it is true, correct, and complete.

Sidney Bones _____ Owner _____ 1 /29/ 07 Sidney Bones
Signature   Title   Month Day Year Printed name (Last, first, middle initial)

Step 10: Mail your application

If you attached additional sheets for any step in this application, please check here. ☐
If you have any questions or need help completing your application, please call us weekdays between 8 a.m. and 5 p.m.

Email: centreg@revenue.state.il.us   **Phone:** 217 785-3707   **Mail:** CENTRAL REGISTRATION DIVISION
ILLINOIS DEPARTMENT OF REVENUE
PO BOX 19476
SPRINGFIELD IL 62794-9476

(REG-1 N-1/00)

State of Illinois   33 South State Street
Department of Employment Security   Chicago, Illinois 60603-2802

Report to Determine Liability Under the
Unemployment Insurance Act

Important: Every newly created employing unit shall file this report within 30 days of the date upon which it commences business. (820 ILCS 405/1800; 56 Ill. Adm. Code 2760.105)

If your only workers are domestic workers, complete a UI-1 DOM Report to Determine Liability for Domestic Employment Under the Unemployment Insurance Act instead of this form.

1. a. Employer Name   Bonus Enterprises

   Doing Business As   Sid's Bones

   b. What is your primary business activity in Illinois?   retail sales

   c. What is your principal product or service? (See examples on pages 4 and 5 of the instructions .)   novelties

   d. If you have more than one product or service, list the top two and indicate the percentage that each contributes to your total revenue:

   _____   % Sales or receipts   _____

   _____   % Sales or receipts   _____

   e. If you know your NAICS Code, enter it here.   453220   If you do not know your NAICS Code, see instructions.

   f. Primary Address   6789 Graves Avenue
                        (Address - Number & Street or Rural Route)

   Chicago   Illinois   60601   Cook   USA
   City/Town   State   ZIP   County   Country   Telephone Number

   g. Business Address   6789 Graves Avenue
                         (Actual physical location - Number & Street or Rural Route - if different from Primary Address

   Chicago   Illinois   60601   Cook   USA
   City/Town   State   ZIP   County   Country   Telephone Number

   h. Do you lease any of your employees (see 56 Ill. Adm. Code 2732.306)?   Yes ☐   No ☒

   If yes, provide the Leasing Company's name, address, telephone number and Unemployment Insurance account number if . available.

2. Enter any employer account number previously assigned to you by the Illinois Department of Employment Security.

   _____

3. Identification number under which you file Employer's Quarterly Federal Tax Return (Form 941)   345-67-8900

214

4. a. Type of Organization (Check One): ☒ Sole Proprietor ☐ Partnership ☐ Corporation ☐ Other (Explain, e.g.,

   Limited Liability Company, Trust, Association, Receivership) _____

   b. If a corporation, date incorporated _____ State in which incorporated _____

   c. Has any form of remuneration, including dividends, been paid to the officers of this corporation? ☐ Yes ☐ No

   d. If you are an LLC, are there any individuals performing services for the organization other than the member manager(s)?

   ☐ Yes ☐ No

   How is the member manager(s) treated for federal tax purposes? ☐ Sole Proprietor ☐ Partner ☐ Other (Explain)

_____

5. Enter the required information for sole proprietor or each partner or officer:

Name	Title	Social Security No.	Residence Address	Residence Telephone No.
Sidney Bones	Owner	123-45-6789	3251 Ulna Lane	312-555-4321
			Chicago, IL 60602	

6. a. Date you first began employing workers in Illinois   1 / 29 / 06

   b. Date of your first payroll in Illinois   2 / 13 / 06

   c. Date you ceased employing workers in Illinois (if applicable)   _____ / _____ / _____

7. Did you acquire your Illinois business or any portion of it by purchase, reorganization or a change in entity; for example, a change from sole proprietor to corporation? ☐ Yes ☐ No   If yes, complete the form **UI-1 S&P, Report to Determine Succession**. Please complete the remainder of the questions on this form as well. Responses to the questions on this form should reflect information relative to the operation of your business **after** the date of acquisition.

----

8. a. Check here ☐ if you employ, have employed or expect to employ one or more workers in domestic service in a private home, local college club or local chapter of a college fraternity or sorority. Otherwise, skip to 9.

   b. Check here ☐ if during the current calendar year or the preceding four calendar years, there was any quarter in which you paid wages of $1,000 or more for domestic service in a private home, local college club or local chapter of a college fraternity or sorority. Otherwise, skip to (c).

   In the space below, circle the first such quarter during that period and indicate the year in which it occurred.

   Jan.-Mar. _____ (year), April-June _____ (year), July-Sept. _____ (year), Oct.-Dec. _____ (year).

   c. Check here ☐ if you expect to pay wages of $1,000 or more for domestic services in a private home, local college club or local chapter of a college fraternity or sorority during any quarter within the current calendar year.

9. a. Check here ☐ if you employ, have employed or expect to employ one or more workers to perform agricultural labor. Otherwise, skip to 10.

   b. Check here ☐ if, during the current calendar year or the preceding four calendar years, there was any quarter in which you paid wages of $20,000 or more for agricultural labor. Otherwise, skip to (c).

   In the space below, circle the first such quarter during that period and indicate the year in which it occurred.

   Jan.-Mar. _____ (year), April-June _____ (year), July-Sept. _____ (year), Oct.-Dec. _____ (year).

   c. Check here ☐ if, you expect to pay wages of $20,000 or more for agricultural labor during any quarter within the current calendar year.

   d. Check here ☐ if, during the period including the current calendar year and the four preceding calendar years, there was any calendar year during which you employed 10 or more individuals to perform agricultural labor for at least 20 weeks (whether or not consecutive). Otherwise, skip to (e).

   In the space below, indicate the first such year and, for that year, circle the quarter that included the 20th week within which you employed 10 more individuals to perform agricultural labor.

   April-June _____ (year), July-Sept. _____ (year), Oct.-Dec. _____ (year).

e. Check here ☐ if you expect to employ 10 or more individuals to perform agricultural labor for at least 20 weeks (whether or not consecutive) during the current calendar year.

f. If you checked (b), (c), (d) or (e), does your business include any retail sales activity? ☐ Yes ☐ No

10. a. Check here ☐ if you are a religious, charitable, educational or other nonprofit organization, as defined in Section 501(c)(3) of the Internal Revenue Code and attach the federal exemption letter. Otherwise, skip to 11.

b. Check here ☐ if, during the period including the current calendar year and the four preceding calendar years, there was any calendar year during which you have had 4 or more individuals performing services in employment in each of at least 20 weeks (whether or not consecutive). Otherwise, skip to (c).

In the space below, indicate the first such year and, for that year, circle the quarter that included the 20th week within which you had 4 or more individuals performing services in employment.

April-June _____ (year), July-Sept. _____ (year), Oct.-Dec. _____ (year).

c. Check here ☐ if you expect to have 4 or more individuals performing services in employment in each of at least 20 weeks (whether or not consecutive) during the current calendar year.

d. Check here ☐ if you wish to be a reimbursable employer. This does not apply to you if you did not check (b) or (c). If you wish to be a reimbursable employer, a **Reimburse Benefits in Lieu of Paying Contributions (UI-5NP)** form will be mailed to you. You must complete this form and return it to this Department.

11. a. Check here ☐ if there was any calendar quarter in either the current calendar year or the preceding four calendar years in which you paid wages of at least $1,500 for services in employment. Otherwise, skip to (b).

In the space below, circle the first such quarter during that period and indicate the year in which it occurred.

Jan.-Mar. _____ (year), April-June _____ (year), July-Sept. _____ (year), Oct.-Dec. _____ (year).

b. Check here ☐ if, within any quarter within the current calendar year, you expect to pay wages of $1,500 or more for services in employment. Please check the appropriate quarter.

Jan.-Mar. ☐ April-June ☐ July-Sept. ☐ Oct.-Dec. ☐

12. a. Check here ☐ if, during the period including the current calendar year and the four preceding calendar years, there was any calendar year in which you have had 1 or more individuals performing services in employment in each of at least 20 weeks (whether or not consecutive). Otherwise, skip to (b).

In the space below, indicate the first such year and, for that year, circle the quarter that included the 20th week within which you had 1 or more individuals performing services in employment.

April-June _____ (year), July-Sept. _____ (year), Oct.-Dec. _____ (year).

b. Check here ☐ if you expect to have 1 or more individuals performing services in employment in each of at least 20 weeks (whether or not consecutive) during the current calendar year.

13. Have you incurred liability under the Federal Unemployment Tax Act (in any state) for any of the last 4 years?

☐ Yes ☒ No If Yes, indicate the year(s) for which you incurred such liability. _____

14. Are there any persons who performed services for you within the current calendar year or the four preceding calendar years, but whom you do not consider to be employees for any reason, including but not limited to, individuals you regard as independent contractors? ☐ Yes ☒ No

If Yes, attach a sheet stating the number of such persons and give details as to the type of service and date such services were performed.

15. Complete the following section only if you have multiple worksites in Illinois.

   The following information is required for reporting statistical data to the federal government. Please complete the information as completely and accurately as possible.

   Enter below the required information for each place of business (worksite) in Illinois (use additional sheets if necessary). Read instructions carefully. If any worksite is engaged in performing support services for other units of the company, please indicate the nature of the activity in "section C-Primary Activity." Examples of support services are Central Administrative Office, Research, Development or Testing, or Storage (warehouse).

a) Physical Location of Each Establishment (Street, City, zip code)	b) County	c) Primary Activity	d) Average Number of Employees

16. If you are determined not liable, based upon the provisions of the Unemployment Insurance Act, you may voluntarily elect coverage under 820 ILCS 405/205 H. Please indicate if you want voluntary coverage. ☒ If checked, we will mail you form **UI-1B, Voluntary Election of Coverage**. Please complete that form and return it to this Department.

Certification: I hereby certify that the information contained in this report and any sheets attached hereto is true and correct. This report must be signed by owner, partner, officer or authorized agent within the employing enterprise. If signed by any other person, a power of attorney must be attached.

Employer Name _____

Signed by *Sidney Bones* _____ Date 1/29/07 _____

Title _____ owner _____

-- Do not write in the area below. For Department use only --

This state agency is requesting information that is necessary to accomplish the statutory purpose as outlined under 820 ILCS 405/100-3200. Disclosure of this information is Required. Failure to disclose this information may result in statutorily prescribed liability and sanction, including penalties and interest.			
	Area	Industry	Source _____ Rec'd Date _____ A/C _____ NL _____ Liab. Date _____ Qtr ____ Sec ____ Analyst _____ Date _____

Illinois Department of Employment Security

INSTRUCTIONS FOR PREPARATION OF UI-1
REPORT TO DETERMINE LIABILITY UNDER
THE ILLINOIS UNEMPLOYMENT INSURANCE ACT

An employing unit must file the Report to Determine Liability even though it may not be liable for payments under the Illinois Unemployment Insurance Act (the Act).

Read the instructions below carefully.

The Guide to the Illinois Unemployment Insurance Act is available on our web site at www.ides.state.il.us. It will assist you in filling out the form.

Type or print in ink your answer to each item that applies. If you need more space, attach additional sheets but mark each "Supplement to UI-1" and sign and date it. Return the completed, signed original to this Department immediately. Retain a copy for your files.

Item No.

1. a. Legal name of employer: If a Sole Proprietor, the owner's name; If a Partnership, the partners' names and type of partnership, such as a general partnership, limited partnership or joint venture; if a Corporation, the corporate name with the word "Corporation," "Incorporated," "Company," "Limited," or its abbreviations; if a Limited Liability Company, the name must contain the phrase Limited Liability Company, or its abbreviation (LLC or L.L.C.). Doing Business as: Enter the trade name of your business. If there is no trade name being used, leave this item blank.

   b. Enter the business activity that produces your major source of income.

   c. & d. List products manufactured, commodities sold, activities engaged in or type of services rendered. See examples of products or services listed after instructions.

   e. **NAICS Code:**
   The North American Industry Classification System (NAICS) was developed jointly by the U.S., Canada and Mexico to improve comparative statistics about business activity across North America. Please enter the 6-digit NAICS code that best describes your primary business activity.

   To find the NAICS code for your business activity, you may contact the U.S. Census Bureau at 1-888-75NAICS or by E-mail at naics@census.gov; or you may go to http://www.census.gov/epcd/www/drnaics.htm.

   f. Enter the address to which your business mail should be delivered. The Department will send correspondence to this address unless you specify special handling for certain forms (See form UI-1M). If this address is different from the address where you conduct your business activities in Illinois, then you must also provide your actual physical location in the Business Address in g.

   g. Enter the address of the physical location (not a post office box) of your Illinois business if this is different from your primary address. If there is no base of operations in Illinois, enter the home address of the primary Illinois employee.

   h. Employee Leasing Company means an individual or an entity which contracts with you to supply or assume responsibility for personnel management of one or more workers to perform services for you on an on-going basis rather than a temporary help arrangement.

UI-1 INST. Pg. 2

3. Enter the **FEDERAL EMPLOYER IDENTIFICATION NUMBER (FEIN)** assigned by the Internal Revenue Service for reporting Social Security, Withholding Tax and Federal Unemployment Tax.

6. a. Enter the date on which you first began employing workers, not the date when wages were first paid.
   b. Enter the date when you first paid wages in the State of Illinois.

8. "Domestic service" means service of a household nature, including service performed by cooks, waiters, butlers, housekeepers, housemothers, governesses, maids, valets, babysitters, janitors, launderers, furnace men, caretakers, handymen, gardeners, footmen, grooms and chauffeurs of automobiles for family use. Service not of a household nature, such as by a private secretary, nurse, tutor or librarian, is not "domestic" service.

   A "private home" is the fixed place of abode of the individual or family for whom the worker is performing services. A separate and distinct dwelling unit maintained by an individual as a residence, such as a hotel room, boat or trailer, can be a "private home." A room or suite in a nursing home can be a "private home," provided that the facts and circumstances of the particular case indicate that such room or suite is, in fact, the place where the individual retains his residence. A home utilized primarily for the purpose of supplying board or lodging to the public as a business enterprise is not a "private home."

   A "local college club" or "local chapter of a college fraternity or sorority" does not include an alumni club or chapter.

9. "Agricultural labor" means all services performed:

   A. On a farm, in the employ of any person, in connection with cultivating the soil or in connection with raising or harvesting any agricultural or horticultural commodity, including the raising, shearing, feeding, caring for, training and management of live stock, bees, poultry and fur-bearing animals and wildlife;

   B. In the employ of the owner or tenant or other operator of a farm, in connection with the operation, management, conservation, improvement or maintenance of such farm and its tools and equipment;

   C. In connection with the ginning of cotton, or the operation or maintenance of ditches, canals, reservoirs or waterways not owned or operated for profit, used exlusively for supplying and storing water for farming purposes;

   D. In the employ of the operator of a farm, or of a group of operators of farms (or a cooperative organization of which such operators are members), in handling, planting , drying, packing, packaging, processing, freezing, grading, storing or delivering to storage or to market or to a carrier for transportation to market, in its unmanufactured state, any agricultural or horticultural commodity; but only if such operator or operators produced more than one-half of the commodity with respect to which such service is performed. The provisions of this subsection shall not be deemed to be applicable with respect to service performed in connection with commercial canning or commercial freezing or in connection with any agricultural or horticultural commodity after its delivery to a terminal market for distribution for consumption.

   For purposes of questions 9 (d) and (e), count each week in which you have employed or will employ 10 or more individuals to perform agricultural labor, whether or not they all worked or will work at the same time during that week and whether or not you employed or will employ the same individuals in each week.

   "Week" means the seven day period, Sunday through Saturday.

10. For purposes of questions 10 (b) and (c), count each week in which you had or expect to have 4 or more individuals performing services in employment, whether or not they all worked or will work at the same time during that week and whether or not you employed or will employ the same individuals in each week.

    "Week" means the seven day period, Sunday through Saturday.

    "Employment" means any service performed by an individual for an employing unit, unless the Unemployment Insurance Act expressly excludes the service from the definition of "employment." It includes service in interstate commerce and service on land which is owned, held or possessed by the United States, and includes all services performed by an officer of a business corporation, without regard to whether such services are executive, managerial or manual in nature, and without regard to whether such officer is or is not a stockholder or a member of the board of directors of the corporation.

UI-1 INST. Pg. 3

Benefit Reimbursable Option:
Each nonprofit organization subject to the Act may, if certain conditions are met, elect to be a reimbursable employer by agreeing, in lieu of paying contributions, to reimburse the State for the actual amount of regular benefits and one half the amount of extended benefits that are charged to it.

11. "Employment" means any service performed by an individual for an employing unit, unless the Unemployment Insurance Act expressly excludes the service from the definition of "employment." It includes service in interstate commerce and service on land which is owned, held or possessed by the United States, and includes all services performed by an officer of a business corporation, without regard to whether such services are executive, managerial or manual in nature, and without regard to whether such officer is or is not a stockholder or a member of the board of directors of the corporation.

12. "Employment" means any service performed by an individual for an employing unit, unless the Unemployment Insurance Act expressly excludes the service from the definition of "employment." It includes service in interstate commerce and service on land which is owned, held or possessed by the United States, and includes all services performed by an officer of a business corporation, without regard to whether such services are executive, managerial or manual in nature, and without regard to whether such officer is or is not a stockholder or a member of the board of directors of the corporation.

For purposes of questions 12 (a) and (b), count each week in which you had or expect to have 1 or more individuals performing services in employment, whether or not they all worked or will work at the same time during that week and whether or not you employed or will employ the same individuals in each week.

"Week" means the seven day period, Sunday through Saturday.

13. If you have been found liable for Federal Unemployment taxes, you become immediately liable to Illinois with your first Illinois payroll.

15. a&b. For two or more places of business in Illinois, enter the number and street or rural route, the city or town, zip code and the Illinois county in which each place of business is located.

d. The average number employed at each address. Include all classes of employees (i.e. administrative, supervisory, clerical, sales, installation, construction, etc.).

16. If an employing unit does not meet the legal definition of employer for unemployment insurance purposes, the employing unit can elect to be fully subject under the Illinois Unemployment Insurance Act with the permission of the Director. An employing unit electing such coverage will not be able to terminate its coverage until January 1 of any calendar year subsequent to two such years of coverage.

If you should need further assistance in filling out this form, you may contact the Employer Hot Line Section at telephone number (312) 793-4880 or (800) 247-4984.

Please make a copy of the completed UI-1 for your records.

UI-1 INST. Pg. 4

EXAMPLES OF PRODUCT OR SERVICE INFORMATION

AGRICULTURAL, FORESTRY, FISHING, AND HUNTING includes establishments primarily engaged in agricultural production including growing crops, raising animals, harvesting timber and harvesting fish and other animals from farms, ranches or the animals' natural habitats.

MINING includes the extraction of naturally occurring mineral solids, such as coal and ore; liquid minerals, such as crude petroleum; and gases, such as natural gas; and beneficiating (e.g., crushing, screening, washing and flotation) and other preparation at the mine site, or as part of mining activity.

UTILITIES includes generating, transmitting and/or distributing electricity, gas, steam and water and removing sewage through a permanent infrastructure of lines, mains and pipe.

CONSTRUCTION includes those establishments which perform new work, additions, alterations, installations or maintenance and repairs. Heavy construction, other than buildings, are located here, e.g. streets and highways, sewers and drainage. This sector also includes contractors, subcontractors and specialty trade contractors.

MANUFACTURING includes the mechanical, physical or chemical transformation of material, substances or components into new products. The new product may be finished and ready for utilization or consumption, or it may be semifinished to become input for an establishment engaged in further manufacturing.

WHOLESALE TRADE establishments or individuals are primarily engaged in the selling of merchandise to other businesses. The wholesale merchant has possession of the merchandise being sold and typically operates out of a warehouse. An agent / broker arranges for the purchase or sale of goods owned by others. Business to business electronic markets, i.e. via the internet, are also included.

RETAIL TRADE are those engaged in retailing merchandise generally in small quantities to the general public and providing services incidental to the sale of the merchandise.

TRANSPORTATION includes industries providing transportation of passengers and cargo; warehousing and storage of goods; scenic and sightseeing transportation and support activities related to modes of transportation.

INFORMATION sector establishments are involved in distributing information and cultural products, providing the means to transmit these products as data or communications, and processing data. Examples include newspaper, book and software publishers; television, radio and internet broadcasters; wire and wireless telecommunications; cable services, data processing and related services and internet service providers.

FINANCE AND INSURANCE includes establishments that are involved in the creation, liquidation or change in ownership of financial assets and/or facilitating financial transactions. Examples are banks; savings institutions; credit unions; personal credit institutions; insurance carriers, agents and brokers; commodity and security brokers; and health and welfare funds.

REAL ESTATE AND RENTAL AND LEASING includes establishments involved in renting, leasing, or otherwise allowing the use of tangible (real estate and equipment) or intangible assets (patents and trademarks) and providing related services.

PROFESSIONAL, SCIENTIFIC, AND TECHNICAL SERVICES are those establishments that specialize in performing professional, scientific and technical services for others. These activities require a high degree of expertise and training.

MANAGEMENT OF COMPANIES AND ENTERPRISES are those businesses engaged in the holding of securities of companies and enterprises for the purpose of owning a controlling interest or influencing management decisions. Also included are establishments that administer, oversee and manage other establishments of the same company or enterprise and normally undertake strategic, organizational planning and decision- making roles.

UI-1 INST. Pg. 5

ADMINISTRATIVE AND SUPPORT AND WASTE MANAGEMENT AND REMEDIATION SERVICES include activities related to performing routine support activities for the day-to-day operations of other organizations. Other activities included in this sector are security and surveillance services, cleaning, waste collection and waste disposal systems.

EDUCATIONAL SERVICES include establishments that provide instruction, training and support services in a wide variety of subjects. This instruction and training is provided by specialized establishments, such as schools, colleges, universities, and training centers. Also included are trade schools, apprenticeship training, professional and management development training and educational testing services.

HEALTH CARE AND SOCIAL ASSISTANCE include businesses involved in providing health care and social assistance for individuals.

ARTS, ENTERTAINMENT, AND RECREATION are organizations that are operating or providing services to meet varied cultural, entertainment, and recreational interests of their patrons.

ACCOMMODATION AND FOOD SERVICES are responsible for providing customers with lodging and/or preparing meals, snacks, and beverages for immediate consumption.

OTHER SERVICES (EXCEPT PUBLIC ADMINISTRATION) include organizations that are responsible for providing services, not elsewhere specified, including repairs, religious activities, grant making, advocacy, laundry and dry-cleaning services, personal care, death care, pet care, domestic service and other personal services.

PUBLIC ADMINISTRATION includes the administration, management, and oversight of public programs by Federal, State, and local governments.

This page is intentionally left blank.

Illinois Withholding Allowance Worksheet

General Information

Complete this worksheet to figure your total withholding allowances.

Everyone must complete Step 1.

Complete Step 2 if
- you (or your spouse) are age 65 or older or legally blind, or
- you wrote an amount on Line 4 of the Deductions and Adjustments Worksheet for federal Form W-4.

If you have more than one job or your spouse works, you should figure the total number of allowances you are entitled to claim. Your withholding usually will be more accurate if you claim all of your allowances on the Form IL-W-4 for the highest-paying job and claim zero on all of your other IL-W-4 forms.

You may reduce the number of allowances or request that your employer withhold an additional amount from your pay, which may help avoid having too little tax withheld.

Step 1: Figure your basic personal allowances (including allowances for dependents)

Check all that apply:
- ☐ No one else can claim me as a dependent.
- ☐ I can claim my spouse as a dependent.

1 Write the total number of boxes you checked.   **1** _1_

2 Write the number of dependents (other than you or your spouse) you will claim on your tax return.   **2** _0_

3 Add Lines 1 and 2. Write the result. This is the total number of basic personal allowances to which you are **entitled**.   **3** _1_

4 If you want to have additional Illinois Income Tax withheld from your pay, you may reduce the number of basic personal allowances or have an additional amount withheld. Write the total number of basic personal allowances you elect to claim on Line 4 and on Form IL-W-4, Line 1.   **4** _1_

Step 2: Figure your additional allowances

Check all that apply:
- ☐ I am 65 or older.
- ☐ My spouse is 65 or older.
- ☐ I am legally blind.
- ☐ My spouse is legally blind.

5 Write the total number of boxes you checked.   **5** _0_

6 Write any amount that you reported on Line 4 of the Deductions and Adjustments Worksheet for federal Form W-4.   **6** _0_

7 Divide Line 6 by 1,000. Round to the nearest whole number. Write the result on Line 7.   **7** _0_

8 Add Lines 5 and 7. Write the result. This is the total number of additional allowances to which you are **entitled**.   **8** _0_

9 If you want to have additional Illinois Income Tax withheld from your pay, you may reduce the number of additional allowances or have an additional amount withheld. Write the total number of additional allowances you elect to claim on Line 9 and on Form IL-W-4, Line 2.   **9** _0_

Note: If you have non-wage income and you expect to owe Illinois Income Tax on that income, you may choose to have an additional amount withheld from your pay. On Line 3 of Form IL-W-4, write the additional amount you want your employer to withhold.

✂ — — — — — — — — Cut here and give the certificate to your employer. Keep the top portion for your records. — — — — — — — — ✂

Illinois Department of Revenue
IL-W-4 Employee's Illinois Withholding Allowance Certificate

0 2 0 . 1 1 . 3 4 5 6
Social Security number

Jonathan Marrow
Name

101 Fossil Drive
Street address

Chicago   IL   60606
City   State   ZIP

Check the box if you are exempt from federal and Illinois Withholding Income Tax. ☐

1 Write the total number of basic allowances that you are claiming (Step 1, Line 4, of the worksheet).   **1** _1_

2 Write the total number of additional allowances that you are claiming (Step 2, Line 9, of the worksheet).   **2** _0_

3 Write the additional amount you want withheld (deducted) from each pay.   **3** _0_

I certify that I am entitled to the number of withholding allowances claimed on this certificate.   *Jonathan Marrow*   1/29/06
Your signature   Date

Employer: Keep this certificate with your records. If you have referred the employee's federal certificate to the Internal Revenue Service (IRS) and the IRS has notified you to disregard it, you may also be required to disregard this certificate. Even if you are not required to refer the employee's federal certificate to the IRS, you may still be required to refer this certificate to the Illinois Department of Revenue for inspection. See Illinois Income Tax Regulations 86 Ill. Adm. Code 100.7110.

This form is authorized as outlined by the Illinois Income Tax Act. Disclosure of this information is REQUIRED. Failure to provide information could result in a penalty. This form has been approved by the Forms Management Center.   IL-492-0039

IL-W-4 (R-12/05)

Illinois Department of Revenue

Form IL-W-4 Employee's Illinois Withholding Allowance Certificate and Instructions

Who must complete this form?

If you are an employee, you must complete this form so your employer can withhold the correct amount of Illinois Income Tax from your pay. The amount withheld from your pay depends, in part, on the number of allowances you claim on this form.

Even if you claimed exemption from withholding on your federal Form W-4, U.S. Employee's Withholding Allowance Certificate, because you do not expect to owe any federal income tax, you may be required to have Illinois Income Tax withheld from your pay. If you are claiming exempt status (see Page 8, IL-700) from Illinois Withholding you must check the exempt status box on the IL-W-4.

Note: If you do not file a completed Form IL-W-4 with your employer, if you fail to sign the form or to include all necessary information, or if you alter the form, your employer must withhold Illinois income tax on the entire amount of your compensation, without allowing any exemptions.

When must I file?

You must file Form IL-W-4 when Illinois Income Tax is required to be withheld from compensation that you receive as an employee. You should complete this form and give it to your employer on or before the date you start working for your employer. You may file a new Form IL-W-4 any time your withholding allowances increase. If the number of your previously claimed allowances decreases, you **must** file a new Form IL-W-4 within 10 days. However, the death of a spouse or a dependent does not affect your withholding allowances until the next tax year.

When does my Form IL-W-4 take effect?

If you do not already have a Form IL-W-4 on file with this employer, this form will be effective for the first payment of compensation made to you after this form is filed. If you already have a Form IL-W-4 on file with this employer, your employer may allow any change you file on this form to become effective immediately, but is not required by law to change your withholding until the first payment of compensation made to you after the first day of the next calendar quarter (that is, January 1, April 1, July 1 or October 1) that falls at least 30 days after the date you file the change with your employer.

Example: If you have a baby and file a new Form IL-W-4 with your employer to claim an additional exemption for the baby, your employer may immediately change the withholding for all future payments of compensation. However, if you file the new form on September 1, your employer does not have to change your withholding until the first payment of compensation made to you after October 1. If you file the new form on September 2, your employer does not have to change your withholding until the first payment of compensation made to you after December 31.

How long is Form IL-W-4 valid?

Your Form IL-W-4 remains valid until a new form you have filed takes effect or until your employer is required by the Department to disregard it. Your employer is required to disregard your Form IL-W-4 if you claim total exemption from Illinois income tax withholding, but you have not filed a federal Form W-4 claiming total exemption. Also, if the Internal Revenue Service has instructed your employer to disregard your federal Form W-4, your employer must also disregard your Form IL-W-4. Finally, if you claim 15 or more exemptions on your Form IL-W-4 without claiming at least the same number of exemptions on your federal Form W-4, and your employer is not required to refer your federal Form W-4 to the Internal Revenue Service for review, your employer must refer your Form IL-W-4 to the Department for review. In that case, your Form IL-W-4 will be effective unless and until the Department notifies your employer to disregard it.

What is an "exemption"?

An "exemption" is a dollar amount on which you do not have to pay Illinois Income Tax. Therefore, your employer will withhold Illinois Income Tax based on your compensation minus the exemptions to which you are entitled.

What is an "allowance"?

The dollar amount that is exempt from Illinois Income Tax is based on the number of allowances you claim on this form. As an employee, you receive one allowance unless you are claimed as a dependent on another person's tax return (e.g., your parents claim you as a dependent on their tax return). If you are married, you may claim additional allowances for your spouse and any dependents that you are entitled to claim for federal income tax purposes. You also receive additional allowances if you or your spouse are age 65 or older, or if you or your spouse are legally blind.

How do I figure the correct number of allowances?

Complete the worksheet on the back of this page to figure the correct number of allowances you are entitled to claim. Give your completed Form IL-W-4 to your employer. Keep the worksheet for your records.

Note: If you have more than one job or your spouse works, you should figure the total number of allowances you are entitled to claim. Your withholding usually will be more accurate if you claim all of your allowances on the Form IL-W-4 for the highest-paying job and claim zero on all of your other IL-W-4 forms.

What if I underpay my tax?

If the amount withheld from your compensation is not enough to cover your tax liability for the year, (e.g., you have non-wage income, such as interest or dividends), you may reduce the number of allowances or request that your employer withhold an additional amount from your pay. Otherwise, you may owe additional tax at the end of the year. If you do not have enough tax withheld from your pay, and you owe more than $500 tax at the end of the year, you may owe a late-payment penalty. You should either increase the amount you have withheld from your pay, or you must make estimated tax payments.

You may be assessed a **late-payment penalty** if your required estimated payments are not paid in full by the due dates.

Note: You may still owe this penalty for an earlier quarter, even if you pay enough tax later to make up the underpayment from a previous quarter.

For additional information on penalties, see Publication 103, Uniform Penalties and Interest. Call **1 800 356-6302** to receive a copy of this publication.

Where do I get help?

- Visit our web site at **tax.illinois.gov**
- Call our Taxpayer Assistance Division at **1 800 732-8866** or **217 782-3336**
- Call our TDD (telecommunications device for the deaf) at **1 800 544-5304**
- Write to
  **ILLINOIS DEPARTMENT OF REVENUE
  PO BOX 19044
  SPRINGFIELD IL 62794-9044**

Illinois Department of Revenue

CRT-61 Certificate of Resale

Step 1: Identify the seller

1 Name Harry's Wholesale Novelties

2 Business address 6699 Wahoo Drive

Chicago   IL   60606
City   State   Zip

Step 2: Identify the purchaser

3 Name Sid's Bones

4 Business address 6789 Graves Avenue

Chicago   IL   60601
City   State   Zip

5 Complete the information below. Check only one box.

[X] The purchaser is registered as a retailer with the Illinois
     Department of Revenue. 2 4 6 8 - 1 3 5 7 .
                                    Registration number

[ ] The purchaser is registered as a reseller with the Illinois
     Department of Revenue. __ __ __ __ - __ __ __ __ .
                                    Resale number

[ ] The purchaser is authorized to do business out-of-state and
     will resell and deliver property only to purchasers located
     outside the state of Illinois. See Line 5 instructions.

Step 3: Describe the property

6 Describe the property that is being purchased for resale or
   list the invoice number and the date of purchase.
   Boxes of novelty toys, e.g.

   alien keychains, mini card deck,

   etc.

Step 4: Complete for blanket certificates

7 Complete the information below. Check only one box.

[X] I am the identified purchaser, and I certify that all of the
     purchases that I make from this seller are for resale.

[ ] I am the identified purchaser, and I certify that the following
     percentage, _____ %, of all of the purchases that I make
     from this seller are for resale.

Step 5: Purchaser's signature

I certify that I am purchasing the property described in Step 3
from the stated seller for the purpose of resale.

Sidney Bones   1 /29/ 2007
Purchaser's signature   Date

**Note: It is the seller's responsibility to verify that the
purchaser's Illinois registration or Illinois resale number is
valid and active.**

General information

When is a Certificate of Resale required?
Generally, a Certificate of Resale is required for proof that no tax
is due on any sale that is made tax-free as a sale for resale. The
purchaser, at the seller's request, must provide the information
that is needed to complete this certificate.

Who keeps the Certificate of Resale?
The seller must keep the certificate. We may request it as proof
that no tax was due on the sale of the specified property.
Do not mail the certificate to us.

Can other forms be used?
Yes. You can use other forms or statements in place of this
certificate but whatever you use as proof that a sale was made for
resale must contain
- the seller's name and address;
- the purchaser's name and address;
- a description of the property being purchased;
- a statement that the property is being purchased for resale;
- the purchaser's signature and date of signing; and
- either an Illinois registration number, an Illinois resale number, or
  a certification of resale to an out-of-state purchaser.

Note: A purchase order signed by the purchaser may be used as
a Certificate of Resale if it contains all of the above required
information.

CRT-61 (R-04/02)
IL-492-3850

When is a blanket certificate of resale used?
The purchaser may provide a blanket certificate of resale to any
seller from whom all purchases made are sales for resale. A
blanket certificate can also specify that a percentage of the
purchases made from the identified seller will be for resale. In
either instance, blanket certificates should be kept up-to-date. If a
specified percentage changes, a new certificate should be
provided. Otherwise, all certificates should be updated at least
every three years.

Specific instructions

Step 1: Identify the seller
Lines 1 and 2 Write the seller's name and mailing address.

Step 2: Identify the purchaser
Lines 3 and 4 Write the purchaser's name and mailing address.

Line 5 Check the statement that applies to the purchaser's
business, and provide any additional requested information.
Note: A statement by the purchaser that property will be sold for
resale will not be accepted by the department without supporting
evidence (*e.g.*, proof of out-of-state registration).

Step 3: Describe the property
Line 6 On the lines provided, briefly describe the tangible
personal property that was purchased for resale or list the invoice
number and date of purchase.

Step 4: Complete for blanket certificates
Line 7 The purchaser must check the statement that applies,
and provide any additional requested information.

Step 5: Purchaser's signature
The purchaser must sign and date the form.

Blank Forms

The following forms may be photocopied or removed from this book and used immediately. Some of the tax forms explained in this book are not included here because you should use original returns or other forms provided by the IRS (940, 941; Federal Tax Deposit Coupon Form 8109-B) or the Illinois Department of Revenue (quarterly unemployment compensation form).

These forms are included on the following pages.

FORM **BCA 2.10** (rev. Dec. 2003)
ARTICLES OF INCORPORATION
Business Corporation Act

Jesse White, Secretary of State
Department of Business Services
Springfield, IL 62756
Telephone (217) 782-9522
         (217) 782-6961
http://www.cyberdriveillinois.com

Remit payment in the form of a cashier's
check, certified check, money order
or an Illinois attorney's or CPA's check
payable to the Secretary of State.
SEE NOTE 1 TO DETERMINE FEES!

Filing Fee: $150.00 Franchise Tax $_____   Total $_____   File #_____   Approved:

——————————Submit in duplicate ————————Type or Print clearly in black ink——————Do not write above this line————————

1.   CORPORATE NAME: _____

      _____
      (The corporate name must contain the word "corporation", "company," "Incorporated," "limited" or an abbreviation thereof.)

2.   Initial Registered Agent: _____

	First Name	Middle Initial	Last name

      Initial Registered Office: _____

Number	Street	Suite #	(A P.O. BOX ALONE IS NOT ACCEPTABLE)

IL

City	ZIP Code	County

3.   Purpose or purposes for which the corporation is organized:
      (If not sufficient space to cover this point, add one or more sheets of this size.)

      The transaction of any or all lawful businesses for which corporations may be incorporated under the Illinois Business Corporation Act.

4.   Paragraph 1: Authorized Shares, Issued Shares and Consideration Received:

Class	Number of Shares Authorized	Number of Shares Proposed to be Issued	Consideration to be Received Therefor
			$
			TOTAL = $

Paragraph 2: The preferences, qualifications, limitations, restrictions and special or relative rights in respect of the shares of each class are:
(If not sufficient space to cover this point, add one or more sheets of this size.)

C-162.24   (over)

5. *OPTIONAL:* (a) Number of directors constituting the initial board of directors of the corporation:_____ .

(b) Names and addresses of the persons who are to serve as directors until the first annual meeting of shareholders or until their successors are elected and qualify:

Name	Address	City, State, ZIP

6. *OPTIONAL:* (a) It is estimated that the value of all property to be owned by the corporation for the following year wherever located will be: $_____

(b) It is estimated that the value of the property to be located within the State of Illinois during the following year will be: $_____

(c) It is estimated that the gross amount of business that will be transacted by the corporation during the following year will be: $_____

(d) It is estimated that the gross amount of business that will be transacted from places of business in the State of Illinois during the following year will be: $_____

7. *OPTIONAL:* OTHER PROVISIONS

Attach a separate sheet of this size for any other provision to be included in the Articles of Incorporation, e.g., authorizing preemptive rights, denying cumulative voting, regulating internal affairs, voting majority requirements, fixing a duration other than perpetual, etc.

8. **NAME(S) & ADDRESS(ES) OF INCORPORATOR(S)**

The undersigned incorporator(s) hereby declare(s), under penalties of perjury, that the statements made in the foregoing Articles of Incorporation are true.

Dated _____ , _____
(Month & Day)   Year

Signature and Name	**Address**
1._____	1._____
Signature	Street
_____	_____
(Type or Print Name)	City/Town State ZIP Code
2._____	2._____
Signature	Street
_____	_____
(Type or Print Name)	City/Town State ZIP Code
3._____	3._____
Signature	Street
_____	_____
(Type or Print Name)	City/Town State ZIP Code

(Signatures must be in **BLACK INK** on original document. Carbon copy, photocopy or rubber stamp signatures may only be used on conformed copies.)

NOTE: If a corporation acts as incorporator, the name of the corporation and the state of incorporation shall be shown and the execution shall be by a duly authorized corporate officer. Type or print officer's name and title beneath signature.

Note 1: Fee Schedule
The initial franchise tax is assessed at the rate of 15/100 of 1 percent ($1.50 per $1,000) on the paid-in capital represented in this State. (Minimum initial franchise tax is $25)

The filing fee is $150

The **minimum total due** (franchise tax + filing fee) is $175.

Note 2: Return to:

_____
(Firm name)

_____
(Attention)

_____
(Mailing Address)

_____
(City, State, ZIP Code)

Form **BCA-4.15/4.20**
(Rev. Jan. 2003)

**APPLICATION TO ADOPT,
CHANGE OR CANCEL,
AN ASSUMED CORPORATE NAME**

File # _____

Jesse White
Secretary of State
Department of Business Services
Springfield, IL 62756
Telephone (217) 782-9520
www.cyberdriveillinois.com

Remit payment in check or money
order, payable to "Secretary of State".

SUBMIT IN DUPLICATE

This space for use by
Secretary of State

Date

Filing Fee
(See Note Below)
Approved:

1.   CORPORATE NAME: _____
_____

2.   State or Country of Incorporation:_____
_____

3.   Date incorporated *(if an Illinois corporation)* or date authorized to transact business in Illinois *(if a foreign corporation):* _____, _____.
                                          (Month & Day)   (Year)

      (Complete No. 4 and No. 5 if adopting or changing an assumed corporate name.)

4.   The corporation intends to adopt and to transact business under the assumed corporate name of:
_____

5.   The right to use the assumed corporate name shall be effective from the date this application is filed by the Secretary of State until _____, _____ , the first day of the corporation's anniversary
                                          (Month & Day)   (Year)
      month in the next year which is evenly divisible by five.

      (Complete No. 6 if changing or cancelling an assumed corporate name.)

6.   The corporation intends to cease transacting business under the assumed corporate name of:
_____

7.   The undersigned corporation has caused this statement to be signed by a duly authorized officer who affirms, under penalties of perjury, that the facts stated herein are true.

      Dated _____ , _____   _____
                    (Month & Day)   (Year)   (Exact Name of Corporation)

                  _____
                    (Any Authorized Officer's Signature)

                  _____
                    (Type or Print Name and Title)

NOTE: The filing fee to adopt an assumed corporate name is $150 if the current year ends with either 0 or 5, $120 if the current year ends with either 1 or 6, $90 if the current year ends with either 2 or 7, $60 if the current year ends with either 3 or 8, $30 if the current year ends with either 4 or 9.
         The fee for cancelling an assumed corporate name is $5.00.
         The fee to change an assumed name is $25.00.

C-148.15

This page is intentionally left blank.

State of Illinois
Trademark or Servicemark
Application

This space for use by Secretary of State

Complete and return with $10 fee and three specimens to:

Secretary of State
Department of Business Services
Trademark Division
3rd Floor, Howlett Building
Springfield, IL 62756

217-524-0400
www.cyberdriveillinois.com

Must be typewritten or legibly printed in black ink.

This application must be accompanied by three specimens of the mark and a $10 filing fee payable to the Secretary of State. Please paperclip specimens to the application. DO NOT GLUE OR STAPLE.

Send a separate check for each application. This will prevent the return of multiple applications for correction.

Items 1–4 refer to Registrant

1. Name of Registrant (Owner of the Mark) _____

2. Mailing Address _____
    Street

    _____
    City, State, ZIP Code

3. Is Registrant a (check one)
    - ❏ Corporation   ❏ Union   ❏ General Partnership   ❏ Limited Liability Partnership (LLP)
    - ❏ Individual   ❏ Association ❏ Limited Partnership (LP) ❏ Limited Liability Company (LLC)
    - ❏ Other (specify) _____

4. a) If a Corporation, LP, LLP or LLC, in what state is it organized? _____
    b) If an LP or LLP, what is the name of one of the general partners? _____

---

5. Name of mark _____
    Does the mark involve a design or logo?   ❏ Yes   ❏ No
    If yes, briefly describe major features of design _____

6. Describe the specific goods or services in connection with which mark is used (provided by the mark)

    _____

    _____

---

7. Class No. _____ (One classification number only; classes are listed on the back. The Secretary of State will fill in the answer if no answer is given and has the right to change the classification if that furnished by the applicant is not correct. Each classification requires a separate application, set of three specimens and fee.)

8. a) If a **Trademark**, check how the mark is used (check as many as apply). Mark is applied:
   - ❐ directly to the goods
   - ❐ on documents, wrappers or articles delivered in connection with the service rendered
   - ❐ in another fashion, please specify _____

   OR

   b) If a **Servicemark**, check how the mark is used (check as many as apply). Mark is displayed:
   - ❐ in advertisements of the service
   - ❐ on documents, wrappers or articles delivered in connection with the service rendered
   - ❐ in another fashion, please specify _____

9. Date of the first use of mark by applicant or predecessor. Mark must be used in Illinois prior to registration. (If first use of mark was in Illinois, use same date in both A and B.)

   a) Anywhere _____   b) In Illinois _____

Month, Day, Year   Month, Day, Year

10. If either of the above first uses was by a predecessor of the applicant, state which use or uses were by a predecessor and identify predecessor _____

The applicant hereby appoints the Secretary of State of Illinois as agent for service of process in an action relating only to the registration, which may be issued pursuant to this application, if the renewal registrant be, or shall become, a non-resident individual, or foreign partnership, limited liability company, association, or corporation not licensed to do business in the State, or cannot be found in this State.

The undersigned hereby declares, under penalty of perjury, that the statements made in the foregoing application are true, and that to his/her knowledge no other person has registered the mark, either federally or in this State, or has the right to use the mark either in the identical form thereof or in such near resemblance thereto as to be likely, when applied to the goods or services of such other person, to cause confusion or to cause mistake, or to deceive.

X _____   _____

Signature of Applicant   Type or Print Name of Applicant

_____   _____

Official Capacity   Contact Phone Number

The following general classes of goods and services are established for convenience of administration of this Act, not to limit or extend the applicant's or registrant's rights. A single application for registration of a mark may include any or all goods or services upon which the mark is actually being used and which are comprised in a single class. In no event shall a single application include goods or services upon which the mark is being used and which fall within different classes.

Classification of Goods for Trademarks

1 Chemicals	12 Vehicles	23 Yarns and threads
2 Paints	13 Firearms	24 Fabrics
3 Cosmetics and cleaning preparations	14 Jewelry	25 Clothing
4 Lubricants and fuels	15 Musical instruments	26 Fancy goods
5 Pharmaceuticals	16 Paper goods and printed matter	27 Floor coverings
6 Metal goods	17 Rubber goods	28 Toys and sporting goods
7 Machinery	18 Leather goods	29 Meals and processed foods
8 Hand tools	19 Non-metallic building materials	30 Staple foods
9 Electrical and scientific apparatus	20 Furniture and articles not otherwise classified	31 Natural agricultural products
10 Medical apparatus	21 Housewares and glass	32 Light beverages
11 Environmental control apparatus	22 Cordage and fibers	33 Wine and spirits
		34 Smoker's articles

Classification of Services for Servicemarks

35 Advertising and business	39 Transportation and storage	43 Restaurants, hotels, motels and boarding
36 Insurance and financial	40 Treatment of materials	44 Medical, veterinary, beauty care and forestry
37 Building construction and repair	41 Education and entertainment	45 Personal, social and security
38 Telecommunications	42 Scientific technological or legal	

Department of Homeland Security
U.S. Citizenship and Immigration Services

OMB No. 1615-0047; Expires 03/31/07

Employment Eligibility Verification

Please read instructions carefully before completing this form. The instructions must be available during completion of this form. ANTI-DISCRIMINATION NOTICE: It is illegal to discriminate against work eligible individuals. Employers CANNOT specify which document(s) they will accept from an employee. The refusal to hire an individual because of a future expiration date may also constitute illegal discrimination.

Section 1. Employee Information and Verification. To be completed and signed by employee at the time employment begins.

Print Name: Last	First	Middle Initial	Maiden Name

Address (Street Name and Number)	Apt. #	Date of Birth (month/day/year)

City	State	Zip Code	Social Security #

I am aware that federal law provides for imprisonment and/or fines for false statements or use of false documents in connection with the completion of this form.

I attest, under penalty of perjury, that I am (check one of the following):

☐ A citizen or national of the United States
☐ A Lawful Permanent Resident (Alien #) A _____
☐ An alien authorized to work until _____

(Alien # or Admission #) _____

Employee's Signature	Date (month/day/year)

Preparer and/or Translator Certification. *(To be completed and signed if Section 1 is prepared by a person other than the employee.) I attest, under penalty of perjury, that I have assisted in the completion of this form and that to the best of my knowledge the information is true and correct.*

Preparer's/Translator's Signature	Print Name

Address (Street Name and Number, City, State, Zip Code)	Date (month/day/year)

Section 2. Employer Review and Verification. To be completed and signed by employer. Examine one document from List A OR examine one document from List B and one from List C, as listed on the reverse of this form, and record the title, number and expiration date, if any, of the document(s).

List A	OR	List B	AND	List C
Document title: _____		_____		_____
Issuing authority: _____		_____		_____
Document #: _____		_____		_____
Expiration Date (if any): _____		_____		_____
Document #: _____				
Expiration Date (if any): _____				

CERTIFICATION - I attest, under penalty of perjury, that I have examined the document(s) presented by the above-named employee, that the above-listed document(s) appear to be genuine and to relate to the employee named, that the employee began employment on *(month/day/year)* _____ **and that to the best of my knowledge the employee is eligible to work in the United States. (State employment agencies may omit the date the employee began employment.)**

Signature of Employer or Authorized Representative	Print Name	Title

Business or Organization Name	Address (Street Name and Number, City, State, Zip Code)	Date (month/day/year)

Section 3. Updating and Reverification. To be completed and signed by employer.

A. New Name (if applicable)	B. Date of Rehire (month/day/year) (if applicable)

C. If employee's previous grant of work authorization has expired, provide the information below for the document that establishes current employment eligibility.

Document Title: _____	Document #: _____	Expiration Date (if any): _____

I attest, under penalty of perjury, that to the best of my knowledge, this employee is eligible to work in the United States, and if the employee presented document(s), the document(s) I have examined appear to be genuine and to relate to the individual.

Signature of Employer or Authorized Representative	Date (month/day/year)

NOTE: This is the 1991 edition of the Form I-9 that has been rebranded with a current printing date to reflect the recent transition from the INS to DHS and its components.

Form I-9 (Rev. 05/31/05)Y Page 2

LISTS OF ACCEPTABLE DOCUMENTS

LIST A

Documents that Establish Both Identity and Employment Eligibility

OR

1. U.S. Passport (unexpired or expired)

2. Certificate of U.S. Citizenship *(Form N-560 or N-561)*

3. Certificate of Naturalization *(Form N-550 or N-570)*

4. Unexpired foreign passport, with *I-551 stamp or* attached *Form I-94* indicating unexpired employment authorization

5. Permanent Resident Card or Alien Registration Receipt Card with photograph *(Form I-151 or I-551)*

6. Unexpired Temporary Resident Card *(Form I-688)*

7. Unexpired Employment Authorization Card *(Form I-688A)*

8. Unexpired Reentry Permit *(Form I-327)*

9. Unexpired Refugee Travel Document *(Form 1-571)*

10. Unexpired Employment Authorization Document issued by DHS that contains a photograph *(Form I-688B)*

LIST B

Documents that Establish Identity

AND

1. Driver's license or ID card issued by a state or outlying possession of the United States provided it contains a photograph or information such as name, date of birth, gender, height, eye color and address

2. ID card issued by federal, state or local government agencies or entities, provided it contains a photograph or information such as name, date of birth, gender, height, eye color and address

3. School ID card with a photograph

4. Voter's registration card

5. U.S. Military card or draft record

6. Military dependent's ID card

7. U.S. Coast Guard Merchant Mariner Card

8. Native American tribal document

9. Driver's license issued by a Canadian government authority

For persons under age 18 who are unable to present a document listed above:

10. School record or report card

11. Clinic, doctor or hospital record

12. Day-care or nursery school record

LIST C

Documents that Establish Employment Eligibility

1. U.S. social security card issued by the Social Security Administration *(other than a card stating it is not valid for employment)*

2. Certification of Birth Abroad issued by the Department of State *(Form FS-545 or Form DS-1350)*

3. Original or certified copy of a birth certificate issued by a state, county, municipal authority or outlying possession of the United States bearing an official seal

4. Native American tribal document

5. U.S. Citizen ID Card *(Form I-197)*

6. ID Card for use of Resident Citizen in the United States *(Form I-179)*

7. Unexpired employment authorization document issued by DHS *(other than those listed under List A)*

Illustrations of many of these documents appear in Part 8 of the Handbook for Employers (M-274)

Department of Homeland Security
U.S. Citizenship and Immigration Services

OMB No. 1615-0047; Expires 03/31/07

Employment Eligibility Verification

INSTRUCTIONS
PLEASE READ ALL INSTRUCTIONS CAREFULLY BEFORE COMPLETING THIS FORM.

Anti-Discrimination Notice. It is illegal to discriminate against any individual (other than an alien not authorized to work in the U.S.) in hiring, discharging, or recruiting or referring for a fee because of that individual's national origin or citizenship status. It is illegal to discriminate against work eligible individuals. Employers **CANNOT** specify which document(s) they will accept from an employee. The refusal to hire an individual because of a future expiration date may also constitute illegal discrimination.

Section 1- Employee.
All employees, citizens and noncitizens, hired after November 6, 1986, must complete Section 1 of this form at the time of hire, which is the actual beginning of employment. **The employer is responsible for ensuring that Section 1 is timely and properly completed.**

Preparer/Translator Certification.
The Preparer/Translator Certification must be completed if Section 1 is prepared by a person other than the employee. A preparer/translator may be used only when the employee is unable to complete Section 1 on his/her own. However, the employee must still sign Section 1 personally.

Section 2 - Employer.
For the purpose of completing this form, the term "employer" includes those recruiters and referrers for a fee who are agricultural associations, agricultural employers or farm labor contractors.

Employers must complete Section 2 by examining evidence of identity and employment eligibility within three (3) business days of the date employment begins. If employees are authorized to work, but are unable to present the required document(s) within three business days, they must present a receipt for the application of the document(s) within three business days and the actual document(s) within ninety (90) days. However, if employers hire individuals for a duration of less than three business days, Section 2 must be completed at the time employment begins. **Employers must record: 1)** document title; **2)** issuing authority; **3)** document number, **4)** expiration date, if any; and **5)** the date employment begins. Employers must sign and date the certification. Employees must present original documents. Employers may, but are not required to, photocopy the document(s) presented. These photocopies may only be used for the verification process and must be retained with the I-9. **However, employers are still responsible for completing the I-9.**

Section 3 - Updating and Reverification.
Employers must complete Section 3 when updating and/or reverifying the I-9. Employers must reverify employment eligibility of their employees on or before the expiration date recorded in Section 1. Employers **CANNOT** specify which document(s) they will accept from an employee.

- If an employee's name has changed at the time this form is being updated/reverified, complete Block A.

- If an employee is rehired within three (3) years of the date this form was originally completed and the employee is still eligible to be employed on the same basis as previously indicated on this form (updating), complete Block B and the signature block.

- If an employee is rehired within three (3) years of the date this form was originally completed and the employee's work authorization has expired **or** if a current employee's work authorization is about to expire (reverification), complete Block B and:

- examine any document that reflects that the employee is authorized to work in the U.S. (see List A **or** C),

- record the document title, document number and expiration date (if any) in Block C, and

- complete the signature block.

Photocopying and Retaining Form I-9. A blank I-9 may be reproduced, provided both sides are copied. The Instructions must be available to all employees completing this form. Employers must retain completed I-9s for three (3) years after the date of hire or one (1) year after the date employment ends, whichever is later.

For more detailed information, you may refer to the Department of Homeland Security (DHS) Handbook for Employers, (Form M-274). You may obtain the handbook at your local U.S. Citizenship and Immigration Services (USCIS) office.

Privacy Act Notice. The authority for collecting this information is the Immigration Reform and Control Act of 1986, Pub. L. 99-603 (8 USC 1324a).

This information is for employers to verify the eligibility of individuals for employment to preclude the unlawful hiring, or recruiting or referring for a fee, of aliens who are not authorized to work in the United States.

This information will be used by employers as a record of their basis for determining eligibility of an employee to work in the United States. The form will be kept by the employer and made available for inspection by officials of the U.S. Immigration and Customs Enforcement, Department of Labor and Office of Special Counsel for Immigration Related Unfair Employment Practices.

Submission of the information required in this form is voluntary. However, an individual may not begin employment unless this form is completed, since employers are subject to civil or criminal penalties if they do not comply with the Immigration Reform and Control Act of 1986.

Reporting Burden. We try to create forms and instructions that are accurate, can be easily understood and which impose the least possible burden on you to provide us with information. Often this is difficult because some immigration laws are very complex. Accordingly, the reporting burden for this collection of information is computed as follows: **1)** learning about this form, 5 minutes; **2)** completing the form, 5 minutes; and **3)** assembling and filing (recordkeeping) the form, 5 minutes, for an average of 15 minutes per response. If you have comments regarding the accuracy of this burden estimate, or suggestions for making this form simpler, you can write to U.S. Citizenship and Immigration Services, Regulatory Management Division, 111 Massachuetts Avenue, N.W., Washington, DC 20529. OMB No. 1615-0047.

NOTE: This is the 1991 edition of the Form I-9 that has been rebranded with a current printing date to reflect the recent transition from the INS to DHS and its components.

EMPLOYERS MUST RETAIN COMPLETED FORM I-9
PLEASE DO NOT MAIL COMPLETED FORM I-9 TO ICE OR USCIS

Form I-9 (Rev. 05/31/05)Y

This page is intentionally left blank.

Form **SS-4**	**Application for Employer Identification Number**	OMB No. 1545-0003

Form **SS-4**

(Rev. February 2006)
Department of the Treasury
Internal Revenue Service

Application for Employer Identification Number

(For use by employers, corporations, partnerships, trusts, estates, churches, government agencies, Indian tribal entities, certain individuals, and others.)

▶ See separate instructions for each line.   ▶ Keep a copy for your records.

OMB No. 1545-0003

EIN

Type or print clearly.

1 Legal name of entity (or individual) for whom the EIN is being requested

2 Trade name of business (if different from name on line 1)

3 Executor, administrator, trustee, "care of" name

4a Mailing address (room, apt., suite no. and street, or P.O. box)

5a Street address (if different) (Do not enter a P.O. box.)

4b City, state, and ZIP code

5b City, state, and ZIP code

6 County and state where principal business is located

7a Name of principal officer, general partner, grantor, owner, or trustor

7b SSN, ITIN, or EIN

8a **Type of entity** (check only one box)
☐ Sole proprietor (SSN) _____
☐ Partnership
☐ Corporation (enter form number to be filed) ▶ _____
☐ Personal service corporation
☐ Church or church-controlled organization
☐ Other nonprofit organization (specify) ▶ _____
☐ Other (specify) ▶

☐ Estate (SSN of decedent) _____
☐ Plan administrator (SSN) _____
☐ Trust (SSN of grantor) _____
☐ National Guard   ☐ State/local government
☐ Farmers' cooperative   ☐ Federal government/military
☐ REMIC   ☐ Indian tribal governments/enterprises
Group Exemption Number (GEN) ▶ _____

8b If a corporation, name the state or foreign country (if applicable) where incorporated

State	Foreign country

9 **Reason for applying** (check only one box)
☐ Started new business (specify type) ▶ _____
☐ Hired employees (Check the box and see line 12.)
☐ Compliance with IRS withholding regulations
☐ Other (specify) ▶

☐ Banking purpose (specify purpose) ▶ _____
☐ Changed type of organization (specify new type) ▶ _____
☐ Purchased going business
☐ Created a trust (specify type) ▶ _____
☐ Created a pension plan (specify type) ▶ _____

10 Date business started or acquired (month, day, year). See instructions.

11 Closing month of accounting year

12 First date wages or annuities were paid (month, day, year). **Note.** If applicant is a withholding agent, enter date income will first be paid to nonresident alien. (month, day, year) . . . . ▶

13 Highest number of employees expected in the next 12 months (enter -0- if none).

Do you expect to have $1,000 or less in employment tax liability for the calendar year? ☐ **Yes** ☐ **No.** (If you expect to pay $4,000 or less in wages, you can mark yes.)

Agricultural	Household	Other

14 Check **one** box that best describes the principal activity of your business.
☐ Construction   ☐ Rental & leasing   ☐ Transportation & warehousing
☐ Real estate   ☐ Manufacturing   ☐ Finance & insurance
☐ Health care & social assistance   ☐ Wholesale–agent/broker
☐ Accommodation & food service   ☐ Wholesale–other   ☐ Retail
☐ Other (specify)

15 Indicate principal line of merchandise sold, specific construction work done, products produced, or services provided.

16a Has the applicant ever applied for an employer identification number for this or any other business? . . . . . ☐ **Yes** ☐ **No**
Note. If "Yes," please complete lines 16b and 16c.

16b If you checked "Yes" on line 16a, give applicant's legal name and trade name shown on prior application if different from line 1 or 2 above.
Legal name ▶   Trade name ▶

16c Approximate date when, and city and state where, the application was filed. Enter previous employer identification number if known.

Approximate date when filed (mo., day, year)	City and state where filed	Previous EIN

Third Party Designee

Complete this section **only** if you want to authorize the named individual to receive the entity's EIN and answer questions about the completion of this form.

Designee's name	Designee's telephone number (include area code) ( )
Address and ZIP code	Designee's fax number (include area code) ( )

Under penalties of perjury, I declare that I have examined this application, and to the best of my knowledge and belief, it is true, correct, and complete.

Name and title (type or print clearly) ▶

Applicant's telephone number (include area code) ( )

Applicant's fax number (include area code) ( )

Signature ▶   Date ▶

For Privacy Act and Paperwork Reduction Act Notice, see separate instructions.   Cat. No. 16055N   Form **SS-4** (Rev. 2-2006)

Do I Need an EIN?

File Form SS-4 if the applicant entity does not already have an EIN but is required to show an EIN on any return, statement, or other document.[1] See also the separate instructions for each line on Form SS-4.

IF the applicant...	AND...	THEN...
Started a new business	Does not currently have (nor expect to have) employees	Complete lines 1, 2, 4a–8a, 8b (if applicable), and 9–16c.
Hired (or will hire) employees, including household employees	Does not already have an EIN	Complete lines 1, 2, 4a–6, 7a–b (if applicable), 8a, 8b (if applicable), and 9–16c.
Opened a bank account	Needs an EIN for banking purposes only	Complete lines 1–5b, 7a–b (if applicable), 8a, 9, and 16a–c.
Changed type of organization	Either the legal character of the organization or its ownership changed (for example, you incorporate a sole proprietorship or form a partnership)[2]	Complete lines 1–16c (as applicable).
Purchased a going business[3]	Does not already have an EIN	Complete lines 1–16c (as applicable).
Created a trust	The trust is other than a grantor trust or an IRA trust[4]	Complete lines 1–16c (as applicable).
Created a pension plan as a plan administrator[5]	Needs an EIN for reporting purposes	Complete lines 1, 3, 4a–b, 8a, 9, and 16a–c.
Is a foreign person needing an EIN to comply with IRS withholding regulations	Needs an EIN to complete a Form W-8 (other than Form W-8ECI), avoid withholding on portfolio assets, or claim tax treaty benefits[6]	Complete lines 1–5b, 7a–b (SSN or ITIN optional), 8a–9, and 16a–c.
Is administering an estate	Needs an EIN to report estate income on Form 1041	Complete lines 1, 2, 3, 4a–6, 8a, 9-11, 12-15 (if applicable), and 16a–c.
Is a withholding agent for taxes on non-wage income paid to an alien (i.e., individual, corporation, or partnership, etc.)	Is an agent, broker, fiduciary, manager, tenant, or spouse who is required to file Form 1042, Annual Withholding Tax Return for U.S. Source Income of Foreign Persons	Complete lines 1, 2, 3 (if applicable), 4a–5b, 7a–b (if applicable), 8a, 9, and 16a–c.
Is a state or local agency	Serves as a tax reporting agent for public assistance recipients under Rev. Proc. 80-4, 1980-1 C.B. 581[7]	Complete lines 1, 2, 4a–5b, 8a, 9, and 16a–c.
Is a single-member LLC	Needs an EIN to file Form 8832, Entity Classification Election, for filing employment tax returns, **or** for state reporting purposes[8]	Complete lines 1–16c (as applicable).
Is an S corporation	Needs an EIN to file Form 2553, Election by a Small Business Corporation[9]	Complete lines 1–16c (as applicable).

[1] For example, a sole proprietorship or self-employed farmer who establishes a qualified retirement plan, or is required to file excise, employment, alcohol, tobacco, or firearms returns, must have an EIN. A partnership, corporation, REMIC (real estate mortgage investment conduit), nonprofit organization (church, club, etc.), or farmers' cooperative must use an EIN for any tax-related purpose even if the entity does not have employees.

[2] However, do not apply for a new EIN if the existing entity only (a) changed its business name, (b) elected on Form 8832 to change the way it is taxed (or is covered by the default rules), or (c) terminated its partnership status because at least 50% of the total interests in partnership capital and profits were sold or exchanged within a 12-month period. The EIN of the terminated partnership should continue to be used. See Regulations section 301.6109-1(d)(2)(iii).

[3] Do not use the EIN of the prior business unless you became the "owner" of a corporation by acquiring its stock.

[4] However, grantor trusts that do not file using Optional Method 1 and IRA trusts that are required to file Form 990-T, Exempt Organization Business Income Tax Return, must have an EIN. For more information on grantor trusts, see the Instructions for Form 1041.

[5] A plan administrator is the person or group of persons specified as the administrator by the instrument under which the plan is operated.

[6] Entities applying to be a Qualified Intermediary (QI) need a QI-EIN even if they already have an EIN. See Rev. Proc. 2000-12.

[7] See also *Household employer* on page 3. **Note.** State or local agencies may need an EIN for other reasons, for example, hired employees.

[8] Most LLCs do not need to file Form 8832. See *Limited liability company (LLC)* on page 4 for details on completing Form SS-4 for an LLC.

[9] An existing corporation that is electing or revoking S corporation status should use its previously-assigned EIN.

Instructions for Form SS-4

 Department of the Treasury
Internal Revenue Service

(Rev. February 2006)

Application for Employer Identification Number

Section references are to the Internal Revenue Code unless otherwise noted.

General Instructions

Use these instructions to complete Form SS-4, Application for Employer Identification Number. Also see *Do I Need an EIN?* on page 2 of Form SS-4.

Purpose of Form

Use Form SS-4 to apply for an employer identification number (EIN). An EIN is a nine-digit number (for example, 12-3456789) assigned to sole proprietors, corporations, partnerships, estates, trusts, and other entities for tax filing and reporting purposes. The information you provide on this form will establish your business tax account.

 An EIN is for use in connection with your business activities only. Do not use your EIN in place of your social security number (SSN).

Reminders

Apply online. Generally, you can apply for and receive an EIN online using the Internet. See *How To Apply* below.

File only one Form SS-4. Generally, a sole proprietor should file only one Form SS-4 and needs only one EIN, regardless of the number of businesses operated as a sole proprietorship or trade names under which a business operates. However, if the proprietorship incorporates or enters into a partnership, a new EIN is required. Also, each corporation in an affiliated group must have its own EIN.

EIN applied for, but not received. If you do not have an EIN by the time a return is due, write "Applied For" and the date you applied in the space shown for the number. Do not show your SSN as an EIN on returns.

If you do not have an EIN by the time a tax deposit is due, send your payment to the Internal Revenue Service Center for your filing area as shown in the instructions for the form that you are filing. Make your check or money order payable to the "United States Treasury" and show your name (as shown on Form SS-4), address, type of tax, period covered, and date you applied for an EIN.

Federal tax deposits. New employers that have a federal tax obligation will be pre-enrolled in the Electronic Federal Tax Payment System (EFTPS). EFTPS allows you to make all of your federal tax payments online at *www.eftps.gov* or by telephone. Shortly after we have assigned you your EIN, you will receive instructions by mail for activating your EFTPS enrollment. You will also receive an EFTPS Personal Identification Number (PIN) that you will use to make your payments, as well as instructions for obtaining an Internet password you will need to make payments online.

If you are not required to make deposits by EFTPS, you can use Form 8109, Federal Tax Deposit (FTD) Coupon, to make deposits at an authorized depositary. If you would like to receive Form 8109, call 1-800-829-4933. Allow 5 to 6 weeks for delivery. For more information on federal tax deposits, see Pub. 15 (Circular E).

How To Apply

You can apply for an EIN online, by telephone, by fax, or by mail depending on how soon you need to use the EIN. Use only one method for each entity so you do not receive more than one EIN for an entity.

Online. Generally, you can receive your EIN by Internet and use it immediately to file a return or make a payment. Go to the IRS website at *www.irs.gov/businesses* and click on Employer ID Numbers.

Applicants that may not apply online. The online application process is not yet available to:
- Applicants with foreign addresses (including Puerto Rico),
- Limited Liability Companies (LLCs) that have not yet determined their entity classification for federal tax purposes (see *Limited liability company (LLC)* on page 4),
- Real Estate Investment Conduits (REMICs),
- State and local governments,
- Federal Government/Military, and
- Indian Tribal Governments/Enterprises.

Telephone. You can receive your EIN by telephone and use it immediately to file a return or make a payment. Call the IRS at 1-800-829-4933. (International applicants must call 215-516-6999.) The hours of operation are 7:00 a.m. to 10.00 p.m. local time (Pacific time for Alaska and Hawaii). The person making the call must be authorized to sign the form or be an authorized designee. See *Signature* and *Third Party Designee* on page 6. Also see the *TIP* below.

If you are applying by telephone, it will be helpful to complete Form SS-4 before contacting the IRS. An IRS representative will use the information from the Form SS-4 to establish your account and assign you an EIN. Write the number you are given on the upper right corner of the form and sign and date it. Keep this copy for your records.

If requested by an IRS representative, mail or fax (facsimile) the signed Form SS-4 (including any Third Party Designee authorization) within 24 hours to the IRS address provided by the IRS representative.

 Taxpayer representatives can apply for an EIN on behalf of their client and request that the EIN be faxed to their client on the same day. **Note.** *By using this procedure, you are authorizing the IRS to fax the EIN without a cover sheet.*

Fax. Under the Fax-TIN program, you can receive your EIN by fax within 4 business days. Complete and fax Form SS-4 to the IRS using the Fax-TIN number listed on page 2 for your state. A long-distance charge to callers outside of the local calling area will apply. Fax-TIN

Cat. No. 62736F

numbers can only be used to apply for an EIN. The numbers may change without notice. Fax-TIN is available 24 hours a day, 7 days a week.

Be sure to provide your fax number so the IRS can fax the EIN back to you.

Note. By using this procedure, you are authorizing the IRS to fax the EIN without a cover sheet.

Mail. Complete Form SS-4 at least 4 to 5 weeks before you will need an EIN. Sign and date the application and mail it to the service center address for your state. You will receive your EIN in the mail in approximately 4 weeks. See also *Third Party Designee* on page 6.

Call 1-800-829-4933 to verify a number or to ask about the status of an application by mail.

Where to Fax or File

If your principal business, office or agency, or legal residence in the case of an individual, is located in:	Fax or file with the "Internal Revenue Service Center" at:
Connecticut, Delaware, District of Columbia, Florida, Georgia, Maine, Maryland, Massachusetts, New Hampshire, New Jersey, New York, North Carolina, Ohio, Pennsylvania, Rhode Island, South Carolina, Vermont, Virginia, West Virginia	Attn: EIN Operation Holtsville, NY 11742 Fax-TIN: 631-447-8960
Illinois, Indiana, Kentucky, Michigan	Attn: EIN Operation Cincinnati, OH 45999 Fax-TIN: 859-669-5760
Alabama, Alaska, Arizona, Arkansas, California, Colorado, Hawaii, Idaho, Iowa, Kansas, Louisiana, Minnesota, Mississippi, Missouri, Montana, Nebraska, Nevada, New Mexico, North Dakota, Oklahoma, Oregon, South Dakota, Tennessee, Texas, Utah, Washington, Wisconsin, Wyoming	Attn: EIN Operation Philadelphia, PA 19255 Fax-TIN: 859-669-5760
If you have no legal residence, principal place of business, or principal office or agency in any state:	Attn: EIN Operation Philadelphia, PA 19255 Fax-TIN: 215-516-1040

How To Get Forms and Publications

Phone. Call 1-800-TAX-FORM (1-800-829-3676) to order forms, instructions, and publications. You should receive your order or notification of its status within 10 workdays.

Internet. You can access the IRS website 24 hours a day, 7 days a week at *www.irs.gov* to download forms, instructions, and publications.

CD-ROM. For small businesses, return preparers, or others who may frequently need tax forms or publications, a CD-ROM containing over 2,000 tax products (including many prior year forms) can be purchased from the National Technical Information Service (NTIS).

To order Pub. 1796, IRS Tax Products CD, call 1-877-CDFORMS (1-877-233-6767) toll free or connect to *www.irs.gov/cdorders*.

Tax Help for Your Business

IRS-sponsored Small Business Workshops provide information about your federal and state tax obligations. For information about workshops in your area, call 1-800-829-4933.

Related Forms and Publications

The following forms and instructions may be useful to filers of Form SS-4.
● Form 990-T, Exempt Organization Business Income Tax Return.
● Instructions for Form 990-T.
● Schedule C (Form 1040), Profit or Loss From Business.
● Schedule F (Form 1040), Profit or Loss From Farming.
● Instructions for Form 1041 and Schedules A, B, D, G, I, J, and K-1, U.S. Income Tax Return for Estates and Trusts.
● Form 1042, Annual Withholding Tax Return for U.S. Source Income of Foreign Persons.
● Instructions for Form 1065, U.S. Return of Partnership Income.
● Instructions for Form 1066, U.S. Real Estate Mortgage Investment Conduit (REMIC) Income Tax Return.
● Instructions for Forms 1120 and 1120-A.
● Form 2553, Election by a Small Business Corporation.
● Form 2848, Power of Attorney and Declaration of Representative.
● Form 8821, Tax Information Authorization.
● Form 8832, Entity Classification Election.

For more information about filing Form SS-4 and related issues, see:
● Pub. 51 (Circular A), Agricultural Employer's Tax Guide;
● Pub. 15 (Circular E), Employer's Tax Guide;
● Pub. 538, Accounting Periods and Methods;
● Pub. 542, Corporations;
● Pub. 557, Tax-Exempt Status for Your Organization;
● Pub. 583, Starting a Business and Keeping Records;
● Pub. 966, The Secure Way to Pay Your Federal Taxes for Business and Individual Taxpayers;
● Pub. 1635, Understanding Your EIN;
● Package 1023, Application for Recognition of Exemption Under Section 501(c)(3) of the Internal Revenue Code; and
● Package 1024, Application for Recognition of Exemption Under Section 501(a).

Specific Instructions

Print or type all entries on Form SS-4. Follow the instructions for each line to expedite processing and to avoid unnecessary IRS requests for additional information. Enter "N/A" (nonapplicable) on the lines that do not apply.

Line 1 — Legal name of entity (or individual) for whom the EIN is being requested. Enter the legal name of the entity (or individual) applying for the EIN exactly as it appears on the social security card, charter, or other applicable legal document. An entry is required.

Individuals. Enter your first name, middle initial, and last name. If you are a sole proprietor, enter your individual name, not your business name. Enter your business name on line 2. Do not use abbreviations or nicknames on line 1.

Trusts. Enter the name of the trust.

Estate of a decedent. Enter the name of the estate. For an estate that has no legal name, enter the name of the decedent followed by "Estate."

Partnerships. Enter the legal name of the partnership as it appears in the partnership agreement.

Corporations. Enter the corporate name as it appears in the corporate charter or other legal document creating it.

Plan administrators. Enter the name of the plan administrator. A plan administrator who already has an EIN should use that number.

Line 2 — Trade name of business. Enter the trade name of the business if different from the legal name. The trade name is the "doing business as " (DBA) name.

 Use the full legal name shown on line 1 on all tax returns filed for the entity. (However, if you enter a trade name on line 2 and choose to use the trade name instead of the legal name, enter the trade name on all returns you file.) To prevent processing delays and errors, always use the legal name only (or the trade name only) on all tax returns.

Line 3 — Executor, administrator, trustee, "care of" name. Trusts enter the name of the trustee. Estates enter the name of the executor, administrator, or other fiduciary. If the entity applying has a designated person to receive tax information, enter that person's name as the "care of" person. Enter the individual's first name, middle initial, and last name.

Lines 4a-b — Mailing address. Enter the mailing address for the entity's correspondence. If line 3 is completed, enter the address for the executor, trustee or "care of" person. Generally, this address will be used on all tax returns.

TIP *File Form 8822, Change of Address, to report any subsequent changes to the entity's mailing address.*

Lines 5a-b — Street address. Provide the entity's physical address only if different from its mailing address shown in lines 4a-b. Do not enter a P.O. box number here.

Line 6 — County and state where principal business is located. Enter the entity's primary physical location.

Lines 7a-b — Name of principal officer, general partner, grantor, owner, or trustor. Enter the first name, middle initial, last name, and SSN of (a) the principal officer if the business is a corporation, (b) a general partner if a partnership, (c) the owner of an entity that is disregarded as separate from its owner (disregarded entities owned by a corporation enter the corporation's name and EIN), or (d) a grantor, owner, or trustor if a trust.

If the person in question is an alien individual with a previously assigned individual taxpayer identification number (ITIN), enter the ITIN in the space provided and submit a copy of an official identifying document. If necessary, complete Form W-7, Application for IRS Individual Taxpayer Identification Number, to obtain an ITIN.

You must enter an SSN, ITIN, or EIN unless the only reason you are applying for an EIN is to make an entity classification election (see Regulations sections 301.7701-1 through 301.7701-3) and you are a nonresident alien or other foreign entity with no effectively connected income from sources within the United States.

Line 8a — Type of entity. Check the box that best describes the type of entity applying for the EIN. If you are an alien individual with an ITIN previously assigned to you, enter the ITIN in place of a requested SSN.

 This is not an election for a tax classification of an entity. See Limited liability company (LLC) *on page 4.*

Other. If not specifically listed, check the "Other" box, enter the type of entity and the type of return, if any, that will be filed (for example, "Common Trust Fund, Form 1065" or "Created a Pension Plan"). Do not enter "N/A." If you are an alien individual applying for an EIN, see the *Lines 7a-b* instructions above.

- **Household employer.** If you are an individual, check the "Other" box and enter "Household Employer" and your SSN. If you are a state or local agency serving as a tax reporting agent for public assistance recipients who become household employers, check the "Other" box and enter "Household Employer Agent." If you are a trust that qualifies as a household employer, you do not need a separate EIN for reporting tax information relating to household employees; use the EIN of the trust.
- **QSub.** For a qualified subchapter S subsidiary (QSub) check the "Other" box and specify "QSub."
- **Withholding agent.** If you are a withholding agent required to file Form 1042, check the "Other" box and enter "Withholding Agent."

Sole proprietor. Check this box if you file Schedule C, C-EZ, or F (Form 1040) and have a qualified plan, or are required to file excise, employment, alcohol, tobacco, or firearms returns, or are a payer of gambling winnings. Enter your SSN (or ITIN) in the space provided. If you are a nonresident alien with no effectively connected income from sources within the United States, you do not need to enter an SSN or ITIN.

Corporation. This box is for any corporation other than a personal service corporation. If you check this box, enter the income tax form number to be filed by the entity in the space provided.

 If you entered "1120S" after the "Corporation" checkbox, the corporation must file Form 2553 no later than the 15th day of the 3rd month of the tax year the election is to take effect. Until Form 2553 has been received and approved, you will be considered a Form 1120 filer. See the Instructions for Form 2553.

Personal service corporation. Check this box if the entity is a personal service corporation. An entity is a personal service corporation for a tax year only if:
- The principal activity of the entity during the testing period (prior tax year) for the tax year is the performance of personal services substantially by employee-owners, and
- The employee-owners own at least 10% of the fair market value of the outstanding stock in the entity on the last day of the testing period.

Personal services include performance of services in such fields as health, law, accounting, or consulting. For more information about personal service corporations, see the Instructions for Forms 1120 and 1120-A and Pub. 542.

Other nonprofit organization. Check this box if the nonprofit organization is other than a church or church-controlled organization and specify the type of nonprofit organization (for example, an educational organization).

 If the organization also seeks tax-exempt status, you must file either Package 1023 or Package 1024. See Pub. 557 for more information.

If the organization is covered by a group exemption letter, enter the four-digit group exemption number (GEN). (Do not confuse the GEN with the nine-digit EIN.) If you do not know the GEN, contact the parent organization. Get Pub. 557 for more information about group exemption numbers.

If the organization is a section 527 political organization, check the box for *Other nonprofit organization* and specify "section 527 organization" in the space to the right. To be recognized as exempt from tax, a section 527 political organization must electronically file Form 8871, Political Organization Notice of Section 527 Status, within 24 hours of the date on which the organization was established. The organization may also have to file Form 8872, Political Organization Report of Contributions and Expenditures. See *www.irs.gov/polorgs* for more information.

Plan administrator. If the plan administrator is an individual, enter the plan administrator's SSN in the space provided.

REMIC. Check this box if the entity has elected to be treated as a real estate mortgage investment conduit (REMIC). See the Instructions for Form 1066 for more information.

State/local government. If you are a government employer and you are not sure of your social security and Medicare coverage options, go to *www.ncsssa.org/ssaframes.html* to obtain the contact information for your state's Social Security Administrator.

Limited liability company (LLC). An LLC is an entity organized under the laws of a state or foreign country as a limited liability company. For federal tax purposes, an LLC may be treated as a partnership or corporation or be disregarded as an entity separate from its owner.

By default, a domestic LLC with only one member is disregarded as an entity separate from its owner and must include all of its income and expenses on the owner's tax return (for example, Schedule C (Form 1040)). Also by default, a domestic LLC with two or more members is treated as a partnership. A domestic LLC may file Form 8832 to avoid either default classification and elect to be classified as an association taxable as a corporation. For more information on entity classifications (including the rules for foreign entities), see the instructions for Form 8832.

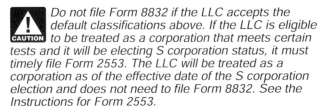 *Do not file Form 8832 if the LLC accepts the default classifications above. If the LLC is eligible to be treated as a corporation that meets certain tests and it will be electing S corporation status, it must timely file Form 2553. The LLC will be treated as a corporation as of the effective date of the S corporation election and does not need to file Form 8832. See the Instructions for Form 2553.*

Complete Form SS-4 for LLCs as follows.

• A single-member domestic LLC that accepts the default classification (above) does not need an EIN and generally should not file Form SS-4. Generally, the LLC should use the name and EIN of its owner for all federal tax purposes. However, the reporting and payment of employment taxes for employees of the LLC may be made using the name and EIN of either the owner or the LLC as explained in Notice 99-6. You can find Notice 99-6 on page 12 of Internal Revenue Bulletin 1999-3 at *www.irs.gov/pub/irs-irbs/irb99-03.pdf.* (**Note.** If the LLC applicant indicates in box 13 that it has employees or expects to have employees, the owner (whether an individual or other entity) of a single-member domestic LLC will also be assigned its own EIN (if it does not already have one) even if the LLC will be filing the employment tax returns.)

• A single-member, domestic LLC that accepts the default classification (above) and wants an EIN for filing employment tax returns (see above) or non-federal purposes, such as a state requirement, must check the "Other" box and write "Disregarded Entity" or, when applicable, "Disregarded Entity — Sole Proprietorship" in the space provided.

• A multi-member, domestic LLC that accepts the default classification (above) must check the "Partnership" box.

• A domestic LLC that will be filing Form 8832 to elect corporate status must check the "Corporation" box and write in "Single-Member" or "Multi-Member" immediately below the "form number" entry line.

Line 9 — Reason for applying. Check only one box. Do not enter "N/A."

Started new business. Check this box if you are starting a new business that requires an EIN. If you check this box, enter the type of business being started. Do not apply if you already have an EIN and are only adding another place of business.

Hired employees. Check this box if the existing business is requesting an EIN because it has hired or is hiring employees and is therefore required to file employment tax returns. Do not apply if you already have an EIN and are only hiring employees. For information on employment taxes (for example, for family members), see Pub. 15 (Circular E).

 You may have to make electronic deposits of all depository taxes (such as employment tax, excise tax, and corporate income tax) using the Electronic Federal Tax Payment System (EFTPS). See Federal tax deposits on page 1; section 11, Depositing Taxes, of Pub. 15 (Circular E); and Pub. 966.

Created a pension plan. Check this box if you have created a pension plan and need an EIN for reporting purposes. Also, enter the type of plan in the space provided.

 Check this box if you are applying for a trust EIN when a new pension plan is established. In addition, check the "Other" box in line 8a and write "Created a Pension Plan" in the space provided.

Banking purpose. Check this box if you are requesting an EIN for banking purposes only, and enter the banking purpose (for example, a bowling league for depositing dues or an investment club for dividend and interest reporting).

Changed type of organization. Check this box if the business is changing its type of organization. For example, the business was a sole proprietorship and has been incorporated or has become a partnership. If you check this box, specify in the space provided (including available space immediately below) the type of change made. For example, "From Sole Proprietorship to Partnership."

Purchased going business. Check this box if you purchased an existing business. Do not use the former owner's EIN unless you became the "owner" of a corporation by acquiring its stock.

Created a trust. Check this box if you created a trust, and enter the type of trust created. For example, indicate if the trust is a nonexempt charitable trust or a split-interest trust.

Exception. Do not file this form for certain grantor-type trusts. The trustee does not need an EIN for the trust if the trustee furnishes the name and TIN of the grantor/owner and the address of the trust to all payors. However, grantor trusts that do not file using Optional Method 1 and IRA trusts that are required to file Form 990-T, Exempt Organization Business Income Tax Return, must have an EIN. For more information on grantor trusts, see the Instructions for Form 1041.

TIP *Do not check this box if you are applying for a trust EIN when a new pension plan is established. Check "Created a pension plan."*

Other. Check this box if you are requesting an EIN for any other reason; and enter the reason. For example, a newly-formed state government entity should enter "Newly-Formed State Government Entity" in the space provided.

Line 10 — Date business started or acquired. If you are starting a new business, enter the starting date of the business. If the business you acquired is already operating, enter the date you acquired the business. If you are changing the form of ownership of your business, enter the date the new ownership entity began. Trusts should enter the date the trust was funded. Estates should enter the date of death of the decedent whose name appears on line 1 or the date when the estate was legally funded.

Line 11 — Closing month of accounting year. Enter the last month of your accounting year or tax year. An accounting or tax year is usually 12 consecutive months, either a calendar year or a fiscal year (including a period of 52 or 53 weeks). A calendar year is 12 consecutive months ending on December 31. A fiscal year is either 12 consecutive months ending on the last day of any month other than December or a 52-53 week year. For more information on accounting periods, see Pub. 538.

Individuals. Your tax year generally will be a calendar year.

Partnerships. Partnerships must adopt one of the following tax years.
• The tax year of the majority of its partners.
• The tax year common to all of its principal partners.
• The tax year that results in the least aggregate deferral of income.
• In certain cases, some other tax year.

See the Instructions for Form 1065 for more information.

REMICs. REMICs must have a calendar year as their tax year.

Personal service corporations. A personal service corporation generally must adopt a calendar year unless it meets one of the following requirements.
• It can establish a business purpose for having a different tax year.
• It elects under section 444 to have a tax year other than a calendar year.

Trusts. Generally, a trust must adopt a calendar year except for the following trusts.
• Tax-exempt trusts.
• Charitable trusts.
• Grantor-owned trusts.

Line 12 — First date wages or annuities were paid. If the business has employees, enter the date on which the business began to pay wages. If the business does not plan to have employees, enter "N/A."

Withholding agent. Enter the date you began or will begin to pay income (including annuities) to a nonresident alien. This also applies to individuals who are required to file Form 1042 to report alimony paid to a nonresident alien.

Line 13 — Highest number of employees expected in the next 12 months. Complete each box by entering the number (including zero ("-0-")) of "Agricultural," "Household," or "Other" employees expected by the applicant in the next 12 months. Check the appropriate box to indicate if you expect your annual employment tax liability to be $1,000 or less. Generally, if you pay $4,000 or less in wages subject to social security and Medicare taxes and federal income tax withholding, you are likely to pay $1,000 or less in employment taxes.

For more information on employment taxes, see Pub. 15 (Circular E); or Pub. 51 (Circular A) if you have agricultural employees (farmworkers).

Lines 14 and 15. Check the one box in line 14 that best describes the principal activity of the applicant's business. Check the "Other" box (and specify the applicant's principal activity) if none of the listed boxes applies. You must check a box.

Use line 15 to describe the applicant's principal line of business in more detail. For example, if you checked the "Construction" box in line 14, enter additional detail such as "General contractor for residential buildings" in line 15. An entry is required.

Construction. Check this box if the applicant is engaged in erecting buildings or engineering projects, (for example, streets, highways, bridges, tunnels). The term "Construction" also includes special trade contractors, (for example, plumbing, HVAC, electrical, carpentry, concrete, excavation, etc. contractors).

Real estate. Check this box if the applicant is engaged in renting or leasing real estate to others; managing, selling, buying or renting real estate for others; or providing related real estate services (for example, appraisal services).

Rental and leasing. Check this box if the applicant is engaged in providing tangible goods such as autos, computers, consumer goods, or industrial machinery and equipment to customers in return for a periodic rental or lease payment.

Manufacturing. Check this box if the applicant is engaged in the mechanical, physical, or chemical transformation of materials, substances, or components into new products. The assembling of component parts of manufactured products is also considered to be manufacturing.

Transportation & warehousing. Check this box if the applicant provides transportation of passengers or cargo; warehousing or storage of goods; scenic or sight-seeing transportation; or support activities related to transportation.

Finance & insurance. Check this box if the applicant is engaged in transactions involving the creation, liquidation, or change of ownership of financial assets and/or facilitating such financial transactions; underwriting annuities/insurance policies; facilitating such underwriting by selling insurance policies; or by providing other insurance or employee-benefit related services.

Health care and social assistance. Check this box if the applicant is engaged in providing physical, medical, or psychiatric care or providing social assistance activities such as youth centers, adoption agencies, individual/family services, temporary shelters, daycare, etc.

Accommodation & food services. Check this box if the applicant is engaged in providing customers with lodging, meal preparation, snacks, or beverages for immediate consumption.

Wholesale–agent/broker. Check this box if the applicant is engaged in arranging for the purchase or sale of goods owned by others or purchasing goods on a commission basis for goods traded in the wholesale market, usually between businesses.

Wholesale–other. Check this box if the applicant is engaged in selling goods in the wholesale market generally to other businesses for resale on their own account, goods used in production, or capital or durable nonconsumer goods.

Retail. Check this box if the applicant is engaged in selling merchandise to the general public from a fixed store; by direct, mail-order, or electronic sales; or by using vending machines.

Other. Check this box if the applicant is engaged in an activity not described above. Describe the applicant's principal business activity in the space provided.

Lines 16a-c. Check the applicable box in line 16a to indicate whether or not the entity (or individual) applying for an EIN was issued one previously. Complete lines 16b and 16c only if the "Yes" box in line 16a is checked. If the applicant previously applied for more than one EIN, write "See Attached" in the empty space in line 16a and attach a separate sheet providing the line 16b and 16c information for each EIN previously requested.

Third Party Designee. Complete this section only if you want to authorize the named individual to receive the entity's EIN and answer questions about the completion of Form SS-4. The designee's authority terminates at the time the EIN is assigned and released to the designee. You must complete the signature area for the authorization to be valid.

Signature. When required, the application must be signed by (a) the individual, if the applicant is an individual, (b) the president, vice president, or other principal officer, if the applicant is a corporation, (c) a responsible and duly authorized member or officer having

knowledge of its affairs, if the applicant is a partnership, government entity, or other unincorporated organization, or (d) the fiduciary, if the applicant is a trust or an estate. Foreign applicants may have any duly-authorized person, (for example, division manager), sign Form SS-4.

Privacy Act and Paperwork Reduction Act Notice. We ask for the information on this form to carry out the Internal Revenue laws of the United States. We need it to comply with section 6109 and the regulations thereunder, which generally require the inclusion of an employer identification number (EIN) on certain returns, statements, or other documents filed with the Internal Revenue Service. If your entity is required to obtain an EIN, you are required to provide all of the information requested on this form. Information on this form may be used to determine which federal tax returns you are required to file and to provide you with related forms and publications.

We disclose this form to the Social Security Administration (SSA) for their use in determining compliance with applicable laws. We may give this information to the Department of Justice for use in civil and criminal litigation, and to the cities, states, and the District of Columbia for use in administering their tax laws. We may also disclose this information to other countries under a tax treaty, to federal and state agencies to enforce federal nontax criminal laws, and to federal law enforcement and intelligence agencies to combat terrorism.

We will be unable to issue an EIN to you unless you provide all of the requested information that applies to your entity. Providing false information could subject you to penalties.

You are not required to provide the information requested on a form that is subject to the Paperwork Reduction Act unless the form displays a valid OMB control number. Books or records relating to a form or its instructions must be retained as long as their contents may become material in the administration of any Internal Revenue law. Generally, tax returns and return information are confidential, as required by section 6103.

The time needed to complete and file this form will vary depending on individual circumstances. The estimated average time is:

Recordkeeping	8 hrs., 22 min.
Learning about the law or the form	42 min.
Preparing the form	52 min.
Copying, assembling, and sending the form to the IRS	- - - - -

If you have comments concerning the accuracy of these time estimates or suggestions for making this form simpler, we would be happy to hear from you. You can write to Internal Revenue Service, Tax Products Coordinating Committee, SE:W:CAR:MP:T:T:SP, IR-6406, 1111 Constitution Avenue, NW, Washington, DC 20224. Do not send the form to this address. Instead, see *Where to Fax or File* on page 2.

Form SS-8
(Rev. June 2003)
Department of the Treasury
Internal Revenue Service

Determination of Worker Status
for Purposes of Federal Employment Taxes
and Income Tax Withholding

OMB No. 1545-0004

Name of firm (or person) for whom the worker performed services	Worker's name	
Firm's address (include street address, apt. or suite no., city, state, and ZIP code)	Worker's address (include street address, apt. or suite no., city, state, and ZIP code)	
Trade name	Telephone number (include area code) ( )	Worker's social security number
Telephone number (include area code) ( )	Firm's employer identification number	Worker's employer identification number (if any)

If the worker is paid by a firm other than the one listed on this form for these services, enter the name, address, and employer identification number of the payer.

Important Information Needed To Process Your Request

We must have your permission to disclose your name and the information on this form and any attachments to other parties involved with this request. **Do we have your permission to disclose this information?** . . . . ☐ **Yes** ☐ **No**
If you answered "No" or did not mark a box, we will not process your request and will not issue a determination.

You must answer ALL items OR mark them "Unknown" or "Does not apply." If you need more space, attach another sheet.

A This form is being completed by: ☐ Firm ☐ Worker; for services performed _____ to _____ .
(beginning date)   (ending date)

B Explain your reason(s) for filing this form (e.g., you received a bill from the IRS, you believe you received a Form 1099 or Form W-2 erroneously, you are unable to get worker's compensation benefits, you were audited or are being audited by the IRS). ....

C Total number of workers who performed or are performing the same or similar services _____ .
D How did the worker obtain the job? ☐ Application   ☐ Bid   ☐ Employment Agency   ☐ Other (specify) _____ .

E Attach copies of all supporting documentation (contracts, invoices, memos, Forms W-2, Forms 1099, IRS closing agreements, IRS rulings, etc.). In addition, please inform us of any current or past litigation concerning the worker's status. If no income reporting forms (Form 1099-MISC or W-2) were furnished to the worker, enter the amount of income earned for the year(s) at issue $ _____ .
F Describe the firm's business. ....

G Describe the work done by the worker and provide the worker's job title. ....

H Explain why you believe the worker is an employee or an independent contractor. ------------------------
----

I Did the worker perform services for the firm before getting this position? . . . . ☐ **Yes** ☐ **No** ☐ **N/A**
If "Yes," what were the dates of the prior service? --
If "Yes," explain the differences, if any, between the current and prior service. ------------------------
----

J If the work is done under a written agreement between the firm and the worker, attach a copy (preferably signed by both parties). Describe the terms and conditions of the work arrangement. --
----

Part I   Behavioral Control

1   What specific training and/or instruction is the worker given by the firm? ....

2   How does the worker receive work assignments? ....

3   Who determines the methods by which the assignments are performed? ....

4   Who is the worker required to contact if problems or complaints arise and who is responsible for their resolution? ....

5   What types of reports are required from the worker? Attach examples. ....

6   Describe the worker's daily routine (i.e., schedule, hours, etc.). ....

7   At what location(s) does the worker perform services (e.g., firm's premises, own shop or office, home, customer's location, etc.)? ....

8   Describe any meetings the worker is required to attend and any penalties for not attending (e.g., sales meetings, monthly meetings, staff meetings, etc.). ....

9   Is the worker required to provide the services personally? . . . . ☐ Yes ☐ No

10 If substitutes or helpers are needed, who hires them? ....

11 If the worker hires the substitutes or helpers, is approval required? . . . . ☐ Yes ☐ No
    If "Yes," by whom? ....

12 Who pays the substitutes or helpers? ....

13 Is the worker reimbursed if the worker pays the substitutes or helpers? . . . . ☐ Yes ☐ No
    If "Yes," by whom?

Part II   Financial Control

1   List the supplies, equipment, materials, and property provided by each party:
    The firm ....
    The worker ....
    Other party ....

2   Does the worker lease equipment? . . . . ☐ Yes ☐ No
    If "Yes," what are the terms of the lease? (Attach a copy or explanatory statement.) ....

3   What expenses are incurred by the worker in the performance of services for the firm? ....

4   Specify which, if any, expenses are reimbursed by:
    The firm ....
    Other party ....

5   Type of pay the worker receives: ☐ Salary   ☐ Commission   ☐ Hourly Wage   ☐ Piece Work
    ☐ Lump Sum   ☐ Other (specify) ....
    If type of pay is commission, and the firm guarantees a minimum amount of pay, specify amount $ _____ .

6   Is the worker allowed a drawing account for advances? . . . . ☐ Yes ☐ No
    If "Yes," how often? ....
    Specify any restrictions. ....

7   Whom does the customer pay? . . . . ☐ Firm   ☐ Worker
    If worker, does the worker pay the total amount to the firm? ☐ Yes ☐ No   If "No," explain. ....

8   Does the firm carry worker's compensation insurance on the worker? . . . . ☐ Yes ☐ No

9   What economic loss or financial risk, if any, can the worker incur beyond the normal loss of salary (e.g., loss or damage of equipment, material, etc.)? ....

Part III	Relationship of the Worker and Firm

1 List the benefits available to the worker (e.g., paid vacations, sick pay, pensions, bonuses). ....

....

2 Can the relationship be terminated by either party without incurring liability or penalty? . . . . ☐ Yes ☐ No
If "No," explain your answer. ....

....

3 Does the worker perform similar services for others? . . . . ☐ Yes ☐ No
If "Yes," is the worker required to get approval from the firm? . . . . ☐ Yes ☐ No

4 Describe any agreements prohibiting competition between the worker and the firm while the worker is performing services or during any later period. Attach any available documentation. ....

....

5 Is the worker a member of a union? . . . . ☐ Yes ☐ No

6 What type of advertising, if any, does the worker do (e.g., a business listing in a directory, business cards, etc.)? Provide copies, if applicable.

....

7 If the worker assembles or processes a product at home, who provides the materials and instructions or pattern? ....

....

8 What does the worker do with the finished product (e.g., return it to the firm, provide it to another party, or sell it)? ....

....

9 How does the firm represent the worker to its customers (e.g., employee, partner, representative, or contractor)? ....

....

10 If the worker no longer performs services for the firm, how did the relationship end? ....

....

Part IV	For Service Providers or Salespersons- Complete this part if the worker provided a service directly to customers or is a salesperson.

1 What are the worker's responsibilities in soliciting new customers? ....

....

2 Who provides the worker with leads to prospective customers? ....

3 Describe any reporting requirements pertaining to the leads. ....

....

4 What terms and conditions of sale, if any, are required by the firm? ....

5 Are orders submitted to and subject to approval by the firm? . . . . ☐ Yes ☐ No

6 Who determines the worker's territory? ....

7 Did the worker pay for the privilege of serving customers on the route or in the territory? . . . . ☐ Yes ☐ No
If "Yes," whom did the worker pay? ....
If "Yes," how much did the worker pay? . . . . $ _____ .

8 Where does the worker sell the product (e.g., in a home, retail establishment, etc.)? ....

....

9 List the product and/or services distributed by the worker (e.g., meat, vegetables, fruit, bakery products, beverages, or laundry or dry cleaning services). If more than one type of product and/or service is distributed, specify the principal one. ....

....

10 Does the worker sell life insurance full time? . . . . ☐ Yes ☐ No

11 Does the worker sell other types of insurance for the firm? . . . . ☐ Yes ☐ No
If "Yes," enter the percentage of the worker's total working time spent in selling other types of insurance. . . .. _____ %

12 If the worker solicits orders from wholesalers, retailers, contractors, or operators of hotels, restaurants, or other similar establishments, enter the percentage of the worker's time spent in the solicitation. . . . . _____ %

13 Is the merchandise purchased by the customers for resale or use in their business operations? . . . . ☐ Yes ☐ No
Describe the merchandise and state whether it is equipment installed on the customers' premises. ....

....

Part V	Signature (see page 4)

Under penalties of perjury, I declare that I have examined this request, including accompanying documents, and to the best of my knowledge and belief, the facts presented are true, correct, and complete.

Signature ▶ _____ Title ▶ _____ Date ▶ _____
(Type or print name below)

General Instructions

Section references are to the Internal Revenue Code unless otherwise noted.

Purpose

Firms and workers file Form SS-8 to request a determination of the status of a worker for purposes of Federal employment taxes and income tax withholding.

A Form SS-8 determination may be requested only in order to resolve Federal tax matters. If Form SS-8 is submitted for a tax year for which the statute of limitations on the tax return has expired, a determination letter will not be issued. The statute of limitations expires 3 years from the due date of the tax return or the date filed, whichever is later.

The IRS does not issue a determination letter for proposed transactions or on hypothetical situations. We may, however, issue an information letter when it is considered appropriate.

Definition

Firm. For the purposes of this form, the term "firm" means any individual, business enterprise, organization, state, or other entity for which a worker has performed services. The firm may or may not have paid the worker directly for these services. **If the firm was not responsible for payment for services, be sure to enter the name, address, and employer identification number of the payer on the first page of Form SS-8 below the identifying information for the firm and the worker.**

The SS-8 Determination Process

The IRS will acknowledge the receipt of your Form SS-8. Because there are usually two (or more) parties who could be affected by a determination of employment status, the IRS attempts to get information from all parties involved by sending those parties blank Forms SS-8 for completion. The case will be assigned to a technician who will review the facts, apply the law, and render a decision. The technician may ask for additional information from the requestor, from other involved parties, or from third parties that could help clarify the work relationship before rendering a decision. The IRS will generally issue a formal determination to the firm or payer (if that is a different entity), and will send a copy to the worker. A determination letter applies only to a worker (or a class of workers) requesting it, and the decision is binding on the IRS. In certain cases, a formal determination will not be issued. Instead, an information letter may be issued. Although an information letter is advisory only and is not binding on the IRS, it may be used to assist the worker to fulfill his or her Federal tax obligations.

Neither the SS-8 determination process nor the review of any records in connection with the determination constitutes an examination (audit) of any Federal tax return. If the periods under consideration have previously been examined, the SS-8 determination process will not constitute a reexamination under IRS reopening procedures. Because this is not an examination of any Federal tax return, the appeal rights available in connection with an examination do not apply to an SS-8 determination. However, if you disagree with a determination and you have additional information concerning the work relationship that you believe was not previously considered, you may request that the determining office reconsider the determination.

Completing Form SS-8

Answer all questions as completely as possible. Attach additional sheets if you need more space. Provide information for all years the worker provided services for the firm. Determinations are based on the entire relationship between the firm and the worker.

Additional copies of this form may be obtained by calling 1-800-829-4933 or from the IRS website at **www.irs.gov.**

Fee

There is no fee for requesting an SS-8 determination letter.

Signature

Form SS-8 must be signed and dated by the taxpayer. A stamped signature will not be accepted.

The person who signs for a corporation must be an officer of the corporation who has personal knowledge of the facts. If the corporation is a member of an affiliated group filing a consolidated return, it must be signed by an officer of the common parent of the group.

The person signing for a trust, partnership, or limited liability company must be, respectively, a trustee, general partner, or member-manager who has personal knowledge of the facts.

Where To File

Send the completed Form SS-8 to the address listed below for the firm's location. However, for cases involving Federal agencies, send Form SS-8 to the Internal Revenue Service, Attn: CC:CORP:T:C, Ben Franklin Station, P.O. Box 7604, Washington, DC 20044.

Firm's location:	Send to:
Alaska, Arizona, Arkansas, California, Colorado, Hawaii, Idaho, Illinois, Iowa, Kansas, Minnesota, Missouri, Montana, Nebraska, Nevada, New Mexico, North Dakota, Oklahoma, Oregon, South Dakota, Texas, Utah, Washington, Wisconsin, Wyoming, American Samoa, Guam, Puerto Rico, U.S. Virgin Islands	Internal Revenue Service SS-8 Determinations P.O. Box 630 Stop 631 Holtsville, NY 11742-0630
Alabama, Connecticut, Delaware, District of Columbia, Florida, Georgia, Indiana, Kentucky, Louisiana, Maine, Maryland, Massachusetts, Michigan, Mississippi, New Hampshire, New Jersey, New York, North Carolina, Ohio, Pennsylvania, Rhode Island, South Carolina, Tennessee, Vermont, Virginia, West Virginia, all other locations not listed	Internal Revenue Service SS-8 Determinations 40 Lakemont Road Newport, VT 05855-1555

Instructions for Workers

If you are requesting a determination for more than one firm, complete a separate Form SS-8 for each firm.

 Form SS-8 is not a claim for refund of social security and Medicare taxes or Federal income tax withholding.

If the IRS determines that you are an employee, you are responsible for filing an amended return for any corrections related to this decision. A determination that a worker is an employee does not necessarily reduce any current or prior tax liability. For more information, call 1-800-829-1040.

Time for filing a claim for refund. Generally, you must file your claim for a credit or refund within 3 years from the date your original return was filed or within 2 years from the date the tax was paid, whichever is later.

Filing Form SS-8 does not prevent the expiration of the time in which a claim for a refund must be filed. If you are concerned about a refund, and the statute of limitations for filing a claim for refund for the year(s) at issue has not yet expired, you should file **Form 1040X,** Amended U.S. Individual Income Tax Return, to protect your statute of limitations. File a separate Form 1040X for each year.

On the Form 1040X you file, do not complete lines 1 through 24 on the form. Write "Protective Claim" at the top of the form, sign and date it. In addition, you should enter the following statement in Part II, Explanation of Changes to Income, Deductions, and Credits: "Filed Form SS-8 with the Internal Revenue Service Office in (Holtsville, NY; Newport, VT; or Washington, DC; as appropriate). By filing this protective claim, I reserve the right to file a claim for any refund that may be due after a determination of my employment tax status has been completed."

Filing Form SS-8 does not alter the requirement to timely file an income tax return. Do not delay filing your tax return in anticipation of an answer to your SS-8 request. In addition, if applicable, do not delay in responding to a request for payment while waiting for a determination of your worker status.

Instructions for Firms

If a **worker** has requested a determination of his or her status while working for you, you will receive a request from the IRS to complete a Form SS-8. In cases of this type, the IRS usually gives each party an opportunity to present a statement of the facts because any decision will affect the employment tax status of the parties. Failure to respond to this request will not prevent the IRS from issuing a determination letter based on the information he or she has made available so that the worker may fulfill his or her Federal tax obligations. However, the information that you provide is extremely valuable in determining the status of the worker.

If **you** are requesting a determination for a particular class of worker, complete the form for **one** individual who is representative of the class of workers whose status is in question. If you want a written determination for more than one class of workers, complete a separate Form SS-8 for one worker from each class whose status is typical of that class. A written determination for any worker will apply to other workers of the same class if the facts are not materially different for these workers. Please provide a list of names and addresses of all workers potentially affected by this determination.

If you have a reasonable basis for not treating a worker as an employee, you may be relieved from having to pay employment taxes for that worker under section 530 of the 1978 Revenue Act. However, this relief provision cannot be considered in conjunction with a Form SS-8 determination because the determination does not constitute an examination of any tax return. For more information regarding section 530 of the 1978 Revenue Act and to determine if you qualify for relief under this section, you may visit the IRS website at **www.irs.gov.**

Privacy Act and Paperwork Reduction Act Notice. We ask for the information on this form to carry out the Internal Revenue laws of the United States. This information will be used to determine the employment status of the worker(s) described on the form. Subtitle C, Employment Taxes, of the Internal Revenue Code imposes employment taxes on wages. Sections 3121(d), 3306(a), and 3401(c) and (d) and the related regulations define employee and employer for purposes of employment taxes imposed under Subtitle C. Section 6001 authorizes the IRS to request information needed to determine if a worker(s) or firm is subject to these taxes. Section 6109 requires you to provide your taxpayer identification number. Neither workers nor firms are required to request a status determination, but if you choose to do so, you must provide the information requested on this form. Failure to provide the requested information may prevent us from making a status determination. If any worker or the firm has requested a status determination and you are being asked to provide information for use in that determination, you are not required to provide the requested information. However, failure to provide such information will prevent the IRS from considering it in making the status determination. Providing false or fraudulent information may subject you to penalties. Routine uses of this information include providing it to the Department of Justice for use in civil and criminal litigation, to the Social Security Administration for the administration of social security programs, and to cities, states, and the District of Columbia for the administration of their tax laws. We may also disclose this information to Federal and state agencies to enforce Federal nontax criminal laws and to combat terrorism. We may provide this information to the affected worker(s) or the firm as part of the status determination process.

You are not required to provide the information requested on a form that is subject to the Paperwork Reduction Act unless the form displays a valid OMB control number. Books or records relating to a form or its instructions must be retained as long as their contents may become material in the administration of any Internal Revenue law. Generally, tax returns and return information are confidential, as required by section 6103.

The time needed to complete and file this form will vary depending on individual circumstances. The estimated average time is: **Recordkeeping,** 22 hrs.; **Learning about the law or the form,** 47 min.; and **Preparing and sending the form to the IRS,** 1 hr., 11 min. If you have comments concerning the accuracy of these time estimates or suggestions for making this form simpler, we would be happy to hear from you. You can write to the Tax Products Coordinating Committee, Western Area Distribution Center, Rancho Cordova, CA 95743-0001. **Do not** send the tax form to this address. Instead, see **Where To File** on page 4.

This page is intentionally left blank.

Form W-4 (2006)

Purpose. Complete Form W-4 so that your employer can withhold the correct federal income tax from your pay. Because your tax situation may change, you may want to refigure your withholding each year.

Exemption from withholding. If you are exempt, complete only lines 1, 2, 3, 4, and 7 and sign the form to validate it. Your exemption for 2006 expires February 16, 2007. See Pub. 505, Tax Withholding and Estimated Tax.

Note. You cannot claim exemption from withholding if (a) your income exceeds $850 and includes more than $300 of unearned income (for example, interest and dividends) and (b) another person can claim you as a dependent on their tax return.

Basic instructions. If you are not exempt, complete the **Personal Allowances Worksheet** below. The worksheets on page 2 adjust your withholding allowances based on itemized deductions, certain credits, adjustments to income, or two-earner/two-job situations. Complete all worksheets that apply. However, you may claim fewer (or zero) allowances.

Head of household. Generally, you may claim head of household filing status on your tax return only if you are unmarried and pay more than 50% of the costs of keeping up a home for yourself and your dependent(s) or other qualifying individuals. See line E below.

Tax credits. You can take projected tax credits into account in figuring your allowable number of withholding allowances. Credits for child or dependent care expenses and the child tax credit may be claimed using the **Personal Allowances Worksheet** below. See Pub. 919, How Do I Adjust My Tax Withholding, for information on converting your other credits into withholding allowances.

Nonwage income. If you have a large amount of nonwage income, such as interest or dividends, consider making estimated tax payments using Form 1040-ES, Estimated Tax for Individuals. Otherwise, you may owe additional tax.

Two earners/two jobs. If you have a working spouse or more than one job, figure the total number of allowances you are entitled to claim on all jobs using worksheets from only one Form W-4. Your withholding usually will be most accurate when all allowances are claimed on the Form W-4 for the highest paying job and zero allowances are claimed on the others.

Nonresident alien. If you are a nonresident alien, see the Instructions for Form 8233 before completing this Form W-4.

Check your withholding. After your Form W-4 takes effect, use Pub. 919 to see how the dollar amount you are having withheld compares to your projected total tax for 2006. See Pub. 919, especially if your earnings exceed $130,000 (Single) or $180,000 (Married).

Recent name change? If your name on line 1 differs from that shown on your social security card, call 1-800-772-1213 to initiate a name change and obtain a social security card showing your correct name.

Personal Allowances Worksheet (Keep for your records.)

A Enter "1" for **yourself** if no one else can claim you as a dependent . . . . **A** _____

B Enter "1" if:
- You are single and have only one job; or
- You are married, have only one job, and your spouse does not work; or
- Your wages from a second job or your spouse's wages (or the total of both) are $1,000 or less.

B _____

C Enter "1" for your **spouse.** But, you may choose to enter "-0-" if you are married and have either a working spouse or more than one job. (Entering "-0-" may help you avoid having too little tax withheld.) . . . . **C** _____

D Enter number of **dependents** (other than your spouse or yourself) you will claim on your tax return . . . . **D** _____

E Enter "1" if you will file as **head of household** on your tax return (see conditions under **Head of household** above) . **E** _____

F Enter "1" if you have at least $1,500 of **child or dependent care expenses** for which you plan to claim a credit . . **F** _____

(**Note.** Do **not** include child support payments. See **Pub. 503,** Child and Dependent Care Expenses, for details.)

G **Child Tax Credit** (including additional child tax credit):
- If your total income will be less than $55,000 ($82,000 if married), enter "2" for each eligible child.
- If your total income will be between $55,000 and $84,000 ($82,000 and $119,000 if married), enter "1" for each eligible child plus "1" **additional** if you have four or more eligible children. . . . . **G** _____

H Add lines A through G and enter total here. (**Note.** This may be different from the number of exemptions you claim on your tax return.) ▶ **H** _____

For accuracy, complete all worksheets that apply.
- If you plan to **itemize or claim adjustments to income** and want to reduce your withholding, see the **Deductions and Adjustments Worksheet** on page 2.
- If you have **more than one job** or are **married and you and your spouse both work** and the combined earnings from all jobs exceed $35,000 ($25,000 if married) see the **Two-Earner/Two-Job Worksheet** on page 2 to avoid having too little tax withheld.
- If **neither** of the above situations applies, **stop here** and enter the number from line H on line 5 of Form W-4 below.

- **Cut here and give Form W-4 to your employer. Keep the top part for your records.** -

Form **W-4**	**Employee's Withholding Allowance Certificate**	OMB No. 1545-0074
Department of the Treasury Internal Revenue Service	▶ Whether you are entitled to claim a certain number of allowances or exemption from withholding is subject to review by the IRS. Your employer may be required to send a copy of this form to the IRS.	2006

1 Type or print your first name and middle initial.	Last name	**2** Your social security number

Home address (number and street or rural route)	**3** ☐ Single ☐ Married ☐ Married, but withhold at higher Single rate. **Note.** If married, but legally separated, or spouse is a nonresident alien, check the "Single" box.
City or town, state, and ZIP code	**4** If your last name differs from that shown on your social security card, check here. You must call 1-800-772-1213 for a new card. ▶ ☐

5 Total number of allowances you are claiming (from line **H** above **or** from the applicable worksheet on page 2) **5** _____

6 Additional amount, if any, you want withheld from each paycheck . . . . **6** $ _____

7 I claim exemption from withholding for 2006, and I certify that I meet **both** of the following conditions for exemption.
- Last year I had a right to a refund of **all** federal income tax withheld because I had **no** tax liability **and**
- This year I expect a refund of **all** federal income tax withheld because I expect to have **no** tax liability.

If you meet both conditions, write "Exempt" here . . . . ▶ **7**

Under penalties of perjury, I declare that I have examined this certificate and to the best of my knowledge and belief, it is true, correct, and complete.

Employee's signature
(Form is not valid unless you sign it.) ▶ _____   **Date** ▶ _____

8 Employer's name and address (Employer: Complete lines 8 and 10 only if sending to the IRS.)	**9** Office code (optional)	**10** Employer identification number (EIN)

For Privacy Act and Paperwork Reduction Act Notice, see page 2.   Cat. No. 10220Q   Form **W-4** (2006)

Deductions and Adjustments Worksheet

Note. Use this worksheet *only* if you plan to itemize deductions, claim certain credits, or claim adjustments to income on your 2006 tax return.

1 Enter an estimate of your 2006 itemized deductions. These include qualifying home mortgage interest, charitable contributions, state and local taxes, medical expenses in excess of 7.5% of your income, and miscellaneous deductions. (For 2006, you may have to reduce your itemized deductions if your income is over $150,500 ($75,250 if married filing separately). See *Worksheet 3* in Pub. 919 for details.) . . .   **1** $ _____

2 Enter: $10,300 if married filing jointly or qualifying widow(er)
            $ 7,550 if head of household
            $ 5,150 if single or married filing separately   . . . .   **2** $ _____

3 **Subtract** line 2 from line 1. If line 2 is greater than line 1, enter "-0-" . . . . . .   **3** $ _____

4 Enter an estimate of your 2006 adjustments to income, including alimony, deductible IRA contributions, and student loan interest   **4** $ _____

5 **Add** lines 3 and 4 and enter the total. (Include any amount for credits from *Worksheet 7* in Pub. 919) .   **5** $ _____

6 Enter an estimate of your 2006 nonwage income (such as dividends or interest) . . . .   **6** $ _____

7 **Subtract** line 6 from line 5. Enter the result, but not less than "-0-" . . . .   **7** $ _____

8 **Divide** the amount on line 7 by $3,300 and enter the result here. Drop any fraction . . . .   **8** _____

9 Enter the number from the **Personal Allowances Worksheet, line H, page 1** . . . .   **9** _____

10 **Add** lines 8 and 9 and enter the total here. If you plan to use the **Two-Earner/Two-Job Worksheet,** also enter this total on line 1 below. Otherwise, **stop here** and enter this total on Form W-4, line 5, page 1 .   **10** _____

Two-Earner/Two-Job Worksheet (See *Two earners/two jobs* on page 1.)

Note. Use this worksheet *only* if the instructions under line H on page 1 direct you here.

1 Enter the number from line H, page 1 (or from line 10 above if you used the **Deductions and Adjustments Worksheet**)   **1** _____

2 Find the number in **Table 1** below that applies to the **LOWEST** paying job and enter it here . . . .   **2** _____

3 If line 1 is **more than or equal to** line 2, subtract line 2 from line 1. Enter the result here (if zero, enter "-0-") and on Form W-4, line 5, page 1. **Do not** use the rest of this worksheet . . . .   **3** _____

Note. If line 1 is *less than* line 2, enter "-0-" on Form W-4, line 5, page 1. Complete lines 4–9 below to calculate the additional withholding amount necessary to avoid a year-end tax bill.

4 Enter the number from line 2 of this worksheet . . . .   **4** _____

5 Enter the number from line 1 of this worksheet . . . .   **5** _____

6 **Subtract** line 5 from line 4 . . . .   **6** _____

7 Find the amount in **Table 2** below that applies to the **HIGHEST** paying job and enter it here . . . .   **7** $ _____

8 **Multiply** line 7 by line 6 and enter the result here. This is the additional annual withholding needed . .   **8** $ _____

9 **Divide** line 8 by the number of pay periods remaining in 2006. For example, divide by 26 if you are paid every two weeks and you complete this form in December 2005. Enter the result here and on Form W-4, line 6, page 1. This is the additional amount to be withheld from each paycheck . . . .   **9** $ _____

Table 1: Two-Earner/Two-Job Worksheet

Married Filing Jointly						All Others	
If wages from **HIGHEST** paying job are—	AND, wages from **LOWEST** paying job are—	Enter on line 2 above	If wages from **HIGHEST** paying job are—	AND, wages from **LOWEST** paying job are—	Enter on line 2 above	If wages from **LOWEST** paying job are—	Enter on line 2 above
$0 - $42,000	$0 - $4,500	0	$42,001 and over	32,001 - 38,000	6	$0 - $6,000	0
	4,501 - 9,000	1		38,001 - 46,000	7	6,001 - 12,000	1
	9,001 - 18,000	2		46,001 - 55,000	8	12,001 - 19,000	2
	18,001 and over	3		55,001 - 60,000	9	19,001 - 26,000	3
				60,001 - 65,000	10	26,001 - 35,000	4
$42,001 and over	$0 - $4,500	0		65,001 - 75,000	11	35,001 - 50,000	5
	4,501 - 9,000	1		75,001 - 95,000	12	50,001 - 65,000	6
	9,001 - 18,000	2		95,001 - 105,000	13	65,001 - 80,000	7
	18,001 - 22,000	3		105,001 - 120,000	14	80,001 - 90,000	8
	22,001 - 26,000	4		120,001 and over	15	90,001 - 120,000	9
	26,001 - 32,000	5				120,001 and over	10

Table 2: Two-Earner/Two-Job Worksheet

Married Filing Jointly		All Others	
If wages from **HIGHEST** paying job are—	Enter on line 7 above	If wages from **HIGHEST** paying job are—	Enter on line 7 above
$0 - $60,000	$500	$0 - $30,000	$500
60,001 - 115,000	830	30,001 - 75,000	830
115,001 - 165,000	920	75,001 - 145,000	920
165,001 - 290,000	1,090	145,001 - 330,000	1,090
290,001 and over	1,160	330,001 and over	1,160

Printed on recycled paper

Illinois Department of Revenue

REG-1 Illinois Business Registration Application   Station # 925

Step 1:   Read this information first

You may electronically file this form at **www.ILtax.com.** $\equiv$ *Faster and Easier*

To update previously submitted information, call **217 785-3707.**

Do not check here until you have read all of Step 4. ☐

Step 2:   Provide your identification numbers and the reason for your application

Check the best description of why you are completing this application.

____ **First-time registration of your business or organization.** Tell us your federal employer identification number (FEIN). If you have applied for but not yet received your FEIN, write **"applied for."** __ __-__ __ __ __ __ __ __

Starting date of this business in Illinois: ____/____/_____
                                                  Month   Day   Year

____ **Re-applying of a previously registered business.** Tell us the Illinois Business Tax number (IBT no.) and, if applicable, the license number (Lic. no.) assigned to this business.   IBT no.:__ __ __ __-__ __ __ __   Lic. no.: _____

New starting date of this business in Illinois: ____/____/_____
                                                            Month   Day   Year

____ **Organizational change requiring a new Federal Employer Identification number (FEIN).**

What is the effective date of this change?   ____/____/_____
                                                 Month   Day   Year

Is this change the result of a merger or consolidation?   ○ yes   ○ no

Tell us the FEIN and Illinois Business Tax number (IBT no.) previously assigned when you registered this business.

FEIN: __ __-__ __ __ __ __ __ __   IBT no.:__ __ __ __ __-__

Tell us the new FEIN assigned to your business as a result of this change. If you have applied for and not yet received your FEIN, write **"applied for."** FEIN: __ __-__ __ __ __ __ __ __

____ **Add a tax requirement or location for a currently registered business.** Tell us the Illinois Business Tax number (IBT no.) and federal employer identification number (FEIN) currently assigned to this business.

IBT no.:__ __ __ __-__ __ __ __   FEIN. __ __-__ __ __ __ __ __ __

What is the effective date of this update or addition? ____/____/_____
                                                        Month   Day   Year

Step 3:   Identify your business or organization

1   Business' or organization's legal name: _____

Corporate, organization, partnership, or owner's (if sole proprietor) name

2   Doing business as (DBA) or trade name (if different from above):_____

3   Address of your corporate/home office or your principal Illinois business address. The address where you can be contacted.

_____   _____
Street address   Apartment or suite number

_____   _____   _____
City   State   ZIP

(___)___-_____   _____   (___)___-_____   _____
Daytime phone (include area code)   Extension   Fax (include area code)   E-mail address

4   Did you buy this business from someone?   ○ yes   ○ no
If **yes,** write the previous business' name and IBT no.

_____   __ __ __ __-__ __ __
Previous business' name   Previous business' IBT#

5   Check **one** to indicate your type of business ownership (using the federal income tax classification).

____ Sole proprietorship. Is this jointly owned by both husband and wife?   ○ yes   ○ no

____ Corporation (other than an exempt organization)

Tell us the Illinois Corporate File (charter) number issued by the Illinois Secretary of State:_____

Is this a small business corporation (subchapter S)?   ○ yes   ○ no   If **yes,** tell us how many shareholders. _____

____ Partnership. Write the number of general partners._____

____ Trust or estate

____ Exempt organization

____ Governmental agency

Step 4: Describe your business type or activity

1 Describe your business and provide the percentage of each activity used in your description.

_____% _____

_____% _____

2 Check all that apply to your type of business:

☐ **Withholding (employees, dividends, or certain winnings) -** You pay wages, taxable dividends, or wagering transactions in Illinois; *or,* you pay wages to Illinois residents under your state's income tax reciprocity agreement with Illinois.

☐ **Sales -** You sell merchandise. Are **all** of your sales for **resale** or otherwise exempt from sales tax?   ◯ yes   ◯ no
Check **any** that apply to your type of **retail** sales (if applicable).

____ Vehicles, trailers, mobile homes, watercraft, aircraft   ____ Items sold from vending machines.

____ Tires   How many machines will you have? _____

____ Beverages (soft drinks) in closed or sealed containers   ____ Solvents sold to dry cleaners

____ Motor fuel (*e.g.,* gasoline, gasohol, diesel fuel)

Do your sales include purchase orders accepted outside of Illinois and items shipped directly into Illinois?   ◯ yes   ◯ no
If **"yes,"** check the best description of your business.

____ Located in Illinois, including but not limited to an office or agent.

____ **No** location in Illinois but will voluntarily collect sales tax on receipts from sales into Illinois.

☐ **Use -** You buy items for use in Illinois on which you do **not** pay the Illinois sales tax to your supplier. This includes items from your inventory bought tax-free for your own use.

☐ **Services -** You provide services (*e.g.,* repairs, printing, funeral, consulting, barber) and you are **not** a public utility.
Do you transfer or sell items (*e.g.,* parts, paper, chemicals, shampoo) with your service?   ◯ yes   ◯ no

☐ **Motor vehicle renting -** You are in the business of renting motor vehicles (*i.e.,* automobiles, motorcycles, certain vans/ recreational vehicles) for one year or less.

☐ **Water or sewer utility services -** You provide water or sewer utility service in Illinois.

☐ **Hotel/motel operators -** You rent, lease, or let rooms to the public for living quarters for periods of less than 30 days.

☐ **Liquor warehousing (not liquor sales) -** You warehouse or deliver alcoholic liquors for compensation.

☐ **Methane gas landfills -** You are a Qualified Solid Waste Energy Facility (QSWEF).

Below are tax responsibilities that may require additional information. We will contact you for this information. If you check any of the boxes below, please check the "Additional Requirements" box in Step 1 on the front of this application.

☐ **Natural gas -** You sell natural gas, provide natural gas services to persons in Illinois, or purchase natural gas from outside of Illinois for your own use (not for resale). Check all that apply.
How do you sell natural gas or natural gas services? ____ at retail   ____ at resale
Are you a municipal utility?   ◯ yes   ◯ no
Do you purchase natural gas from outside of Illinois for your own use (not for resale) and want to pay the tax directly to us?
◯ yes   ◯ no

☐ **Telecommunications -** You provide telecommunications services in Illinois. How do you sell your service? ____ Retail ____ Resale
Is the only service you provide a paging or wireless service?   ◯ yes   ◯ no

☐ **Cigarette or tobacco products -** You manufacture, wholesale, or distribute cigarettes or tobacco products.
Check all that apply to your business' activities.

Cigarette: ____ Manufacture   ____ Stamp   ____ Distribute

Tobacco products: ____ Distribute   ____ Retail (purchase from distributors and tax is **not** or will **not** be paid)

☐ **Motor fuel, aviation fuels and kerosene -** Check the activities which apply to your business.

____ Distributor - **not** from retail outlets   ____ Compressed gas sales - highway use **only**   ____ Bulk storage plants - **not** at retail outlets

____ Retail outlet **only**   ____ Manufacturing   ____ Gas/motor fuel blending   ____ Importing   ____ Exporting

☐ **Electricity services -** You deliver electricity to persons in Illinois for their own use.
How do you sell your service?   ____ Retail   ____ Resale
Check **any** that apply to your type of business:

____ Electric cooperative   ____ Municipal utility

____ Self-assessing purchaser of electricity for **nonresidential use** who elects to pay the Electricity Excise Tax directly to us.

☐ **Gaming events -** You operate gaming (*i.e.,* bingo, charitable games, pull tabs) events or are a premise provider, supplier, or manufacturer of equipment used during gaming events. Check **all** that pertains to your organization or business.

____ organization operating an event   ____ supplier or manufacturer of gaming equipment   ____ premise provider for events

Step 5: Describe your business

1 Check **all** that apply to your Illinois business activity. ___ **Retail** ___ **Wholesale** ___ **Service** ___ **Manufacturing/production**

2 Check **all** that apply to your type of business.

___ Advertising, business services
___ Auto supplies
___ Books, jewelry, gifts, cameras
___ Building trades, construction, contractors
___ Clothing and accessories
___ Coin-operated amusement devices
___ Communication
___ Computers/programming/design/software
___ Dental, medical services/facilities
___ Dept. store/general merchandise
___ Drinking places
___ Eating places
___ Electric
___ Electronics, TVs, music, instruments
___ Forestry, livestock, agriculture, fishing

___ Furniture, flooring, appliances
___ Gasoline, other petroleum products
___ Grocery items
___ Hardware
___ Homes - mobile/modular
___ Hotel/motel
___ Leasing/renting equipment
___ Liquor
___ Lumber, building materials
___ Machines, parts, equipment
___ Mail order, direct/vending sales
___ Medical supplies
___ Metals, rubber, plastic
___ Mining, coal, other minerals
___ Natural gas

___ Not-for-profit business/organization
___ Nursery, florists, garden supplies
___ Other manufacturing not listed: _____
___ Other retail not listed: _____
___ Other services not listed: _____
___ Other wholesale not listed: _____
___ Paper, textiles, printing, chemicals
___ Pharmaceuticals/drug stores
___ Public administration, government
___ Real estate, insurance, finance
___ Renting vehicles
___ Sporting goods, bicycles, toys
___ Tobacco products
___ Transportation
___ Vehicles, boats, motorcycles
___ Water, sewer

Step 6: Identify your business location

Do **not** complete this step unless your location is in Illinois and your business activities include sales (including vehicle sales), use, service, hotel/motel operations, telecommunications, motor vehicle renting, electricity services, natural gas, or liquor warehousing. Write your business name, address (even if it is the same as identified in Step 3), and the date the location started doing business. **Note:** Township information is required for all Madison or St. Clair County locations in Illinois.

Location 1: Is this the same address as the address in Step 3?   ○ yes   ○ no

Check **all** that apply to this location's type of activity.

___ Sales, Use, Service   ___ Motor vehicle renting   ___ Telecommunications   ___ Electricity services
___ Vehicle sales   ___ Liquor warehousing   ___ Hotel/motel operator   ___ Natural gas

Name: _____   Starting date: ___/___/_____

<small>Doing business as (DBA) or trade name if different from the name you provided in Step 3</small>   <small>Month Day   Year</small>

_____
<small>Street address (Do **not** use PO Box), include apartment or suite number (if applicable)</small>

_____ **Illinois** _____
<small>City</small>   <small>State</small>   <small>ZIP</small>

County: _____   Township: _____   (___)___-_____ Ext:_____   (___)___-_____
<small>Daytime phone (include area code)</small>   <small>Fax (include area code)</small>

a Check the best *physical* description of this location: ☐ permanent   ☐ one that will change (*e.g.*, fairs, flea market)

b Check the best description of this location in regards to the city, village, or town limits listed above: ☐ inside   ☐ outside

Location 2:

Check **all** that apply to this location's type of activity.

___ Sales, Use, Service   ___ Motor vehicle renting   ___ Telecommunications   ___ Electricity services
___ Vehicle sales   ___ Liquor warehousing   ___ Hotel/motel operator   ___ Natural gas

Name: _____   Starting date: ___/___/_____

<small>Doing business as (DBA) or trade name if different from the name you provided in Step 3</small>   <small>Month Day   Year</small>

_____
<small>Street address (Do **not** use PO Box), include apartment or suite number (if applicable)</small>

_____ **Illinois** _____
<small>City</small>   <small>State</small>   <small>ZIP</small>

County: _____   Township: _____   (___)___-_____ Ext:_____   (___)___-_____
<small>Daytime phone (include area code)</small>   <small>Fax (include area code)</small>

a Check the best *physical* description of this location: ☐ permanent   ☐ one that will change (*e.g.*, fairs, flea market)

b Check the best description of this location in regards to the city, village, or town limits listed above: ☐ inside   ☐ outside

Additional locations:

___ Check if you need to identify more locations. Attach a separate sheet containing all of the required information in a similar format.

Tell us your **total** number of Illinois locations. _____

Step 7: Identify your officers and owners

1   If your business is a **corporation, subchapter S corporation, or nonprofit organization,** print the legal name and SSN of each officer.

President

_____   ___ - ___ - ___
Legal name (Last, first, middle initial)   SSN

Vice-President

_____   ___ - ___ - ___
Legal name (Last, first, middle initial)   SSN

Secretary

_____   ___ - ___ - ___
Legal name (Last, first, middle initial)   SSN

Treasurer/Comptroller

_____   ___ - ___ - ___
Legal name (Last, first, middle initial)   SSN

2   Is your business a limited liability company?   ◯ yes   ◯ no
If **yes**, attach a list designating each manager and member by name and SSN or FEIN.

3   If your corporation is owned (over 50 percent) by another business, print the legal name and FEIN of the owning entity.

_____   ___ - _____
Owning entity name   FEIN

4   If your business is a **sole proprietorship, trust/estate, or partnership,** provide the legal name and SSN or FEIN of each owner, trustee/ executor, or general partner. **Note:** If you need to identify more, attach additional sheets with the required information in a similar format.

_____   ___ - ___ - ___
Legal name (Last, first, middle initial)   SSN

_____   ___ - ___ - ___
Legal name (Last, first, middle initial)   SSN

_____   ___ - _____
Business name of your owner   FEIN

Step 8: Tell us your mailing address

Complete this information **only** if you want your tax forms and correspondence mailed to an address other than the one listed in Step 3.
Note: All notices and bills (containing confidential tax information), refunds, certificates, and tax forms will be sent to this address.

_____   _____
In-care-of name. Please print.   Street address

_____   _____   _____
City   State   ZIP

Step 9: Sign below

1   **Person responsible for filing returns and paying taxes:** If in Step 4, "Withholding," "Sales," "Use," "Service," "Motor vehicle renting," or "Hotel/motel" was checked, the person(s) that will be personally responsible for filing returns and paying the tax due **must** complete the following information. This signature is required in addition to the signature in Item 2 of this step. The same person can sign both statements. **Note:** If you need to identify more, attach sheets with the required information in a similar format.

Check tax responsibility(ies):   ❑ Withholding   ❑ Sales, Use, or Services   ❑ Motor vehicle renting   ❑ Hotel/motel

_____   ___/___/___   _____   ___ - ___ - ___
Signature   Month Day Year   Printed name (Last, first, middle initial)   SSN

_____   _____   _____   _____
Street address   City   State   ZIP

Check tax responsibility(ies):   ❑ Withholding   ❑ Sales, Use, or Services   ❑ Motor vehicle renting   ❑ Hotel/motel

_____   ___/___/___   _____   ___ - ___ - ___
Signature   Month Day Year   Printed name (Last, first, middle initial)   SSN

_____   _____   _____   _____
Street address   City   State   ZIP

2   **This must be completed by the person completing this application and verifying the information.** Signature stamps are **not** acceptable. _Under penalties of perjury, I state that I have examined this information and, to the best of my knowledge, it is true, correct, and complete._

_____   _____   ___/___/___   _____
Signature   Title   Month Day Year   Printed name (Last, first, middle initial)

Step 10: Mail your application

If you attached additional sheets for any step in this application, please check here.   ❑

If you have any questions or need help completing your application, please call us weekdays between 8 a.m. and 5 p.m.

   Email: centreg@revenue.state.il.us   **Phone:** 217 785-3707   **Mail:** CENTRAL REGISTRATION DIVISION
                                                               ILLINOIS DEPARTMENT OF REVENUE
                                                               PO BOX 19476
                                                               SPRINGFIELD IL 62794-9476

State of Illinois
Department of Employment Security

33 South State Street
Chicago, Illinois 60603-2802

Report to Determine Liability Under the
Unemployment Insurance Act

Important: Every newly created employing unit shall file this report within 30 days of the date upon which it commences business. (820 ILCS 405/1800; 56 Ill. Adm. Code 2760.105)

If your only workers are domestic workers, complete a UI-1 DOM Report to Determine Liability for Domestic Employment Under the Unemployment Insurance Act instead of this form.

1. a. Employer Name _____

   Doing Business As _____

   b. What is your primary business activity in Illinois? _____

   c. What is your principal product or service? (See examples on pages 4 and 5 of the instructions .) _____

   d. If you have more than one product or service, list the top two and indicate the percentage that each contributes to your total revenue:

   _____   % Sales or receipts _____

   _____   % Sales or receipts _____

   e. If you know your NAICS Code, enter it here. _____ If you do not know your NAICS Code, see instructions.

   f. Primary Address _____

   (Address - Number & Street or Rural Route)

City/Town	State	ZIP	County	Country	Telephone Number

   g. Business Address _____

   (Actual physical location - Number & Street or Rural Route - if different from Primary Address

City/Town	State	ZIP	County	Country	Telephone Number

   h. Do you lease any of your employees (see 56 Ill. Adm. Code 2732.306)?   Yes ☐   No ☐

   If yes, provide the Leasing Company's name, address, telephone number and Unemployment Insurance account number if . available. _____

2. Enter any employer account number previously assigned to you by the Illinois Department of Employment Security.

_____

3. Identification number under which you file Employer's Quarterly Federal Tax Return (Form 941) _____

4. a. Type of Organization (Check One): ☐ Sole Proprietor ☐ Partnership ☐ Corporation ☐ Other (Explain, e.g., Limited Liability Company, Trust, Association, Receivership) _____

b. If a corporation, date incorporated _____ State in which incorporated _____

c. Has any form of remuneration, including dividends, been paid to the officers of this corporation? ☐ Yes ☐ No

d. If you are an LLC, are there any individuals performing services for the organization other than the member manager(s)?

☐ Yes ☐ No

How is the member manager(s) treated for federal tax purposes? ☐ Sole Proprietor ☐ Partner ☐ Other (Explain)

_____

5. Enter the required information for sole proprietor or each partner or officer:

Name	Title	Social Security No.	Residence Address	Residence Telephone No.

6. a. Date you first began employing workers in Illinois _____ / _____ / _____

b. Date of your first payroll in Illinois _____ / _____ / _____

c. Date you ceased employing workers in Illinois (if applicable) _____ / _____ / _____

7. Did you acquire your Illinois business or any portion of it by purchase, reorganization or a change in entity; for example, a change from sole proprietor to corporation? ☐ Yes ☐ No If yes, complete the form **UI-1 S&P, Report to Determine Succession**. Please complete the remainder of the questions on this form as well. Responses to the questions on this form should reflect information relative to the operation of your business **after** the date of acquisition.

8. a. Check here ☐ if you employ, have employed or expect to employ one or more workers in domestic service in a private home, local college club or local chapter of a college fraternity or sorority. Otherwise, skip to 9.

b. Check here ☐ if during the current calendar year or the preceding four calendar years, there was any quarter in which you paid wages of $1,000 or more for domestic service in a private home, local college club or local chapter of a college fraternity or sorority. Otherwise, skip to (c).

In the space below, circle the first such quarter during that period and indicate the year in which it occurred.

Jan.-Mar. _____ (year), April-June _____ (year), July-Sept. _____ (year), Oct.-Dec. _____ (year).

c. Check here ☐ if you expect to pay wages of $1,000 or more for domestic services in a private home, local college club or local chapter of a college fraternity or sorority during any quarter within the current calendar year.

9. a. Check here ☐ if you employ, have employed or expect to employ one or more workers to perform agricultural labor. Otherwise, skip to 10.

b. Check here ☐ if, during the current calendar year or the preceding four calendar years, there was any quarter in which you paid wages of $20,000 or more for agricultural labor. Otherwise, skip to (c).

In the space below, circle the first such quarter during that period and indicate the year in which it occurred.

Jan.-Mar. _____ (year), April-June _____ (year), July-Sept. _____ (year), Oct.-Dec. _____ (year).

c. Check here ☐ if, you expect to pay wages of $20,000 or more for agricultural labor during any quarter within the current calendar year.

d. Check here ☐ if, during the period including the current calendar year and the four preceding calendar years, there was any calendar year during which you employed 10 or more individuals to perform agricultural labor for at least 20 weeks (whether or not consecutive). Otherwise, skip to (e).

In the space below, indicate the first such year and, for that year, circle the quarter that included the 20th week within which you employed 10 more individuals to perform agricultural labor.

April-June _____ (year), July-Sept. _____ (year), Oct.-Dec. _____ (year).

e. Check here ☐ if you expect to employ 10 or more individuals to perform agricultural labor for at least 20 weeks (whether or not consecutive) during the current calendar year.

f. If you checked (b), (c), (d) or (e), does your business include any retail sales activity? ☐ Yes ☐ No

10. a. Check here ☐ if you are a religious, charitable, educational or other nonprofit organization, as defined in Section 501(c)(3) of the Internal Revenue Code and attach the federal exemption letter. Otherwise, skip to 11.

b. Check here ☐ if, during the period including the current calendar year and the four preceding calendar years, there was any calendar year during which you have had 4 or more individuals performing services in employment in each of at least 20 weeks (whether or not consecutive). Otherwise, skip to (c).

In the space below, indicate the first such year and, for that year, circle the quarter that included the 20th week within which you had 4 or more individuals performing services in employment.

April-June _____ (year), July-Sept. _____ (year), Oct.-Dec. _____ (year).

c. Check here ☐ if you expect to have 4 or more individuals performing services in employment in each of at least 20 weeks (whether or not consecutive) during the current calendar year.

d. Check here ☐ if you wish to be a reimbursable employer. This does not apply to you if you did not check (b) or (c). If you wish to be a reimbursable employer, a **Reimburse Benefits in Lieu of Paying Contributions (UI-5NP)** form will be mailed to you. You must complete this form and return it to this Department.

11. a. Check here ☐ if there was any calendar quarter in either the current calendar year or the preceding four calendar years in which you paid wages of at least $1,500 for services in employment. Otherwise, skip to (b).

In the space below, circle the first such quarter during that period and indicate the year in which it occurred.

Jan.-Mar. _____ (year), April-June _____ (year), July-Sept. _____ (year), Oct.-Dec. _____ (year).

b. Check here ☐ if, within any quarter within the current calendar year, you expect to pay wages of $1,500 or more for services in employment. Please check the appropriate quarter.

Jan.-Mar. ☐ April-June ☐ July-Sept. ☐ Oct.-Dec. ☐

12. a. Check here ☐ if, during the period including the current calendar year and the four preceding calendar years, there was any calendar year in which you have had 1 or more individuals performing services in employment in each of at least 20 weeks (whether or not consecutive). Otherwise, skip to (b).

In the space below, indicate the first such year and, for that year, circle the quarter that included the 20th week within which you had 1 or more individuals performing services in employment.

April-June _____ (year), July-Sept. _____ (year), Oct.-Dec. _____ (year).

b. Check here ☐ if you expect to have 1 or more individuals performing services in employment in each of at least 20 weeks (whether or not consecutive) during the current calendar year.

13. Have you incurred liability under the Federal Unemployment Tax Act (in any state) for any of the last 4 years?

☐ Yes ☐ No If Yes, indicate the year(s) for which you incurred such liability. _____

14. Are there any persons who performed services for you within the current calendar year or the four preceding calendar years, but whom you do not consider to be employees for any reason, including but not limited to, individuals you regard as independent contractors? ☐ Yes ☐ No

If Yes, attach a sheet stating the number of such persons and give details as to the type of service and date such services were performed.

15. Complete the following section only if you have multiple worksites in Illinois.

The following information is required for reporting statistical data to the federal government. Please complete the information as completely and accurately as possible.

Enter below the required information for each place of business (worksite) in Illinois (use additional sheets if necessary). Read instructions carefully. If any worksite is engaged in performing support services for other units of the company, please indicate the nature of the activity in "section C-Primary Activity." Examples of support services are Central Administrative Office, Research, Development or Testing, or Storage (warehouse).

a) Physical Location of Each Establishment (Street, City, zip code)	b) County	c) Primary Activity	d) Average Number of Employees

16. If you are determined not liable, based upon the provisions of the Unemployment Insurance Act, you may voluntarily elect coverage under 820 ILCS 405/205 H. Please indicate if you want voluntary coverage. ☐ If checked, we will mail you form **UI-1B, Voluntary Election of Coverage**. Please complete that form and return it to this Department.

Certification: I hereby certify that the information contained in this report and any sheets attached hereto is true and correct. This report must be signed by owner, partner, officer or authorized agent within the employing enterprise. If signed by any other person, a power of attorney must be attached.

Employer Name _____

Signed by _____ Date _____

Title _____

-- Do not write in the area below. For Department use only --

This state agency is requesting information that is necessary to accomplish the statutory purpose as outlined under 820 ILCS 405/100-3200. Disclosure of this information is Required. Failure to disclose this information may result in statutorily prescribed liability and sanction, including penalties and interest.	Area	Industry	Source _____ Rec'd Date _____ A/C _____ NL _____ Liab. Date _____ Qtr _____ Sec _____ Analyst _____ Date _____

UI-1 INSTRUCTIONS

Illinois Department of Employment Security

INSTRUCTIONS FOR PREPARATION OF UI-1
REPORT TO DETERMINE LIABILITY UNDER
THE ILLINOIS UNEMPLOYMENT INSURANCE ACT

An employing unit must file the Report to Determine Liability even though it may not be liable for payments under the Illinois Unemployment Insurance Act (the Act).

Read the instructions below carefully.

The Guide to the Illinois Unemployment Insurance Act is available on our web site at www.ides.state.il.us. It will assist you in filling out the form.

Type or print in ink your answer to each item that applies. If you need more space, attach additional sheets but mark each "Supplement to UI-1" and sign and date it. Return the completed, signed original to this Department immediately. Retain a copy for your files.

Item No.

1. a. Legal name of employer: If a Sole Proprietor, the owner's name; If a Partnership, the partners' names and type of partnership, such as a general partnership, limited partnership or joint venture; if a Corporation, the corporate name with the word "Corporation," "Incorporated," "Company," "Limited," or its abbreviations; if a Limited Liability Company, the name must contain the phrase Limited Liability Company, or its abbreviation (LLC or L.L.C.). Doing Business as: Enter the trade name of your business. If there is no trade name being used, leave this item blank.

   b. Enter the business activity that produces your major source of income.

   c. & d. List products manufactured, commodities sold, activities engaged in or type of services rendered. See examples of products or services listed after instructions.

   e. **NAICS Code:**
   The North American Industry Classification System (NAICS) was developed jointly by the U.S., Canada and Mexico to improve comparative statistics about business activity across North America. Please enter the 6-digit NAICS code that best describes your primary business activity.

   To find the NAICS code for your business activity, you may contact the U.S. Census Bureau at 1-888-75NAICS or by E-mail at naics@census.gov; or you may go to http://www.census.gov/cpcd/www/drnaics.htm.

   f. Enter the address to which your business mail should be delivered. The Department will send correspondence to this address unless you specify special handling for certain forms (See form UI-1M). If this address is different from the address where you conduct your business activities in Illinois, then you must also provide your actual physical location in the Business Address in g.

   g. Enter the address of the physical location (not a post office box) of your Illinois business if this is different from your primary address. If there is no base of operations in Illinois, enter the home address of the primary Illinois employee.

   h. Employee Leasing Company means an individual or an entity which contracts with you to supply or assume responsibility for personnel management of one or more workers to perform services for you on an on-going basis rather than a temporary help arrangement.

UI-1 INST. Pg. 2

3. Enter the **FEDERAL EMPLOYER IDENTIFICATION NUMBER (FEIN)** assigned by the Internal Revenue Service for reporting Social Security, Withholding Tax and Federal Unemployment Tax.

6. a. Enter the date on which you first began employing workers, not the date when wages were first paid.
   b. Enter the date when you first paid wages in the State of Illinois.

8. "Domestic service" means service of a household nature, including service performed by cooks, waiters, butlers, housekeepers, housemothers, governesses, maids, valets, babysitters, janitors, launderers, furnace men, caretakers, handymen, gardeners, footmen, grooms and chauffeurs of automobiles for family use. Service not of a household nature, such as by a private secretary, nurse, tutor or librarian, is not "domestic" service.

   A "private home" is the fixed place of abode of the individual or family for whom the worker is performing services. A separate and distinct dwelling unit maintained by an individual as a residence, such as a hotel room, boat or trailer, can be a "private home." A room or suite in a nursing home can be a "private home," provided that the facts and circumstances of the particular case indicate that such room or suite is, in fact, the place where the individual retains his residence. A home utilized primarily for the purpose of supplying board or lodging to the public as a business enterprise is not a "private home."

   A "local college club" or "local chapter of a college fraternity or sorority" does not include an alumni club or chapter.

9. "Agricultural labor" means all services performed:

   A. On a farm, in the employ of any person, in connection with cultivating the soil or in connection with raising or harvesting any agricultural or horticultural commodity, including the raising, shearing, feeding, caring for, training and management of live stock, bees, poultry and fur-bearing animals and wildlife;

   B. In the employ of the owner or tenant or other operator of a farm, in connection with the operation, management, conservation, improvement or maintenance of such farm and its tools and equipment;

   C. In connection with the ginning of cotton, or the operation or maintenance of ditches, canals, reservoirs or waterways not owned or operated for profit, used exlusively for supplying and storing water for farming purposes;

   D. In the employ of the operator of a farm, or of a group of operators of farms (or a cooperative organization of which such operators are members), in handling, planting , drying, packing, packaging, processing, freezing, grading, storing or delivering to storage or to market or to a carrier for transportation to market, in its unmanufactured state, any agricultural or horticultural commodity; but only if such operator or operators produced more than one-half of the commodity with respect to which such service is performed. The provisions of this subsection shall not be deemed to be applicable with respect to service performed in connection with commercial canning or commercial freezing or in connection with any agricultural or horticultural commodity after its delivery to a terminal market for distribution for consumption.

   For purposes of questions 9 (d) and (e), count each week in which you have employed or will employ 10 or more individuals to perform agricultural labor, whether or not they all worked or will work at the same time during that week and whether or not you employed or will employ the same individuals in each week.

   "Week" means the seven day period, Sunday through Saturday.

10. For purposes of questions 10 (b) and (c), count each week in which you had or expect to have 4 or more individuals performing services in employment, whether or not they all worked or will work at the same time during that week and whether or not you employed or will employ the same individuals in each week.

    "Week" means the seven day period, Sunday through Saturday.

    "Employment" means any service performed by an individual for an employing unit, unless the Unemployment Insurance Act expressly excludes the service from the definition of "employment." It includes service in interstate commerce and service on land which is owned, held or possessed by the United States, and includes all services performed by an officer of a business corporation, without regard to whether such services are executive, managerial or manual in nature, and without regard to whether such officer is or is not a stockholder or a member of the board of directors of the corporation.

UI-1 INST. Pg. 3

Benefit Reimbursable Option:
Each nonprofit organization subject to the Act may, if certain conditions are met, elect to be a reimbursable employer by agreeing, in lieu of paying contributions, to reimburse the State for the actual amount of regular benefits and one half the amount of extended benefits that are charged to it.

11. "Employment" means any service performed by an individual for an employing unit, unless the Unemployment Insurance Act expressly excludes the service from the definition of "employment." It includes service in interstate commerce and service on land which is owned, held or possessed by the United States, and includes all services performed by an officer of a business corporation, without regard to whether such services are executive, managerial or manual in nature, and without regard to whether such officer is or is not a stockholder or a member of the board of directors of the corporation.

12. "Employment" means any service performed by an individual for an employing unit, unless the Unemployment Insurance Act expressly excludes the service from the definition of "employment." It includes service in interstate commerce and service on land which is owned, held or possessed by the United States, and includes all services performed by an officer of a business corporation, without regard to whether such services are executive, managerial or manual in nature, and without regard to whether such officer is or is not a stockholder or a member of the board of directors of the corporation.

For purposes of questions 12 (a) and (b), count each week in which you had or expect to have 1 or more individuals performing services in employment, whether or not they all worked or will work at the same time during that week and whether or not you employed or will employ the same individuals in each week.

"Week" means the seven day period, Sunday through Saturday.

13. If you have been found liable for Federal Unemployment taxes, you become immediately liable to Illinois with your first Illinois payroll.

15. a&b. For two or more places of business in Illinois, enter the number and street or rural route, the city or town, zip code and the Illinois county in which each place of business is located.

d. The average number employed at each address. Include all classes of employees (i.e. administrative, supervisory, clerical, sales, installation, construction, etc.).

16. If an employing unit does not meet the legal definition of employer for unemployment insurance purposes, the employing unit can elect to be fully subject under the Illinois Unemployment Insurance Act with the permission of the Director. An employing unit electing such coverage will not be able to terminate its coverage until January 1 of any calendar year subsequent to two such years of coverage.

If you should need further assistance in filling out this form, you may contact the Employer Hot Line Section at telephone number (312) 793-4880 or (800) 247-4984.

Please make a copy of the completed UI-1 for your records.

EXAMPLES OF PRODUCT OR SERVICE INFORMATION

AGRICULTURAL, FORESTRY, FISHING, AND HUNTING includes establishments primarily engaged in agricultural production including growing crops, raising animals, harvesting timber and harvesting fish and other animals from farms, ranches or the animals' natural habitats.

MINING includes the extraction of naturally occurring mineral solids, such as coal and ore; liquid minerals, such as crude petroleum; and gases, such as natural gas; and beneficiating (e.g., crushing, screening, washing and flotation) and other preparation at the mine site, or as part of mining activity.

UTILITIES includes generating, transmitting and/or distributing electricity, gas, steam and water and removing sewage through a permanent infrastructure of lines, mains and pipe.

CONSTRUCTION includes those establishments which perform new work, additions, alterations, installations or maintenance and repairs. Heavy construction, other than buildings, are located here, e.g. streets and highways, sewers and drainage. This sector also includes contractors, subcontractors and specialty trade contractors.

MANUFACTURING includes the mechanical, physical or chemical transformation of material, substances or components into new products. The new product may be finished and ready for utilization or consumption, or it may be semifinished to become input for an establishment engaged in further manufacturing.

WHOLESALE TRADE establishments or individuals are primarily engaged in the selling of merchandise to other businesses. The wholesale merchant has possession of the merchandise being sold and typically operates out of a warehouse. An agent / broker arranges for the purchase or sale of goods owned by others. Business to business electronic markets, i.e. via the internet, are also included.

RETAIL TRADE are those engaged in retailing merchandise generally in small quantities to the general public and providing services incidental to the sale of the merchandise.

TRANSPORTATION includes industries providing transportation of passengers and cargo; warehousing and storage of goods; scenic and sightseeing transportation and support activities related to modes of transportation.

INFORMATION sector establishments are involved in distributing information and cultural products, providing the means to transmit these products as data or communications, and processing data. Examples include newspaper, book and software publishers; television, radio and internet broadcasters; wire and wireless telecommunications; cable services, data processing and related services and internet service providers.

FINANCE AND INSURANCE includes establishments that are involved in the creation, liquidation or change in ownership of financial assets and/or facilitating financial transactions. Examples are banks; savings institutions; credit unions; personal credit institutions; insurance carriers, agents and brokers; commodity and security brokers; and health and welfare funds.

REAL ESTATE AND RENTAL AND LEASING includes establishments involved in renting, leasing, or otherwise allowing the use of tangible (real estate and equipment) or intangible assets (patents and trademarks) and providing related services.

PROFESSIONAL, SCIENTIFIC, AND TECHNICAL SERVICES are those establishments that specialize in performing professional, scientific and technical services for others. These activities require a high degree of expertise and training.

MANAGEMENT OF COMPANIES AND ENTERPRISES are those businesses engaged in the holding of securities of companies and enterprises for the purpose of owning a controlling interest or influencing management decisions. Also included are establishments that administer, oversee and manage other establishments of the same company or enterprise and normally undertake strategic, organizational planning and decision- making roles.

UI-1 INST. Pg. 5

ADMINISTRATIVE AND SUPPORT AND WASTE MANAGEMENT AND REMEDIATION SERVICES include activities related to performing routine support activities for the day-to-day operations of other organizations. Other activities included in this sector are security and surveillance services, cleaning, waste collection and waste disposal systems.

EDUCATIONAL SERVICES include establishments that provide instruction, training and support services in a wide variety of subjects. This instruction and training is provided by specialized establishments, such as schools, colleges, universities, and training centers. Also included are trade schools, apprenticeship training, professional and management development training and educational testing services.

HEALTH CARE AND SOCIAL ASSISTANCE include businesses involved in providing health care and social assistance for individuals.

ARTS, ENTERTAINMENT, AND RECREATION are organizations that are operating or providing services to meet varied cultural, entertainment, and recreational interests of their patrons.

ACCOMMODATION AND FOOD SERVICES are responsible for providing customers with lodging and/or preparing meals, snacks, and beverages for immediate consumption.

OTHER SERVICES (EXCEPT PUBLIC ADMINISTRATION) include organizations that are responsible for providing services, not elsewhere specified, including repairs, religious activities, grant making, advocacy, laundry and dry-cleaning services, personal care, death care, pet care, domestic service and other personal services.

PUBLIC ADMINISTRATION includes the administration, management, and oversight of public programs by Federal, State, and local governments.

This page is intentionally left blank.

Illinois Withholding Allowance Worksheet

General Information

Complete this worksheet to figure your total withholding allowances.

Everyone must complete Step 1.

Complete Step 2 if
  • you (or your spouse) are age 65 or older or legally blind, or
  • you wrote an amount on Line 4 of the Deductions and Adjustments Worksheet for federal Form W-4.

If you have more than one job or your spouse works, you should figure the total number of allowances you are entitled to claim. Your withholding usually will be more accurate if you claim all of your allowances on the Form IL-W-4 for the highest-paying job and claim zero on all of your other IL-W-4 forms.

You may reduce the number of allowances or request that your employer withhold an additional amount from your pay, which may help avoid having too little tax withheld.

Step 1: Figure your basic personal allowances (including allowances for dependents)

Check all that apply:
  ☐ No one else can claim me as a dependent.
  ☐ I can claim my spouse as a dependent.

1 Write the total number of boxes you checked.   **1** _____

2 Write the number of dependents (other than you or your spouse) you will claim on your tax return.   **2** _____

3 Add Lines 1 and 2. Write the result. This is the total number of basic personal allowances to which you are **entitled**.   **3** _____

4 If you want to have additional Illinois Income Tax withheld from your pay, you may reduce the number of basic personal allowances or have an additional amount withheld. Write the total number of basic personal allowances you elect to claim on Line 4 and on Form IL-W-4, Line 1.   **4** _____

Step 2: Figure your additional allowances

Check all that apply:
  ☐ I am 65 or older.   ☐ I am legally blind.
  ☐ My spouse is 65 or older.   ☐ My spouse is legally blind.

5 Write the total number of boxes you checked.   **5** _____

6 Write any amount that you reported on Line 4 of the Deductions and Adjustments Worksheet for federal Form W-4.   **6** _____

7 Divide Line 6 by 1,000. Round to the nearest whole number. Write the result on Line 7.   **7** _____

8 Add Lines 5 and 7. Write the result. This is the total number of additional allowances to which you are **entitled**.   **8** _____

9 If you want to have additional Illinois Income Tax withheld from your pay, you may reduce the number of additional allowances or have an additional amount withheld. Write the total number of additional allowances you elect to claim on Line 9 and on Form IL-W-4, Line 2.   **9** _____

Note: If you have non-wage income and you expect to owe Illinois Income Tax on that income, you may choose to have an additional amount withheld from your pay. On Line 3 of Form IL-W-4, write the additional amount you want your employer to withhold.

✂ — — — — — — — —   Cut here and give the certificate to your employer. Keep the top portion for your records.   — — — — — — — — ✂

Illinois Department of Revenue
IL-W-4 Employee's Illinois Withholding Allowance Certificate

___ ___ ___ - ___ ___ - ___ ___ ___ ___
Social Security number

_____
Name

_____
Street address

_____
City   State   ZIP

Check the box if you are exempt from federal and Illinois Withholding Income Tax. ☐

1 Write the total number of basic allowances that you are claiming (Step 1, Line 4, of the worksheet). **1** _____

2 Write the total number of additional allowances that you are claiming (Step 2, Line 9, of the worksheet). **2** _____

3 Write the additional amount you want withheld (deducted) from each pay. **3** _____

I certify that I am entitled to the number of withholding allowances claimed on this certificate.

_____
Your signature   Date

Employer: Keep this certificate with your records. If you have referred the employee's federal certificate to the Internal Revenue Service (IRS) and the IRS has notified you to disregard it, you may also be required to disregard this certificate. Even if you are not required to refer the employee's federal certificate to the IRS, you may still be required to refer this certificate to the Illinois Department of Revenue for inspection. See Illinois Income Tax Regulations 86 Ill. Adm. Code 100.7110.

This form is authorized as outlined by the Illinois Income Tax Act. Disclosure of this information is REQUIRED. Failure to provide information could result in a penalty. This form has been approved by the Forms Management Center.   IL-492-0039

IL-W-4 (R-12/05)

Illinois Department of Revenue

Form IL-W-4 Employee's Illinois Withholding Allowance Certificate and Instructions

Who must complete this form?

If you are an employee, you must complete this form so your employer can withhold the correct amount of Illinois Income Tax from your pay. The amount withheld from your pay depends, in part, on the number of allowances you claim on this form.

Even if you claimed exemption from withholding on your federal Form W-4, U.S. Employee's Withholding Allowance Certificate, because you do not expect to owe any federal income tax, you may be required to have Illinois Income Tax withheld from your pay. If you are claiming exempt status (see Page 8, IL-700) from Illinois Withholding you must check the exempt status box on the IL-W-4.

Note: If you do not file a completed Form IL-W-4 with your employer, if you fail to sign the form or to include all necessary information, or if you alter the form, your employer must withhold Illinois income tax on the entire amount of your compensation, without allowing any exemptions.

When must I file?

You must file Form IL-W-4 when Illinois Income Tax is required to be withheld from compensation that you receive as an employee. You should complete this form and give it to your employer on or before the date you start working for your employer. You may file a new Form IL-W-4 any time your withholding allowances increase. If the number of your previously claimed allowances decreases, you **must** file a new Form IL-W-4 within 10 days. However, the death of a spouse or a dependent does not affect your withholding allowances until the next tax year.

When does my Form IL-W-4 take effect?

If you do not already have a Form IL-W-4 on file with this employer, this form will be effective for the first payment of compensation made to you after this form is filed. If you already have a Form IL-W-4 on file with this employer, your employer may allow any change you file on this form to become effective immediately, but is not required by law to change your withholding until the first payment of compensation made to you after the first day of the next calendar quarter (that is, January 1, April 1, July 1 or October 1) that falls at least 30 days after the date you file the change with your employer.

Example: If you have a baby and file a new Form IL-W-4 with your employer to claim an additional exemption for the baby, your employer may immediately change the withholding for all future payments of compensation. However, if you file the new form on September 1, your employer does not have to change your withholding until the first payment of compensation made to you after October 1. If you file the new form on September 2, your employer does not have to change your withholding until the first payment of compensation made to you after December 31.

How long is Form IL-W-4 valid?

Your Form IL-W-4 remains valid until a new form you have filed takes effect or until your employer is required by the Department to disregard it. Your employer is required to disregard your Form IL-W-4 if you claim total exemption from Illinois income tax withholding, but you have not filed a federal Form W-4 claiming total exemption. Also, if the Internal Revenue Service has instructed your employer to disregard your federal Form W-4, your employer must also disregard your Form IL-W-4. Finally, if you claim 15 or more exemptions on your Form IL-W-4 without claiming at least the same number of exemptions on your federal Form W-4, and your employer is not required to refer your federal Form W-4 to the Internal Revenue Service for review, your employer must refer your Form IL-W-4 to the Department for review. In that case, your Form IL-W-4 will be effective unless and until the Department notifies your employer to disregard it.

What is an "exemption"?

An "exemption" is a dollar amount on which you do not have to pay Illinois Income Tax. Therefore, your employer will withhold Illinois Income Tax based on your compensation minus the exemptions to which you are entitled.

What is an "allowance"?

The dollar amount that is exempt from Illinois Income Tax is based on the number of allowances you claim on this form. As an employee, you receive one allowance unless you are claimed as a dependent on another person's tax return (e.g., your parents claim you as a dependent on their tax return). If you are married, you may claim additional allowances for your spouse and any dependents that you are entitled to claim for federal income tax purposes. You also will receive additional allowances if you or your spouse are age 65 or older, or if you or your spouse are legally blind.

How do I figure the correct number of allowances?

Complete the worksheet on the back of this page to figure the correct number of allowances you are entitled to claim. Give your completed Form IL-W-4 to your employer. Keep the worksheet for your records.

Note: If you have more than one job or your spouse works, you should figure the total number of allowances you are entitled to claim. Your withholding usually will be more accurate if you claim all of your allowances on the Form IL-W-4 for the highest-paying job and claim zero on all of your other IL-W-4 forms.

What if I underpay my tax?

If the amount withheld from your compensation is not enough to cover your tax liability for the year, (e.g., you have non-wage income, such as interest or dividends), you may reduce the number of allowances or request that your employer withhold an additional amount from your pay. Otherwise, you may owe additional tax at the end of the year. If you do not have enough tax withheld from your pay, and you owe more than $500 tax at the end of the year, you may owe a late-payment penalty. You should either increase the amount you have withheld from your pay, or you must make estimated tax payments.

You may be assessed a **late-payment penalty** if your required estimated payments are not paid in full by the due dates.

Note: You may still owe this penalty for an earlier quarter, even if you pay enough tax later to make up the underpayment from a previous quarter.

For additional information on penalties, see Publication 103, Uniform Penalties and Interest. Call **1 800 356-6302** to receive a copy of this publication.

Where do I get help?

- Visit our web site at **tax.illinois.gov**
- Call our Taxpayer Assistance Division at **1 800 732-8866** or **217 782-3336**
- Call our TDD (telecommunications device for the deaf) at **1 800 544-5304**
- Write to
  **ILLINOIS DEPARTMENT OF REVENUE
  PO BOX 19044
  SPRINGFIELD IL 62794-9044**

Illinois Department of Revenue

ST-44 Illinois Use Tax Return

Rev 02
Form 019
RC NS DP CA E S __/__/__

Step 1: Identify yourself

0775-0005

Your name_____

Number and street_____

City, state, ZIP_____

Daytime phone number (_____)_____-_____

Social Security number _____ - ____ - _____
or
FEIN _____ - _____

Step 2: Figure the Illinois Use Tax

(Please round figures to whole dollars.)

1 Write the date of your last purchase of general merchandise   ___/___/_____
   If you are filing on an annual basis, write the year only. Otherwise, write the entire date.   Month   Day   Year

1a Write the total cost of general merchandise
    you purchased outside of Illinois to use in Illinois.   1a _____ |

1b Multiply Line 1a by 6.25% (.0625).   1b _____|_____

2a Write the total cost of qualifying food, drugs, medical appliances,
    and diabetic supplies, such as insulin and syringes, you
    purchased outside of Illinois to use in Illinois.   2a _____|_____

2b Multiply Line 2a by 1% (.01).   2b _____|_____

3 Add Lines 1b and 2b. **This is your use tax on purchases.**   3 _____|_____

4 Write the amount of sales tax you paid to another state (not to another country)
   on the items included on Lines 1a and 2a.   4 _____|_____

Step 3: Figure the total amount you owe

(Please round figures to whole dollars.)

5 Compare Line 3 and Line 4. If Line 4 is equal to or greater than Line 3, you do not
   owe use tax. If Line 3 is greater than Line 4, subtract Line 4 from Line 3.

   This is the total amount you owe.   ➡   5 _____|_____

Step 4: Sign below

Under penalties of perjury, I state that I have examined this return and, to the best of my knowledge, it is true, correct, and complete.

_____
Your signature   Date

See next page for instructions.   ➡

- **DO NOT attach your check OR this form to any other return.**
- **MAKE your check payable to the "Illinois Department of Revenue."**
- **MAIL all other forms separately.**
- **WRITE your SSN and "ST-44" on your check and attach it to this form (ST-44).**
- **MAIL this form (ST-44) to:**   **ILLINOIS DEPARTMENT OF REVENUE**
                               RETAILERS' OCCUPATION TAX
                               SPRINGFIELD, IL 62776-0001

This form is authorized as outlined by the Use Tax Act. Disclosure of this information is REQUIRED. Failure to provide it may result in a penalty. This form has been approved by the Forms Management Center.   IL 492-2302

Use Tax Information and Instructions for Form ST-44

What is a use tax?

A use tax is a tax upon the privilege of using tangible personal property in Illinois. It is designed to distribute the tax burden fairly among Illinois consumers and to assure fair competition between Illinois businesses and out-of-state businesses. Illinois law requires you to pay tax at the Illinois rate when you buy an item from another state or country to use in Illinois.

Is Illinois increasing its efforts to collect use taxes?

Yes, Illinois is increasing its efforts to collect use taxes. Illinois shares sales information with other states and bills Illinois residents for unpaid tax, penalty, and interest. Illinois also gathers information on overseas purchases from the U.S. Customs Service. (Use tax is due whether or not an item has to be declared or is subject to duty tax.) Illinois also encourages out-of-state businesses to register and collect the tax voluntarily as a convenience to their customers. If they do not, we can bill their Illinois customers directly.

What forms are used to report and pay use tax on items purchased from another state or country?

- cigarettes — Form RC-44
- motor vehicles, watercraft, aircraft, or trailers purchased from an out-of-state dealer — Form RUT-25
- purchases made by registered retailers or servicepersons — Form ST-1
- general merchandise (not otherwise specified) and food, drugs, and medical appliances — Form ST-44

What forms are used to report and pay use tax due on certain transactions that occur in Illinois?

- motor vehicle acquired by non-retail purchase — Form RUT-50
- aircraft or watercraft acquired by gift, transfer, or non-retail purchase — Form RUT-75

When do I owe Illinois Use Tax?

You owe Illinois Use Tax and must complete Form ST-44 if the person or business from which you bought general merchandise or food, drugs, and medical appliances did not collect Illinois Sales Tax (*e.g.*, purchases from catalogs, TV advertisements, magazines, the Internet); **and**

- the items purchased are taxable in Illinois;
- you will use or consume these items in Illinois; **and**
- you have not yet paid Illinois Sales Tax or an equivalent amount to another state.

If you paid the Illinois Use Tax due for cigarette purchases when you filed Form RC-44, do not include the cost from those cigarette purchases in the figure you report on Line 1a.

Note: Some out-of-state businesses collect Illinois Sales Tax, and their customers pay the tax just as they would pay state sales tax to an Illinois retailer. You can check your receipt or invoice to determine if Illinois Sales Tax was collected.

When paying use tax on Form ST-44, may I take credit for taxes paid to another country or state?

If you purchase any item from **another country**, you must pay Illinois the full use tax rate.

If you purchase an item from **another state** and you properly paid tax to the other state, you may take credit for the tax paid. If you paid tax at a rate lower than the Illinois rate, you must pay Illinois the difference.

When is Form ST-44 due?

If your total tax liability for the year is

- $600 or less, you may pay the tax for the entire year (January 1 through December 31) by filing Form ST-44 on or before April 15 of the following year; or
- greater than $600, you must pay the tax by the last day of the month following the month in which the purchase was made.

Is there anything else I need to know about completing this form?

- When writing your figures, please use whole dollar amounts by dropping amounts of less than 50 cents and increasing amounts of 50 cents or more to the next higher dollar.
- MAKE your check payable to the "Illinois Department of Revenue."
- DO NOT attach your check OR this form to any other return.
- WRITE your SSN and "ST-44" on your check and attach it to this form (ST-44).
- MAIL all other forms separately.
- MAIL this form (ST-44) to:
  ILLINOIS DEPARTMENT OF REVENUE
  RETAILERS' OCCUPATION TAX
  SPRINGFIELD, IL 62776-0001
- KEEP a copy of your completed return for your records.

What if I do not file my return or pay the use tax due on time?

You owe a **late filing penalty** if you do not file a processable return by the due date and a **late payment penalty** if you do not pay the amount you owe by the due date of the return.

You can also be assessed an **under reporting penalty** if you do not report your entire liability by the due date of your return, a **bad check penalty** if your remittance is not honored by your financial institution, and a **cost of collection fee** if you do not pay the amount you owe within 30 days of the date printed on an assessment.

We will bill you for any amounts owed.

For more information, see Publication 103, Penalties and Interest.

How do I get help?

If you have questions, you may

- visit our web site at **tax.illinois.gov**
- call our Taxpayer Assistance Division at 1 800 732-8866 or 217 782-3336
- call our TDD (telecommunications device for the deaf) at 1 800 544-5304
- write us at
  ILLINOIS DEPARTMENT OF REVENUE
  PO BOX 19044
  SPRINGFIELD IL 62794-9044

ST-44 back (R-12/05)

Illinois Department of Revenue

CRT-61 Certificate of Resale

Step 1: Identify the seller

1 Name _____

2 Business address _____

_____
City   State   Zip

Step 2: Identify the purchaser

3 Name _____

4 Business address _____

_____
City   State   Zip

5 Complete the information below. Check only one box.

☐ The purchaser is registered as a retailer with the Illinois
Department of Revenue. __ __ __ __ - __ __ __ __
                                  Registration number

☐ The purchaser is registered as a reseller with the Illinois
Department of Revenue. __ __ __ __ - __ __ __ __
                                  Resale number

☐ The purchaser is authorized to do business out-of-state and
will resell and deliver property only to purchasers located
outside the state of Illinois. See Line 5 instructions.

Step 3: Describe the property

6 Describe the property that is being purchased for resale or
list the invoice number and the date of purchase.

_____

_____

_____

Step 4: Complete for blanket certificates

7 Complete the information below. Check only one box.

☐ I am the identified purchaser, and I certify that all of the
purchases that I make from this seller are for resale.

☐ I am the identified purchaser, and I certify that the following
percentage, _____ %, of all of the purchases that I make
from this seller are for resale.

Step 5: Purchaser's signature

I certify that I am purchasing the property described in Step 3
from the stated seller for the purpose of resale.

_____ __ /__ /__ __ __ __
Purchaser's signature   Date

**Note: It is the seller's responsibility to verify that the
purchaser's Illinois registration or Illinois resale number is
valid and active.**

General information

When is a Certificate of Resale required?

Generally, a Certificate of Resale is required for proof that no tax
is due on any sale that is made tax-free as a sale for resale. The
purchaser, at the seller's request, must provide the information
that is needed to complete this certificate.

Who keeps the Certificate of Resale?

The seller must keep the certificate. We may request it as proof
that no tax was due on the sale of the specified property.
Do not mail the certificate to us.

Can other forms be used?

Yes. You can use other forms or statements in place of this
certificate but whatever you use as proof that a sale was made for
resale must contain

- the seller's name and address;
- the purchaser's name and address;
- a description of the property being purchased;
- a statement that the property is being purchased for resale;
- the purchaser's signature and date of signing; and
- either an Illinois registration number, an Illinois resale number, or
a certification of resale to an out-of-state purchaser.

Note: A purchase order signed by the purchaser may be used as
a Certificate of Resale if it contains all of the above required
information.

CRT-61 (R-04/02)
IL-492-3850

When is a blanket certificate of resale used?

The purchaser may provide a blanket certificate of resale to any
seller from whom all purchases made are sales for resale. A
blanket certificate can also specify that a percentage of the
purchases made from the identified seller will be for resale. In
either instance, blanket certificates should be kept up-to-date. If a
specified percentage changes, a new certificate should be
provided. Otherwise, all certificates should be updated at least
every three years.

Specific instructions

Step 1: Identify the seller
Lines 1 and 2 Write the seller's name and mailing address.

Step 2: Identify the purchaser
Lines 3 and 4 Write the purchaser's name and mailing address.

Line 5 Check the statement that applies to the purchaser's
business, and provide any additional requested information.
Note: A statement by the purchaser that property will be sold for
resale will not be accepted by the department without supporting
evidence (*e.g.,* proof of out-of-state registration).

Step 3: Describe the property
Line 6 On the lines provided, briefly describe the tangible
personal property that was purchased for resale or list the invoice
number and date of purchase.

Step 4: Complete for blanket certificates
Line 7 The purchaser must check the statement that applies,
and provide any additional requested information.

Step 5: Purchaser's signature
The purchaser must sign and date the form.

This page is intentionally left blank.

IRS Form 8300 (Rev. December 2004)
OMB No. 1545-0892
Department of the Treasury
Internal Revenue Service

Report of Cash Payments Over $10,000 Received in a Trade or Business

▶ See instructions for definition of cash.

▶ Use this form for transactions occurring after December 31, 2004. Do not use prior versions after this date.

For Privacy Act and Paperwork Reduction Act Notice, see page 5.

FinCEN Form 8300 (Rev. December 2004)
OMB No. 1506-0018
Department of the Treasury
Financial Crimes
Enforcement Network

1   Check appropriate box(es) if: **a** ☐ Amends prior report;   **b** ☐ Suspicious transaction.

Part I   Identity of Individual From Whom the Cash Was Received

2   If more than one individual is involved, check here and see instructions . . . . ▶ ☐

3 Last name	4 First name	5 M.I.	6 Taxpayer identification number

7 Address (number, street, and apt. or suite no.)	8 Date of birth . ▶ (see instructions) M M D D Y Y Y Y

9 City	10 State	11 ZIP code	12 Country (if not U.S.)	13 Occupation, profession, or business

14 Identifying document (ID)	a Describe ID ▶ c Number ▶	b Issued by ▶

Part II   Person on Whose Behalf This Transaction Was Conducted

15   If this transaction was conducted on behalf of more than one person, check here and see instructions . . . . . ▶ ☐

16 Individual's last name or Organization's name	17 First name	18 M.I.	19 Taxpayer identification number

20 Doing business as (DBA) name (see instructions)	Employer identification number

21 Address (number, street, and apt. or suite no.)	22 Occupation, profession, or business

23 City	24 State	25 ZIP code	26 Country (if not U.S.)

27 Alien identification (ID)	a Describe ID ▶ c Number ▶	b Issued by ▶

Part III   Description of Transaction and Method of Payment

28 Date cash received M M D D Y Y Y Y	29 Total cash received $ .00	30 If cash was received in more than one payment, check here . . . ▶ ☐	31 Total price if different from item 29 $ .00

32   Amount of cash received (in U.S. dollar equivalent) (must equal item 29) (see instructions):

a U.S. currency $ _____ .00   (Amount in $100 bills or higher $ _____ .00)
b Foreign currency $ _____ .00   (Country ▶ _____)
c Cashier's check(s) $ _____ .00   Issuer's name(s) and serial number(s) of the monetary instrument(s) ▶
d Money order(s) $ _____ .00   _____
e Bank draft(s) $ _____ .00   _____
f Traveler's check(s) $ _____ .00

33   Type of transaction

a ☐ Personal property purchased   f ☐ Debt obligations paid
b ☐ Real property purchased   g ☐ Exchange of cash
c ☐ Personal services provided   h ☐ Escrow or trust funds
d ☐ Business services provided   i ☐ Bail received by court clerks
e ☐ Intangible property purchased   j ☐ Other (specify in item 34) ▶

34   Specific description of property or service shown in 33. Give serial or registration number, address, docket number, etc. ▶ _____

Part IV   Business That Received Cash

35 Name of business that received cash	36 Employer identification number

37 Address (number, street, and apt. or suite no.)	Social security number

38 City	39 State	40 ZIP code	41 Nature of your business

42   Under penalties of perjury, I declare that to the best of my knowledge the information I have furnished above is true, correct, and complete.

Signature ▶ _____ Authorized official   Title ▶ _____

43 Date of signature M M D D Y Y Y Y	44 Type or print name of contact person	45 Contact telephone number ( )

IRS Form **8300** (Rev. 12-2004)   Cat. No. 62133S   FinCEN Form **8300** (Rev. 12-2004)

IRS Form 8300 (Rev. 12-2004)   Page **2**   **FinCEN Form 8300** (Rev. 12-2004)

Multiple Parties
(Complete applicable parts below if box 2 or 15 on page 1 is checked)

Part I   Continued—Complete if box 2 on page 1 is checked

3 Last name	4 First name	5 M.I.	6 Taxpayer identification number

7 Address (number, street, and apt. or suite no.)	8 Date of birth. ▶ (see instructions) M M D D Y Y Y Y

9 City	10 State	11 ZIP code	12 Country (if not U.S.)	13 Occupation, profession, or business

14 Identifying document (ID)	**a Describe ID** ▶	**b Issued by** ▶ ....
	c Number ▶	

3 Last name	4 First name	5 M.I.	6 Taxpayer identification number

7 Address (number, street, and apt. or suite no.)	8 Date of birth. ▶ (see instructions) M M D D Y Y Y Y

9 City	10 State	11 ZIP code	12 Country (if not U.S.)	13 Occupation, profession, or business

14 Identifying document (ID)	**a Describe ID** ▶	**b Issued by** ▶ ....
	c Number ▶	

Part II   Continued—Complete if box 15 on page 1 is checked

16 Individual's last name or Organization's name	17 First name	18 M.I.	19 Taxpayer identification number

20 Doing business as (DBA) name (see instructions)	Employer identification number

21 Address (number, street, and apt. or suite no.)	22 Occupation, profession, or business

23 City	24 State	25 ZIP code	26 Country (if not U.S.)

27 Alien identification (ID)	**a Describe ID** ▶	**b Issued by** ▶ ....
	c Number ▶	

16 Individual's last name or Organization's name	17 First name	18 M.I.	19 Taxpayer identification number

20 Doing business as (DBA) name (see instructions)	Employer identification number

21 Address (number, street, and apt. or suite no.)	22 Occupation, profession, or business

23 City	24 State	25 ZIP code	26 Country (if not U.S.)

27 Alien identification (ID)	**a Describe ID** ▶	**b Issued by** ▶ ....
	c Number ▶	

Comments – Please use the lines provided below to comment on or clarify any information you entered on any line in Parts I, II, III, and IV

_____

_____

_____

_____

_____

IRS Form 8300 (Rev. 12-2004)   **FinCEN Form 8300** (Rev. 12-2004)

IRS Form 8300 (Rev. 12-2004) Page **3** **FinCEN Form 8300** (Rev. 12-2004)

Section references are to the Internal Revenue Code unless otherwise noted.

Important Reminders

● Section 6050I (26 United States Code (U.S.C.) 6050I) and 31 U.S.C. 5331 require that certain information be reported to the IRS and the Financial Crimes Enforcement Network (FinCEN). This information must be reported on IRS/FinCEN Form 8300.

● Item 33 box i is to be checked only by clerks of the court; box d is to be checked by bail bondsmen. See the instructions on page 5.

● For purposes of section 6050I and 31 U.S.C. 5331, the word "cash" and "currency" have the same meaning. See *Cash* under *Definitions* on page 4.

General Instructions

Who must file. Each person engaged in a trade or business who, in the course of that trade or business, receives more than $10,000 in cash in one transaction or in two or more related transactions, must file Form 8300. Any transactions conducted between a payer (or its agent) and the recipient in a 24-hour period are related transactions. Transactions are considered related even if they occur over a period of more than 24 hours if the recipient knows, or has reason to know, that each transaction is one of a series of connected transactions.

Keep a copy of each Form 8300 for 5 years from the date you file it.

Clerks of Federal or State courts must file Form 8300 if more than $10,000 in cash is received as bail for an individual(s) charged with certain criminal offenses. For these purposes, a clerk includes the clerk's office or any other office, department, division, branch, or unit of the court that is authorized to receive bail. If a person receives bail on behalf of a clerk, the clerk is treated as receiving the bail. See the instructions for Item 33 on page 5.

If multiple payments are made in cash to satisfy bail and the initial payment does not exceed $10,000, the initial payment and subsequent payments must be aggregated and the information return must be filed by the 15th day after receipt of the payment that causes the aggregate amount to exceed $10,000 in cash. In such cases, the reporting requirement can be satisfied either by sending a single written statement with an aggregate amount listed or by furnishing a copy of each Form 8300 relating to that payer. Payments made to satisfy separate bail requirements are not required to be aggregated. See Treasury Regulations section 1.6050I-2.

Casinos must file Form 8300 for nongaming activities (restaurants, shops, etc.).

Voluntary use of Form 8300. Form 8300 may be filed voluntarily for any suspicious transaction (see *Definitions*) for use by the IRS, even if the total amount does not exceed $10,000.

Exceptions. Cash is not required to be reported if it is received:

● By a financial institution required to file Form 104, Currency Transaction Report.

● By a casino required to file (or exempt from filing) Form 103, Currency Transaction Report by Casinos, if the cash is received as part of its gaming business.

● By an agent who receives the cash from a principal, if the agent uses all of the cash within 15 days in a second transaction that is reportable on Form 8300 or on Form 104, and discloses all the information necessary to complete Part II of Form 8300 or Form 104 to the recipient of the cash in the second transaction.

● In a transaction occurring entirely outside the United States. See Publication 1544, Reporting Cash Payments Over $10,000 (Received in a Trade or Business), regarding transactions occurring in Puerto Rico, the Virgin Islands, and territories and possessions of the United States.

● In a transaction that is not in the course of a person's trade or business.

When to file. File Form 8300 by the 15th day after the date the cash was received. If that date falls on a Saturday, Sunday, or legal holiday, file the form on the next business day.

Where to file. File the form with the Internal Revenue Service, Detroit Computing Center, P.O. Box 32621, Detroit, MI 48232.

Statement to be provided. You must give a written or electronic statement to each person named on a required Form 8300 on or before January 31 of the year following the calendar year in which the cash is received. The statement must show the name, telephone number, and address of the information contact for the business, the aggregate amount of reportable cash received, and that the information was furnished to the IRS. Keep a copy of the statement for your records.

Multiple payments. If you receive more than one cash payment for a single transaction or for related transactions, you must report the multiple payments any time you receive a total amount that exceeds $10,000 within any 12-month period. Submit the report within 15 days of the date you receive the payment that

causes the total amount to exceed $10,000. If more than one report is required within 15 days, you may file a combined report. File the combined report no later than the date the earliest report, if filed separately, would have to be filed.

Taxpayer identification number (TIN). You must furnish the correct TIN of the person or persons from whom you receive the cash and, if applicable, the person or persons on whose behalf the transaction is being conducted. You may be subject to penalties for an incorrect or missing TIN.

The TIN for an individual (including a sole proprietorship) is the individual's social security number (SSN). For certain resident aliens who are not eligible to get an SSN and nonresident aliens who are required to file tax returns, it is an IRS Individual Taxpayer Identification Number (ITIN). For other persons, including corporations, partnerships, and estates, it is the employer identification number (EIN).

If you have requested but are not able to get a TIN for one or more of the parties to a transaction within 15 days following the transaction, file the report and attach a statement explaining why the TIN is not included.

Exception: *You are not required to provide the TIN of a person who is a nonresident alien individual or a foreign organization if that person does not have income effectively connected with the conduct of a U.S. trade or business and does not have an office or place of business, or fiscal or paying agent, in the United States. See* Publication 1544 *for more information.*

Penalties. You may be subject to penalties if you fail to file a correct and complete Form 8300 on time and you cannot show that the failure was due to reasonable cause. You may also be subject to penalties if you fail to furnish timely a correct and complete statement to each person named in a required report. A minimum penalty of $25,000 may be imposed if the failure is due to an intentional or willful disregard of the cash reporting requirements.

Penalties may also be imposed for causing, or attempting to cause, a trade or business to fail to file a required report; for causing, or attempting to cause, a trade or business to file a required report containing a material omission or misstatement of fact; or for structuring, or attempting to structure, transactions to avoid the reporting requirements. These violations may also be subject to criminal prosecution which, upon conviction, may result in imprisonment of up to 5 years or fines of up to $250,000 for individuals and $500,000 for corporations or both.

Definitions

Cash. The term "cash" means the following:

• U.S. and foreign coin and currency received in any transaction.

• A cashier's check, money order, bank draft, or traveler's check having a face amount of $10,000 or less that is received in a designated reporting transaction (defined below), or that is received in any transaction in which the recipient knows that the instrument is being used in an attempt to avoid the reporting of the transaction under either section 6050I or 31 U.S.C. 5331.

Note. Cash does not include a check drawn on the payer's own account, such as a personal check, regardless of the amount.

Designated reporting transaction. A retail sale (or the receipt of funds by a broker or other intermediary in connection with a retail sale) of a consumer durable, a collectible, or a travel or entertainment activity.

Retail sale. Any sale (whether or not the sale is for resale or for any other purpose) made in the course of a trade or business if that trade or business principally consists of making sales to ultimate consumers.

Consumer durable. An item of tangible personal property of a type that, under ordinary usage, can reasonably be expected to remain useful for at least 1 year, and that has a sales price of more than $10,000.

Collectible. Any work of art, rug, antique, metal, gem, stamp, coin, etc.

Travel or entertainment activity. An item of travel or entertainment that pertains to a single trip or event if the combined sales price of the item and all other items relating to the same trip or event that are sold in the same transaction (or related transactions) exceeds $10,000.

Exceptions. A cashier's check, money order, bank draft, or traveler's check is not considered received in a designated reporting transaction if it constitutes the proceeds of a bank loan or if it is received as a payment on certain promissory notes, installment sales contracts, or down payment plans. See Publication 1544 for more information.

Person. An individual, corporation, partnership, trust, estate, association, or company.

Recipient. The person receiving the cash. Each branch or other unit of a person's trade or business is considered a separate recipient unless the branch receiving the cash (or a central office linking the branches), knows or has reason to know the identity of payers making cash payments to other branches.

Transaction. Includes the purchase of property or services, the payment of debt, the exchange of a negotiable instrument for cash, and the receipt of cash to be held in escrow or trust. A single transaction may not be broken into multiple transactions to avoid reporting.

Suspicious transaction. A transaction in which it appears that a person is attempting to cause Form 8300 not to be filed, or to file a false or incomplete form. The term also includes any transaction in which there is an indication of possible illegal activity.

Specific Instructions

You must complete all parts. However, you may skip Part II if the individual named in Part I is conducting the transaction on his or her behalf only. For voluntary reporting of suspicious transactions, see Item 1 below.

Item 1. If you are amending a prior report, check box 1a. Complete the appropriate items with the correct or amended information only. Complete all of Part IV. Staple a copy of the original report to the amended report.

To voluntarily report a suspicious transaction (see *Definitions*), check box 1b. You may also telephone your local IRS Criminal Investigation Division or call 1-800-800-2877.

Part I

Item 2. If two or more individuals conducted the transaction you are reporting, check the box and complete Part I for any one of the individuals. Provide the same information for the other individual(s) on the back of the form. If more than three individuals are involved, provide the same information on additional sheets of paper and attach them to this form.

Item 6. Enter the taxpayer identification number (TIN) of the individual named. See *Taxpayer identification number (TIN)* on page 3 for more information.

Item 8. Enter eight numerals for the date of birth of the individual named. For example, if the individual's birth date is July 6, 1960, enter 07 06 1960.

Item 13. Fully describe the nature of the occupation, profession, or business (for example, "plumber," "attorney," or "automobile dealer"). Do not use general or nondescriptive terms such as "businessman" or "self-employed."

Item 14. You must verify the name and address of the named individual(s). Verification must be made by examination of a document normally accepted as a means of identification when cashing checks (for example, a driver's license, passport, alien registration card, or other official

document). In item 14a, enter the type of document examined. In item 14b, identify the issuer of the document. In item 14c, enter the document's number. For example, if the individual has a Utah driver's license, enter "driver's license" in item 14a, "Utah" in item 14b, and the number appearing on the license in item 14c.

Note. You must complete all three items (a, b, and c) in this line to make sure that Form 8300 will be processed correctly.

Part II

Item 15. If the transaction is being conducted on behalf of more than one person (including husband and wife or parent and child), check the box and complete Part II for any one of the persons. Provide the same information for the other person(s) on the back of the form. If more than three persons are involved, provide the same information on additional sheets of paper and attach them to this form.

Items 16 through 19. If the person on whose behalf the transaction is being conducted is an individual, complete items 16, 17, and 18. Enter his or her TIN in item 19. If the individual is a sole proprietor and has an employer identification number (EIN), you must enter both the SSN and EIN in item 19. If the person is an organization, put its name as shown on required tax filings in item 16 and its EIN in item 19.

Item 20. If a sole proprietor or organization named in items 16 through 18 is doing business under a name other than that entered in item 16 (e.g., a "trade" or "doing business as (DBA)" name), enter it here.

Item 27. If the person is not required to furnish a TIN, complete this item. See *Taxpayer Identification Number (TIN)* on page 3. Enter a description of the type of official document issued to that person in item 27a (for example, "passport"), the country that issued the document in item 27b, and the document's number in item 27c.

Note. You must complete all three items (a, b, and c) in this line to make sure that Form 8300 will be processed correctly.

Part III

Item 28. Enter the date you received the cash. If you received the cash in more than one payment, enter the date you received the payment that caused the combined amount to exceed $10,000. See *Multiple payments* under *General Instructions* for more information.

Item 30. Check this box if the amount shown in item 29 was received in more than one payment (for example, as installment payments or payments on related transactions).

Item 31. Enter the total price of the property, services, amount of cash exchanged, etc. (for example, the total cost of a vehicle purchased, cost of catering service, exchange of currency) if different from the amount shown in item 29.

Item 32. Enter the dollar amount of each form of cash received. Show foreign currency amounts in U.S. dollar equivalent at a fair market rate of exchange available to the public. The sum of the amounts must equal item 29. For cashier's check, money order, bank draft, or traveler's check, provide the name of the issuer and the serial number of each instrument. Names of all issuers and all serial numbers involved must be provided. If necessary, provide this information on additional sheets of paper and attach them to this form.

Item 33. Check the appropriate box(es) that describe the transaction. If the transaction is not specified in boxes a–i, check box j and briefly describe the transaction (for example, "car lease," "boat lease," "house lease," or "aircraft rental"). If the transaction relates to the receipt of bail by a court clerk, check box i, "Bail received by court clerks." This box is only for use by court clerks. If the transaction relates to cash received by a bail bondsman, check box **d**, "Business services provided."

Part IV

Item 36. If you are a sole proprietorship, you must enter your SSN. If your business also has an EIN, you must provide the EIN as well. All other business entities must enter an EIN.

Item 41. Fully describe the nature of your business, for example, "attorney" or "jewelry dealer." Do not use general or nondescriptive terms such as "business" or "store."

Item 42. This form must be signed by an individual who has been authorized to do so for the business that received the cash.

Comments

Use this section to comment on or clarify anything you may have entered on any line in Parts I, II, III, and IV. For example, if you checked box b (Suspicious transaction) in line 1 above Part I, you may want to explain why you think that the cash transaction you are reporting on Form 8300 may be suspicious.

Privacy Act and Paperwork Reduction Act Notice. Except as otherwise noted, the information solicited on this form is required by the Internal Revenue Service (IRS) and the Financial Crimes Enforcement Network (FinCEN) in order to carry out the laws and regulations of the United States Department of the Treasury. Trades or businesses, except for clerks of criminal courts, are required to provide the information to the IRS and FinCEN under both section 6050I and 31 U.S.C. 5331. Clerks of criminal courts are required to provide the information to the IRS under section 6050I. Section 6109 and 31 U.S.C. 5331 require that you provide your social security number in order to adequately identify you and process your return and other papers. The principal purpose for collecting the information on this form is to maintain reports or records which have a high degree of usefulness in criminal, tax, or regulatory investigations or proceedings, or in the conduct of intelligence or counterintelligence activities, by directing the Federal Government's attention to unusual or questionable transactions.

You are not required to provide information as to whether the reported transaction is deemed suspicious. Failure to provide all other requested information, or providing fraudulent information, may result in criminal prosecution and other penalties under Title 26 and Title 31 of the United States Code.

Generally, tax returns and return information are confidential, as stated in section 6103. However, section 6103 allows or requires the IRS to disclose or give the information requested on this form to others as described in the Code. For example, we may disclose your tax information to the Department of Justice, to enforce the tax laws, both civil and criminal, and to cities, states, the District of Columbia, to carry out their tax laws. We may disclose this information to other persons as necessary to obtain information which we cannot get in any other way. We may disclose this information to Federal, state, and local child support agencies; and to other Federal agencies for the purposes of determining entitlement for benefits or the eligibility for and the repayment of loans. We may also provide the records to appropriate state, local, and foreign criminal law enforcement and regulatory personnel in the performance of their official duties. We may also disclose this information to other countries under a tax treaty, or to Federal and state agencies to enforce Federal nontax criminal laws and to combat terrorism.

The IRS authority to disclose information to combat terrorism expired on December 31, 2003. Legislation is pending that would reinstate this authority. "In addition, FinCEN may provide the information to those officials if they are conducting intelligence or counter-intelligence activities to protect against international terrorism."

You are not required to provide the information requested on a form that is subject to the Paperwork Reduction Act unless the form displays a valid OMB control number. Books or records relating to a form or its instructions must be retained as long as their contents may become material in the administration of any law under Title 26 or Title 31.

The time needed to complete this form will vary depending on individual circumstances. The estimated average time is 21 minutes. If you have comments concerning the accuracy of this time estimate or suggestions for making this form simpler, you can write to the Tax Products Coordinating Committee, Western Area Distribution Center, Rancho Cordova, CA 95743-0001. Do not send this form to this office. Instead, see *Where To File* on page 3.

This page is intentionally left blank.

Form 8850
(Rev. January 2006)
Department of the Treasury
Internal Revenue Service

Pre-Screening Notice and Certification Request for the Work Opportunity and Welfare-to-Work Credits

▶ See separate instructions.

OMB No. 1545-1500

Job applicant: Fill in the lines below and check any boxes that apply. Complete only this side.

Your name _____ Social security number ▶ _____

Street address where you live _____

City or town, state, and ZIP code _____

Telephone number (___) ___ - _____

If you are under age 25, enter your date of birth (month, day, year) ___/___/___

Work Opportunity Credit

1 ☐ Check here if you are a Hurricane Katrina employee. Enter the address of your main home on August 28, 2005, and the state and county or parish in which it was located.

_____

2 ☐ Check here if you received a conditional certification from the state employment security agency (SESA) or a participating local agency for the work opportunity credit.

3 ☐ Check here if **any** of the following statements apply to you.
- I am a member of a family that has received assistance from Temporary Assistance for Needy Families (TANF) for any 9 months during the last 18 months.
- I am a veteran and a member of a family that received food stamps for at least a 3-month period within the last 15 months.
- I was referred here by a rehabilitation agency approved by the state, an employment network under the Ticket to Work program, or the Department of Veterans Affairs.
- I am at least age 18 but **not** age 25 or older and I am a member of a family that:

    a Received food stamps for the last 6 months **or**

    b Received food stamps for at least 3 of the last 5 months, **but** is no longer eligible to receive them.
- Within the past year, I was convicted of a felony or released from prison for a felony **and** during the last 6 months I was a member of a low-income family.
- I received supplemental security income (SSI) benefits for any month ending within the last 60 days.

Welfare-to-Work Credit

4 ☐ Check here if you received a conditional certification from the SESA or a participating local agency for the welfare-to-work credit.

5 ☐ Check here if you are a member of a family that:
- Received TANF payments for at least the last 18 months, **or**
- Received TANF payments for any 18 months beginning after August 5, 1997, **and** the earliest 18-month period beginning after August 5, 1997, ended within the last 2 years, **or**
- Stopped being eligible for TANF payments within the last 2 years because federal or state law limited the maximum time those payments could be made.

All Applicants

Under penalties of perjury, I declare that I gave the above information to the employer on or before the day I was offered a job, and it is, to the best of my knowledge, true, correct, and complete.

Job applicant's signature ▶ _____   **Date** ___/___/___

For Privacy Act and Paperwork Reduction Act Notice, see page 2.   Cat. No. 22851L   Form **8850** (Rev. 01-06)

For Employer's Use Only

Employer's name _____ Telephone no. (___) ___ - _____ EIN ▶ _____

Street address _____

City or town, state, and ZIP code _____

Person to contact, if different from above _____ Telephone no. (___) ___ - _____

Street address _____

City or town, state, and ZIP code _____

If, based on the individual's age and home address, he or she is a member of group 4 or 6 (as described under Members of Targeted Groups in the separate instructions), enter that group number (4 or 6) . . . . ▶ _____

Date applicant: Gave information ___/___/___   Was offered job ___/___/___   Was hired ___/___/___   Started job ___/___/___

Complete Only If Box 1 on Page 1 is Checked

State and county or parish of job _____

☐ Check if the individual was not my employee on August 28, 2005 and this is the first time the employee has been hired by me since August 28, 2005.

Under penalties of perjury, I declare that the applicant completed this form on or before the day a job was offered to the applicant and that the information I have furnished is, to the best of my knowledge, true, correct, and complete. Based on the information the job applicant furnished on page 1, I believe the individual is a member of a targeted group or a long-term family assistance recipient. I hereby request a certification that the individual is a member of a targeted group or a long-term family assistance recipient.

Employer's signature ▶ _____ Title _____ Date ___/___/___

Privacy Act and Paperwork Reduction Act Notice

Section references are to the Internal Revenue Code.

Section 51(d)(12) permits a prospective employer to request the applicant to complete this form and give it to the prospective employer. The information will be used by the employer to complete the employer's federal tax return. Completion of this form is voluntary and may assist members of targeted groups and long-term family assistance recipients in securing employment. Routine uses of this form include giving it to the state employment security agency (SESA), which will contact appropriate sources to confirm that the applicant is a member of a targeted group or a long-term family assistance recipient. This form may also be given to the Internal Revenue Service

for administration of the Internal Revenue laws, to the Department of Justice for civil and criminal litigation, to the Department of Labor for oversight of the certifications performed by the SESA, and to cities, states, and the District of Columbia for use in administering their tax laws. We may also disclose this information to other countries under a tax treaty, to federal and state agencies to enforce federal nontax criminal laws, or to federal law enforcement and intelligence agencies to combat terrorism.

You are not required to provide the information requested on a form that is subject to the Paperwork Reduction Act unless the form displays a valid OMB control number. Books or records relating to a form or its instructions must be retained as long as their contents may become material in the administration of any Internal Revenue law. Generally, tax returns and return information are confidential, as required by section 6103.

The time needed to complete and file this form will vary depending on individual circumstances. The estimated average time is:

Recordkeeping . . . .5 hrs., 30 min.
Learning about the law or the form . . . . 24 min.
Preparing and sending this form to the SESA . . . . 30 min.

If you have comments concerning the accuracy of these time estimates or suggestions for making this form simpler, we would be happy to hear from you. You can write to the Internal Revenue Service, Tax Products Coordinating Committee, SE:W:CAR:MP:T:T:SP, 1111 Constitution Ave. NW, IR-6406, Washington, DC 20224.

Do not send this form to this address. Instead, see *When and Where To File* in the separate instructions.

Instructions for Form 8850

 **Department of the Treasury
Internal Revenue Service**

(Rev. January 2006)

Pre-Screening Notice and Certification Request for the Work Opportunity and Welfare-to-Work Credits

Section references are to the Internal Revenue Code unless otherwise noted.

General Instructions

What's New

● The work opportunity credit and the welfare-to-work credit are now allowed for qualified individuals who begin work for you before January 1, 2006.

TIP *These credits may be extended with respect to employees who began work for you after December 31, 2005. See What's Hot in Tax Forms, Pubs, and Other Tax Products at www.irs.gov/formspubs to find out if the credits have been extended.*

● The Katrina Emergency Relief Act of 2005 added a new targeted group, Hurricane Katrina employee, identified as group 9.

Purpose of Form

Employers use Form 8850 to pre-screen and to make a written request to a state employment security agency (SESA) (unless the employee checks only the Hurricane Katrina employee box) to certify an individual as:

● A member of a targeted group for purposes of qualifying for the work opportunity credit or

● A long-term family assistance recipient for purposes of qualifying for the welfare-to-work credit.

Submitting Form 8850 to the SESA (unless the employee checks only the Hurricane Katrina employee box) is but one step in the process of qualifying for the work opportunity credit or the welfare-to-work credit. The SESA must certify the job applicant is a member of a targeted group or is a long-term family assistance recipient. After starting work, the employee must meet the minimum number-of-hours-worked requirement for the work opportunity credit or the minimum number-of-hours, number-of-days requirement for the welfare-to-work credit. The employer may elect to take the applicable credit by filing Form 5884, Work Opportunity Credit, or Form 8861, Welfare-to-Work Credit.

CAUTION *The certification requirements described above do not apply to Hurricane Katrina employees. For an employer of a Hurricane Katrina employee, this form is used to accept reasonable evidence that the worker is a Hurricane Katrina employee. It is the employer's responsibility to ascertain that the place where the employee lived on August 28, 2005, (the address on line 1 of the form) is in fact in the core disaster area (see pages 2 and 3 for a list of these areas). The employer is not required to ask employees to furnish any documentary evidence.*

Who Should Complete and Sign the Form

The job applicant gives information to the employer on or before the day a job offer is made. This information is entered on Form 8850. Based on the applicant's information, the employer determines whether or not he or she believes the applicant is a member of a targeted group (as defined under Members of Targeted Groups) or a long-term family assistance recipient (as defined under Welfare-to-Work Job Applicants). If the employer believes the applicant is a member of a targeted group or a long-term family assistance recipient, the employer completes the rest of the form no later than the day the job offer is made. Both the job applicant and the employer must sign Form 8850 no later than the date for submitting the form to the SESA.

Instructions for Employer

When and Where To File

Do not file Form 8850 with the Internal Revenue Service. Instead, if required, file it with the work opportunity tax credit (WOTC) coordinator for your SESA no later than the 21st day after the job applicant begins work for you. Although electronic filing of Form 8850 is permitted, at the time these instructions were published, no state was equipped to receive Form 8850 electronically. See Announcement 2002-44 for details. You can find Announcement 2002-44 on page 809 of Internal Revenue Bulletin 2002-17 at *www.irs.gov/pub/irs-irbs/irb02-17.pdf.*

To get the name, address, phone and fax numbers, and email address of the WOTC coordinator for your SESA, visit the Department of Labor Employment and Training Administration (ETA) web site at *www.ows.doleta.gov/employ/tax.asp.*

CAUTION *Never include Form 8850 with a tax return or otherwise send it to the IRS, regardless of the employee's targeted group. Form 8850 should be filed with the state SESA unless the employee checks only the Hurricane Katrina employee box, in which case the employer should keep the Form 8850 for its records.*

Additional Requirements for Certification

In addition to filing Form 8850, you must complete and send to your state's WOTC coordinator either:
- ETA Form 9062, Conditional Certification Form, if the job applicant received this form from a participating agency (e.g., the Jobs Corps) or
- ETA Form 9061, Individual Characteristics Form, if the job applicant did not receive a conditional certification.

You can get ETA Form 9061 from your local public employment service office or you can download it from the ETA web site at *www.ows.doleta.gov/employ/tax.asp*.

Recordkeeping

Keep copies of Forms 8850, along with any transmittal letters that you submit to your SESA, as long as they may be needed for the administration of the Internal Revenue Code provisions relating to the work opportunity credit and the welfare-to-work credit. Records that support these credits usually must be kept for 3 years from the date any income tax return claiming the credits is due or filed, whichever is later.

Hurricane Katrina employee. *Form 8850 should not be filed with the state SESA for employees who only check box 1 on Form 8850. Employers should keep Form 8850 for their records. If a prior version of Form 8850 was sent to the state SESA indicating the employee is a Hurricane Katrina employee, the employer and employee should complete this version of Form 8850 for the employer to retain for its records. Do not attach Form 8850 to a tax return.*

Members of Targeted Groups

A job applicant may be certified as a member of a targeted group if he or she is described in one of the following groups.

1. **Qualified IV-A recipient.** A member of a family receiving assistance under a state plan approved under part A of title IV of the Social Security Act relating to Temporary Assistance for Needy Families (TANF). The assistance must be received for any 9 months during the 18-month period that ends on the hiring date.

2. **Qualified veteran.** A veteran who is a member of a family receiving assistance under the Food Stamp program for at least a 3-month period during the 15-month period ending on the hiring date. See section 51(d)(3). To be considered a veteran, the applicant must:
- Have served on active duty (not including training) in the Armed Forces of the United States for more than 180 days or have been discharged or released from active duty for a service-connected disability and
- Not have a period of active duty (not including training) of more than 90 days that ended during the 60-day period ending on the hiring date.

3. **Qualified ex-felon.** An ex-felon who:
- Has been convicted of a felony under any Federal or state law,
- Is hired not more than 1 year after the conviction or release from prison for that felony, and

- Is a member of a family that had income on an annual basis of 70% or less of the Bureau of Labor Statistics lower living standard during the 6 months immediately preceding the earlier of the month the income determination occurs or the month in which the hiring date occurs.

4. **High-risk youth.** An individual who is at least 18 but not yet 25 on the hiring date and lives within an empowerment zone, enterprise community, or renewal community.

5. **Vocational rehabilitation referral.** An individual who has a physical or mental disability resulting in a substantial handicap to employment and who was referred to the employer upon completion of (or while receiving) rehabilitation services by a rehabilitation agency approved by the state, an employment network under the Ticket to Work program, or the Department of Veterans Affairs.

6. **Summer youth employee.** An individual who:
- Performs services for the employer between May 1 and September 15,
- Is age 16 but not yet age 18 on the hiring date (or if later, on May 1),
- Has never worked for the employer before, and
- Lives within an empowerment zone, enterprise community, or renewal community.

7. **Food stamp recipient.** An individual who:
- Is at least age 18 but not yet age 25 on the hiring date, and
- Is a member of a family that —
a. Has received food stamps for the 6-month period ending on the hiring date or
b. Is no longer eligible for such assistance under section 6(o) of the Food Stamp Act of 1977, but the family received food stamps for at least 3 months of the 5-month period ending on the hiring date.

8. **SSI recipient.** An individual who is receiving supplemental security income benefits under title XVI of the Social Security Act (including benefits of the type described in section 1616 of the Social Security Act or section 212 of Public Law 93-66) for any month ending within the 60-day period ending on the hiring date.

9. **Hurricane Katrina employee.** A Hurricane Katrina employee is:
- A person who, on August 28, 2005, had a main home in the core disaster area and, within a two-year period beginning on this date, is hired to perform services principally in the core disaster area; or
- A person who, on August 28, 2005, had a main home in the core disaster area, was displaced from the main home as a result of Hurricane Katrina, and was hired during the period beginning on August 28, 2005, and ending on December 31, 2005, for a job located outside the core disaster area.

Gulf Opportunity (GO) Zone (Core Disaster Area). The GO Zone (also called the core disaster area) covers the portion of the Hurricane Katrina disaster area determined by the Federal Emergency Management Agency (FEMA) to be eligible for either individual only or both individual and public assistance from the Federal

Government. The GO Zone covers the following areas in three states.

    a. **Alabama.** The counties of Baldwin, Choctaw, Clarke, Greene, Hale, Marengo, Mobile, Pickens, Sumter, Tuscaloosa, and Washington.

    b. **Louisiana.** The parishes of Acadia, Ascension, Assumption, Calcasieu, Cameron, East Baton Rouge, East Feliciana, Iberia, Iberville, Jefferson, Jefferson Davis, Lafayette, Lafourche, Livingston, Orleans, Plaquemines, Pointe Coupee, St. Bernard, St. Charles, St. Helena, St. James, St. John the Baptist, St. Martin, St. Mary, St. Tammany, Tangipahoa, Terrebonne, Vermilion, Washington, West Baton Rouge, and West Feliciana.

    c. **Mississippi.** The counties of Adams, Amite, Attala, Choctaw, Claiborne, Clarke, Copiah, Covington, Forrest, Franklin, George, Greene, Hancock, Harrison, Hinds, Holmes, Humphreys, Jackson, Jasper, Jefferson, Jefferson Davis, Jones, Kemper, Lamar, Lauderdale, Lawrence, Leake, Lincoln, Lowndes, Madison, Marion, Neshoba, Newton, Noxubee, Oktibbeha, Pearl River, Perry, Pike, Rankin, Scott, Simpson, Smith, Stone, Walthall, Warren, Wayne, Wilkinson, Winston, and Yazoo.

Empowerment zones, enterprise communities, and renewal communities. For details on all empowerment zones, enterprise communities, and renewal communities, you can use the RC/EZ/EC Address Locator at *www.hud.gov/crlocator*. For details about empowerment zones, enterprise communities, and renewal communities, call 1-800-998-9999, or contact your SESA. For more information about empowerment zones, enterprise communities, and renewal

communities, see Publication 954, Tax Incentives for Distressed Communities.

 Under section 1400, parts of Washington, DC, are treated as an empowerment zone. For details, use the RC/EZ/EC Address Locator at www.hud.gov/crlocator or see Notice 98-57, on page 9 of Internal Revenue Bulletin 1998-47 at www.irs.gov/pub/irs-irbs/irb98-47.pdf. Also, there are no areas designated in Puerto Rico, Guam, or any U.S. possession.

Welfare-to-Work Job Applicants

An individual may be certified as a long-term family assistance recipient if he or she is a member of a family that:
- Has received TANF payments for at least 18 consecutive months ending on the hiring date, or
- Receives TANF payments for any 18 months (whether or not consecutive) beginning after August 5, 1997, and the earliest 18-month period beginning after August 5, 1997, ended within the last 2 years, or
- Stopped being eligible for TANF payments because Federal or state law limits the maximum period such assistance is payable and the individual is hired not more than 2 years after such eligibility ended.

Member of a family

With respect to the qualified IV-A recipient, qualified veteran, food stamp recipient, and long-term family assistance recipient, an individual whose family receives assistance for the requisite period meets the family assistance requirement of the applicable group if the individual is included on the grant (and thus receives assistance) for some portion of the specified period.

Index